'Atta Girl!

A Celebration of Women in Sport

Previously published as *The Quiet Storm*
Completely revised and updated, 2002

Alexandra Powe Allred

with Karen and Michelle Powe

Wish Publishing
Terre Haute, Indiana
www.wishpublishing.com

LCCN: 2002109920

Edited by Heather Lowhorn
Cover designed by Phil Velikan
Cover photography by Photodisk

Printed in the United States of America
10 9 8 7 6 5 4 3 2 1

Published in the United States by
Wish Publishing
P.O. Box 10337
Terre Haute, IN 47801, USA
www.wishpublishing.com

Distributed in the United States by
Cardinal Publishers Group
7301 Georgetown Road, Suite 118
Indianapolis, Indiana 46268
www.cardinalpub.com

SOC

From Alexandra

This book exists because of two extraordinary ladies — my mother and Holly Kondras. When I came up with the hairbrained idea to try out for the U.S. Bobsled team, Karen Powe helped me get a trainer, provided childcare, and boundless positive energy. In all ways, she is my greatest coach!

I met Holly Kondras in 1997 when she helped publish our first book *The Quiet Storm: A Celebration of Women in Sport*. So dedicated to the concept of this book and the need to celebrate women in sport, she created her own publishing house in honor of women's athletics and encouraged me to re-create '*Atta Girl: A Celebration of Women in Sport*.

To these two women, I must cheer "Atta Girl!" and thank you!

I also need to give an "Atta Boy!" cheer to two wonderful men — my father and my husband.

Marc Powe called me "Sport" all my life, challenged me always in sports and allowed me to believe I actually *could* try out for the U.S. Bobsled team! From 1994–2002, while I had and raised three small children, competed, trained, wrote, ranted, raved, cried, and cheered, my husband was right there. "Atta Boy!"

From Karen

What greater joy is there than to watch your daughters develop into caring, creative women and committed athletes with whom you can share interests, ideas, and love? I have been able to work with my girls to support, in some small way, girls and women who are determined to be all that they can be. My thanks go to my two girls, who are the essence of *Atta Girl!*

From Michelle

To my parents, thank you for letting me dream and, thank you Frank for being you.

Thanks

Nancy Woodhull told us, "I think we're put on earth to make sure that everything carries on — and not that it fails when we are absent." Woodhull devoted her life to shattering the glass ceiling and to bringing along as many women as possible. A founding editor of *USA Today*, a former president of Gannett News Service, and senior vice president of the Freedom Forum, she was a trailblazer for women's rights and for improving perceptions about women in the media.

We were honored that she shared some of her wisdom with us and saddened when she died in 1997 at the age of 52. But her work and her words do live on. And we thank her for her incredible influence and efforts in tearing down stereotypes and barriers.

We also want to thank all the athletes who lent their precious time to us. And special thanks go to the men and women who allowed us to call them again and again, bounce ideas off of them, and ask more questions. The staffs at the Women's Sports Foundation, Winter Sports Foundation, and the governing bodies of U.S. Swim Team, USA Gymnastics, and U.S. Track and Field, and all the other sports mentioned in the book promptly provided information in any way they could. Without these men and women, contacting athletes would have been far more difficult — maybe impossible. Thank you to Dave Weiss of Sports Unlimited for your commitment to women in sport. Thanks to the women of professional football whose hearts are as big as their dreams. A special thanks to the coaching staff of the Austin Rage of the Women's Professional Football League (WPFL). Your love, commitment, dedication and enthusiasm made dreams come true for women who never thought they would be allowed to set foot on a football field.

Thank you, Greg Sun — the best friend of the women's bobsled team and our favorite male bobsledder — for your wis-

It's 20 degrees outside and Karen Powe is playing the broomball game of her life, forever instilling the 'Atta Girl! spirit in her daughters, Michelle and Alex (photo by Marc Powe).

dom and your encouragement and your humor. Thank you, Joey Kilburn, for rising above politics and letting us do what we most wanted to do — slide. And a big thank you to Dr. James Larmour, a doctor with real heart, who keeps Michelle straightened out, neck and all.

The cooperation and support of all these people is what sports is all about. Together, our family, friends, and all the women and men who participated in this book have created something very special for anyone interested in women's athletics.

To all of them — especially our family — thank you for letting us be on your team.

Table of Contents

Foreword by Tori Allen

I was born to run, jump, and climb. In fact, these things are as necessary to my daily life as eating breathing and sleeping. Over the years I have tried many different sports experiences to find the perfect outlet for my insatiable need to be active. Unfortunately (really!), I was born with a genetic code that enabled me to be extremely coordinated, extremely strong, and thus extremely gifted in most of the activities I tried. Often I would take up an activity and, within a month or so, a coach would be talking to my parents about extra lessons and "my future" in the sport. Due to this "gift," it took me awhile to be able to tell the difference between merely enjoying a sport and loving it. For most sports I tried, I found that I truly did enjoy the activity itself. I liked soccer, figure skating, ballet, and basketball all just fine. What I came to realize, though, was that I was only pushing myself to really train to improve in those sports because of the outward pressure of those around me. On the other hand, I eventually discovered a couple sports that I loved—rock climbing and pole vaulting. I knew I was in love with these sports because I wanted to do them all the time. I didn't care if I was good or not, I just wanted to never have to go to sleep because that was taking time away from climbing and vaulting. Now, when I practice these sports, my motivation is entirely within my own heart and body.

My name is Tori Allen, and I am a teenager, a sister, a daughter, a friend, a citizen, a female, a student, and a Christian. Yet, most people only know me as an athlete. Being an athlete has made me a better person in all those other roles due to the character it has built in me and the lessons about life I have learned through my athletic experiences.

Sports are very important to me because they have helped to build my character. My motto for my life as well as my sports is that hard work is the only yellow brick road that leads to my goals and dreams which are my Oz. When I go to the gym to

Tori Allen celebrating a gold medal at the X-Games, 2002 (Photo provided by Dave Weiss of Sports Unlimited).

train for rock climbing, I often get teased for being antisocial because I spend three hours climbing every route in the gym, rather than playing climbing games and gossiping. The thing is, every time I enter the gym, I know that I have a certain amount of time to spend there. It is up to me to decide how I spend it. The way I figure it, if I don't earn my opportunities, then those opportunities will belong to someone else, so I spend my time working as hard as I can.

Being so active also makes me very impatient. I want things now and when that doesn't happen, I go into action to speed up the process. As a pole vaulter, I have learned that improvement comes only from fine-tuning minute details such as the tilt of my head at the moment I plant my pole in the box. Of course, all last season, my head tilt was not right so I had to spend an entire season working on tilting it a new way—or un-tilting it. I won't say I wasn't frustrated, because I was. I felt like I was working on something insignificant, and meanwhile, my vault heights plateaued.

I never wanted to actually quit vaulting during the head-tilt-fixing time, but I did want to work on something else. Although, we did fine-tune other areas as well, this head tilt seemed to be my coach's obsession. Well, when summer arrived, my head tilt had improved as well as my vault heights. Both the patience and the perseverance paid off with a national age-group record height and a gold medal at the USATF Jr. Olympics. Even though I am still tempted to play instead of

Allen at the Junior Olympics (photo courtesy of Tori Allen).

train or rush ahead and forget about the details or even give up on a certain thing that seems too hard, I am a better person in all areas of my life because of my new appreciation for hard work, patience, and perseverance that I learned through my involvement in sports.

In addition to building my character, sports have played an important role in my life in other ways. The most obvious way is that my participation in sports has improved my overall physical fitness. Not only am I better fit now, but I know more about what it takes to have a healthy body. I know what foods provide me the energy and nutrition I need and I know how much of each of those I should eat each day in order to fuel my body. I also have acquired active habits that will keep me from becoming a lifelong couch potato. I roller blade instead of watching TV and I bike to climbing instead of driving. Fitness is all about making good decisions and sports have taught me what those decisions are.

Sports have also provided me the opportunity not just to succeed but to fail as well. Since adversity and failure are natural parts of anyone's life, I have been fortunate to learn how to handle these challenges through my involvement in sports. Even though I earned a national title and broke a national record in vault this summer, I still failed to reach a personal goal of vaulting 11'6". Failure is not a huge motivator to persevere, yet my failure in this goal has helped me to refocus. I am learning to look at aspects of achievement that are not just measured by medals and tape measures. As a goal-directed person, this is a slow, hard lesson that failure and sports are teaching me.

Finally, my involvement in sports has provided me with the opportunity to hold positions of leadership within my sport and community as well the privilege of being seen as a role model among my peers. I have been able to inspire other young girls to take up climbing and to shoot for earning a spot on the U.S. Junior team. I have been a voice for the rights of girls to pole vault in Indiana since pole vault is only a recognized high school sport for boys in my state and not girls. I have even been able to promote a family-focused film festival and to talk to elementary school kids about the importance of good character, all because of my involvement in sports. Fitness, adversity, and opportunity are all examples of how my involvement in sports has impacted who I am and my future.

Like I said earlier, I am a sister and a daughter as well as an athlete. It is important to me to be good at these roles because my family is a top priority in my life. Even though my sports do not take priority over my family, they have definitely enhanced my family life. Being so athletic makes me want to constantly be moving. This is great for my family because we are active together and keep each other accountable for making healthy decisions.

My brother is two years younger than I and he is an athlete as well. I love having an athletic brother because our time together is spent riding bikes, throwing a football, playing frisbee golf, and swimming. He even rock climbs and pole vaults so that provides us with some common ground on which to build our relationship.

My parents know how committed I am to being an elite athlete and they see how much time and thought I put into my training. They respect me for my dedication and they see me making hard choices between going out with friends or getting to bed early before a meet. They tell me all the time how mature, responsible, and reliable I am, and they give me freedom to make choices outside of my athletic involvement because I have earned their trust. Overall, my involvement in sports has brought me closer to my family. I appreciate the sacrifices they make for me, and I depend on them to support me in the good and the hard times. They have never let me down.

Finding reliable, mature friends who care about me as Tori the teen and not Tori, that famous climber girl, has been one of the biggest challenges I've faced recently. Thankfully, I have three people who don't care about my accolades and who are confident enough with themselves to allow our friendship to ebb and flow with my travel schedule without trying to cling to me or playing gossip games in my absence. They give me space to be me and are honest enough to help me work on problem areas in my life. Also, since I have very little free time to just hang out, I make a point to spend quality time with these few select people. I know that taking time to really talk and share and be accountable has made our friendship grow deep and real in a limited time frame. In this way, my crazy training and travel schedule for my sports has enhanced my closest friendships.

Outside of these best friends, I hang out with a bunch of people I would call my peer group. I am thankful for the character that my sports involvement has built in me because it has given me the self-confidence to stand up to any given group of my peers and say no to an activity or attitude that they are pushing that goes against anything I stand for. In addition, my status as a serious athlete allows me to break the barrier of stereotypes or cliques and to lead the way in changing attitudes and actions in the halls of my school. My ultimate goal is for others to see the courage I have to be different, and then for them to feel inspired to act out their convictions as well. I know that this courage inside of me can be directly traced to the confidence I have gained through competition and taking risks in pole vaulting and rock climbing.

Boys. Most coaches can tell you the story of at least one very talented girl that they coached who got distracted by boys and lost focus. Hopefully, those stories are becoming things of the past. For me, being a dedicated athlete has given me a greater respect for my body. Not only do I not want anyone else to have any claim of ownership on my body but, also, I am proud of the way I look. I used to get comments from guys in the weight room all the time about how I was going to look like a guy one day or that it just wasn't normal for a girl to do what I did. Yet, because I persevered, I now see myself on even ground with my male peers. In fact, since I have to vault on the boys track team, I proved just how even that ground was last year by winning the boys' freshman county meet in the pole vault. I can see the respect among my teammates growing each day as I match them workout for workout. No, I don't lift the same amount of weight as they do but I do train with the same intensity.

In addition to respecting my body and building a mutual respect with the guys around me, my athletic experience has taught me to respect my future. In relation to boys, this means precisely that, it's MY future. My future does not depend on a boy to give me status, worth, or value. Therefore, all my relationships with boys start with an admiration of the talents and the goals of the other. If that is not there, I do not allow a relationship/friendship to develop. I have some of the most amazing friends who are guys. They tell me that I am not like other girls. I know that is not true, it's just that I am one of the few who caught their attention as an athlete first and a female second.

I am excited about the future. Of course, I am excited about possibly representing my country in an Olympic event one day but there is much more to my future than that. I can't wait to be a mom so that I can give my daughters opportunities to find activities that they love. I can't wait to be a teacher so that I can set up sports experiences in my class in order to show the girls the potential that is locked in their bodies. I can't wait to be a coach of an elite female athlete in either climbing or pole vault so that I can pass on the things I've learned to someone traveling along the same path I am traveling. I can't wait for next spring when I can go to the middle schools and recruit some girls to come work out with me and give pole vault a try.

I can't wait for next month when I can go to the youth center in the inner city and watch the girls there overcome their fears as they climb things on the wall that they thought were impossible. I can't wait for tomorrow when I can go to the gym and coach two budding rock stars who see me as their hero when really they are mine. I just can't wait. My sports have given so much to me that I just can't wait for each day to come so that I can share all those gifts.

In closing, I guess that is the biggest lesson I've learned of all—don't be selfish. If I am having fun, I try to let others know it. If I appreciate someone's help, I thank them. If I just go out there each day and rack up medals and records but I don't leave a trail for others to follow, the victories are empty and meaningless and will fade with time. So, I wake up each day ready to pass on whatever that day shares with me so that someone else can enjoy it too. For me, that means sharing my sports—passing it on.

Tori Allen
August 2002

Photo opposite by Dave Weiss, Sports Unlimited

Introduction

From the beginning of this project, we were struck by the instant bond and camaraderie we felt with the women we interviewed. Initially, we were surprised by how much each woman opened up, talking for long periods of time. We wondered, didn't these women have strong familial and filial support groups? But we soon realized that this open communication and cooperation was indicative of something much deeper, much more relevant than talking about sports. Every athlete conveyed a feeling of goodwill and trust toward fellow female athletes, a special bond between sportswomen. We came to realize that what we, the authors, have experienced as bobsledders is not isolated to our sport; rather, our frustrations and joys and the sisterhood that has developed among us are representative of the experiences of female athletes generally.

More than just teammates, the girls and women who train and compete together share a very special, family-like relationship. U.S. Olympic basketball player Teresa Edwards, the only basketball player — male or female — to compete in four Olympics sums it up well: "The joy of the party is just being with each other. It's a family atmosphere." [1]

An example of the relationship that develops is demonstrated by the following story. U.S. bobsledders Liz Parr-Smestad and Alexandra Powe-Allred were working as a team in Calgary in November 1995, alternating driving and braking for each other. The Calgary track descends a mountain through 14 curves. During one trip down, before curve seven, the women's bobsled flipped over. Gravity dragged Alex out of the sled and onto the track, while Liz was able to slip under the front of the bob, forced to ride out the crash through every twist and turn of the tracks. What happened next left track workers laughing and all saying the same thing: Men would never have done that.

When Alex stopped sliding and was able to stand again (and pull her pants up), she spied pieces of the sled on the track. Her mind raced. Where was Liz, and was she hurt? Alex began sprinting down the track without spikes, defying gravity and ice. Meanwhile Liz had been helped out of the capsized bobsled at the end of the run. Her first words were, "Where's Alex?" She was assured by the first-aid officials that Alex was OK. In truth, a bobsled truck was following Alex down the mountain, unable to keep up with her. Never mind that Liz had torn the ligaments from her sternum or that Alex had ice burns from sliding down the track. As Alex rounded the finish curve, and she and Liz saw each other, the two women ran toward one another while everyone else listened to the track announcer's commentary on the public address system: "She's coming around finish ... Smooooth exit out of finish curve ... They've seen each other ... Now the other American woman is coming toward her brake ... They haaaave contact. It's a hug!"

Beyond the strong sense of family among female athletes, there is also a sense of responsibility toward young female hopefuls. This was demonstrated by the wide, enthusiastic response we received from so many celebrated athletes, coaches, sports commentators, entertainers, and businesswomen who credited sports for having given them the competitive skills needed to succeed in sports and business. These women were eager to tell their stories and extol the benefits of sports and to help inspire and raise the chances for success and happiness among today's girls and young women.

Olympic gold-medallist swimmer Janet Evans agreed to an interview because she believes in the importance of sports for females and wants "to give back to young kids. We didn't have books like this when I was younger," she says. "It's important to have female role models."

When Olympic basketball star Dawn Staley forced a bus driver to stop for a small girl who had been chasing the team for an autograph, she was demonstrating that sense of responsibility and inclusiveness. "You never know," says teammate Sheryl Swoopes, "it might change [that little girl's] life. We didn't have anybody to look up to — positive, female role models in sports. Now little girls can choose ... ."[2] Indeed, little girls today can choose from an impressive pool of women to inspire them — women from all backgrounds, sports, and professions.

The title *'Atta Girl!* came to us because, as athletes, it is the best thing to hear from a coach, a fan or, better yet, a teammate. As a coach, it is meant as a great compliment and, now, having stood on the sidelines of some of the most intense, nail-biting, emotionally draining little league soccer games for two budding soccer jocks, this mother/aunt/grandmother trio of authors has burst forward with wild chants of "'Atta girl," as our hearts swell. Could there be any greater sports chant than that? Maybe. If it comes unexpectedly from a teammate. As you will later read, as Alexandra faces the daunting task of making and playing for a professional women's football league and Michelle and Karen try to muscle their way into the locker room of professional soccer players Mia Hamm, Brandi Chastain, and Carla Overbeck (to name a few), the cheers from peers can be the most powerful words ever uttered. They reaffirm to us that what we are doing and feeling is important.

But "'Atta girl!" is so much more than a sports fan chant. It is an attitude we need and must adopt in the workplace, the classroom, in the locker room, and on the fields. As much as we — as female athletes — are growing and exploring new options in the world of sport, we are under siege with regard to what the perfect female body looks like and why we should all want to obtain the perfect body. While cosmetic surgery and eating disorders are on the rise in this country — as is obesity — we need to partake in backslapping, congratulatory "atta girls!" as much as possible. Truly, our futures are at stake.

In 1992, a widely publicized report from the American Association of University Women (AAUW) documented disturbing statistics of self-esteem among middle school girls along with gender inequities in the classroom. Shortly thereafter, the book *Reviving Ophelia* by Mary Pipher came out discussing the "look-obsessed, media-saturated, girl-poisoning" culture we live in and how this culture is harming adolescent girls. Much has changed since that time. In a 2000 study conducted by the New York City-based Girl Scout Research Institute, over 93 percent of the girls surveyed intended to go to college and 76 percent said they were going to have careers. Girl Power is on the move! But it is important to note two things: this new girl power attitude didn't just appear from thin air, and there is still more work to be done in the gender equity game. For this reason, we need to celebrate our sisters who have blazed trails for us and note the work that still needs to be done. As we talked to more and more athletes and businesswomen, we realized that these amazing pioneers have done so much for us. They have knocked down barriers in their paths and blown apart stereotypes and images — producing a kind of rain and a life that grows after the storm is gone, bringing new hope to others.

That hope was illustrated during the 1996 Olympic Games in Atlanta, marked as "The Year of the Women." Since then there has been no turning back. It was a women's sporting event in 1999 that would capture the attention of almost everyone in the Western Hemisphere — the Women's 1999 World Cup for soccer. Scratch that. It was a worldwide event. Some 90,000 screaming fans made it the largest non-football event in the U.S. Many celebrities, including the president of the United States, were in attendance — making it, what the women from the U.S. Soccer team would later tell us, one of the most exciting, nerve-wracking experiences of their lives. Mia Hamm told us even she never would have believed so many fans would show up for a soccer game. But she and her teammates had become the darlings of the sport world.

More girls than ever are playing recreational sports. While ballet and cheerleading squads continue to be filled (a good thing), girls are signing up for softball, baseball, and soccer. Stories of girls playing hockey and football are more commonplace, giving us more hope that the playing fields are evening up and little girls really can grow up to be anyone they want. But there are still hurdles. Just when the going gets good, we find out about a small town in Texas where the high school girls are not allowed to play softball on the high school fields. Those fields are earmarked for the boys. Instead, the girls are bussed to the city's recreational fields to play. These are high school athletes who are not given proper coaches and will never have the chance to show college recruiters what they can do.

Yet this is a time to celebrate what has been done and forge ahead for our sister athletes. This really is an exciting time and we feel that we were fortunate enough to have been standing on the threshold of positive change. While promoting our sport of bobsledding, we were in attendance at the '96 Atlanta Games and saw the tide turn for women in sport. The world began to see what we've known for years: Female athletes are fun and exciting to watch! The world got to watch and fall in love with the group hugs, diving belly slides, victory dances, and cartwheels. Bob Hunter of the *Columbus Dispatch* put it this way: "When NBC finally got around to giving us more than a quick peek at the U.S. Olympic women's basketball team, we discovered why the network didn't put it on more often than it did. After all the hype NBC had given the men's Dream Team, it probably was embarrassed that the women played harder and with more emotion than the men, and that their games were a lot more exciting."[3] Olympic host Bob Costas repeated with some humor a viewer's comment about the Centennial Games: "You mean there are men competing, too?"

Of course, there are two sides to every coin. Reporter Cecil Harris observed: "There is no acceptable reason why women's soccer and women's softball didn't exist as Olympic sports until this year. Nor is there an acceptable reason why U.S. women still do not have money-earning opportunities in sports after their Olympic experiences end ... If the International Olympic Committee truly cared about promoting women at the Games, it wouldn't sanction inclusion of the NBA's multimillionaires."

Harris acknowledges that "things are improving, especially for U.S. women." But, he continues, "The Year of the Women at the Olympics? Not yet. That would require an almost equal number of male and female athletes with achievers of both genders praised for their efforts ... The Olympics have yet to reach that stage of maturity."[4]

Oh, but we are there. Do we have room to grow? Of course. But female athletes have firmly and definitively made their mark in the media and in the perception of the average sports fan. In the last few years, it has been female athletes, not males, who have graced the covers of such magazines as *Time, Newsweek, Health, TV Guide*, and a variety of business magazines. The U.S. women's soccer team, U.S. sprinter Marion Jones, and professional female boxers Laila Ali and Jacqai Frazier have captured the attention of the public. But, now the female athlete faces still another obstacle: not can she play, but what sport is acceptable and how she should play it! Step by step, play by play, one exceptional athletic feat after another, we are breaking down those barriers as well.

What has been dubbed as one of the greatest sports moments was in 1999 when the U.S. women's soccer team faced off against China in sudden death — a kick-off. The game ended in a tie as well as the overtime, leaving players, coaches, and fans so emotionally exhausted, it just didn't seem like it could get any more intense. A scoreless game went into overtime and, finally, into a shoot-out. It was so excruciatingly exhausting and exciting and overwhelming no one could believe it was happening, no one could look away. China shot first. It scored. Carla Overbeck

Soccer stud Brandi Chastain (photo by AP/Worldwide Photo).

shot and scored for the U.S. China shot and scored. Joy Fawcett went for the U.S. Another score! China was up. As U.S. goalkeeper Briana Scurry would later tell it, she had a feeling about the next kicker. She blocked the shot and 90,000 fans (plus over 40 million television viewers) went nuts. Kristine Lily put the U.S. up with a lead, scoring the next shot. China shot and scored again, leaving Mia Hamm to step up. She buried it in the bottom right corner, but China paid us back with the same shot. It was up to Brandi Chastain — the final shooter — to determine the outcome of the game. Mia Hamm and several other players have said that as soon as Chastain walked up to the ball they knew the U.S. was going to win. There was a confidence, a girl power that exuded from Chastain.

Personally, we never saw that. In fact, many people didn't see it. We all had our faces buried in our hands. If she missed, it would be another shoot-out and most of the viewing public was going to have to be hospitalized for extreme suspense trauma. If she made it ... well, dare any of us think it possible. There we were, millions of us were holding our breaths, crossing our fingers, and fighting back tears. Chastain took her shot. Score! The place went nuts. The U.S. team piled out on to the field and, there, in the midst of the insanity, Chastain did the unimaginable. She did the most cool, liberating, atta girl! thing ever done in the history of women's sports. She ripped off her shirt, fell to her knees, and flexed her well-toned, beautiful, tanned muscles for all the free world to see, marvel at, and celebrate. Posters of her pumping her fists were created overnight, magazine covers were made, and more girls than ever suddenly dreamed bigger, better, more fanciful than ever dreams. Michael Jordan, who? Suddenly, she was the single most-talked-about, sought-after, photographed athlete in the world.

'Atta girl!

For that moment, watching her pump her fists and flex her muscles, it was so much more than scoring a goal and winning a game. It was so much more than winning a World Cup. Her actions were a pure celebration of women in sport and how very, very far we've come. In that moment of splendor, we were lucky enough to have been watching as a family. We cried for our own advances and for what was to come for our daughters/nieces/granddaughters. Courage, innerstrength, and self-sufficiency are ours for the taking. *'Atta Girl!* tells girls and women of all ages and backgrounds how to embrace this power without having to lose their femininity, friends, or themselves.

Indeed, girls today benefit from the work of pioneers. So many battles have already been fought for them — fought and

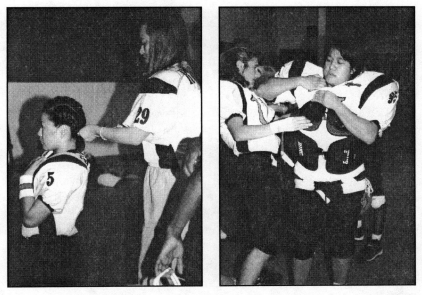

Left, Linebacker Ana Rosales braids teammate Tokie Ogita's hair before their professional debut. Right, Minori "Samoan" Jorel gets help with her pads (photos by Alexandra Powe Allred).

won. But there are still existing prejudices against females in sports, as in society, and a disproportionate number of girls drop out of sports by age 14. This is particularly tragic since these sports dropouts also drop out of high school more often, tend to abuse drugs and alcohol, and have more unwanted pregnancies than their sports-minded classmates.

One reason so many quit sports is negative pressure. As Donna Lopiano, executive director of the Women's Sports Foundation explains it, puberty is an especially difficult time for girls. "When [the adolescent girl] gets into puberty, she cares more about what her friends think, she is extremely vulnerable. Another girl can come up to her and say, 'You may score 20 points, but I have more dates.' Or a boy could say, 'I don't like a girl who has muscles.'" And the pressure does not go away with adolescence. But the girl who is able to withstand the pressure is more likely to grow into a confident and successful woman."

Historically, women have been discouraged from being assertive, "especially in business where they don't want to be labeled the big bitch," says sport psychologist Shelley Shaffer. "But once you've fought your way onto the playing field," Shaffer says, "you develop this sense of confidence and poise, that you have just as much right to be here as anyone else. And that carries over to the workplace, the community, and social settings."[5]

The women interviewed in this book reflect that philosophy. They speak candidly about the challenges they have faced as female athletes and professionals and how they have handled those challenges. They share stories — some funny, some sad, some inspirational — with which the reader can relate, stories we hope will serve as a catharsis for the wounded female ego and a catalyst for continuing efforts toward progress.

Our subjects' experiences have tended to begin with difficult non-sports challenges that carry over into their athletic lives, then arrive at some payoff. This book follows a similar pattern: what girls and women are up against when they choose to pursue athletics, how they overcome both non-sport and athletic challenges, and how they are rewarded. The rewards are many and varied.

Along the way, we also discovered how much fun we are all having — and should be having — enjoying sports and each other and, in some cases, rediscovering ourselves. For Michelle and Alex, perhaps one of the more enjoyable times in bobsledding was summer training camp. There were very few people in the training center, leaving us to ourselves. We were hard-working athletes and dedicated teammates but, shhhh, we also had fun doing things we would have never done in high school or college for fear of what others might have thought of us.

Picture this: For three days, power lifter and bobsledder Krista Ford has complained that she wanted a candy bar (something not provided by the training center's cafeteria). One of our teammates went into town and bought her a Butterfinger. After a hard day of pushing the dry-land sled, we dragged back to our room and found rock-solid, 185-pound Krista standing in our doorway, taunting us with her candy bar. "I've got a Buuuuutterfinger. I've got a Buuuuuttergfinger." As Alex walked by, she snatched it out of Krista's hand and tossed it to Michelle.

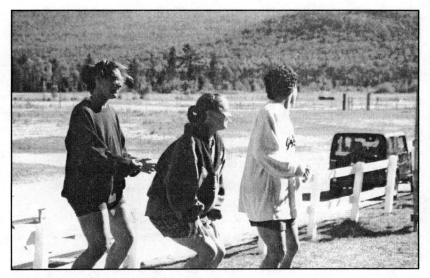

Future gold medalist Jill Bakken playing with teammates at the Olympic Training Center (photo by Alexandra Powe Allred).

Suddenly, Michelle jumped onto her bed, tossing it over Krista's head to fellow driver Jill Bakken. Alex, Michelle, and Jill then proceeded to tease one of the most powerful women in the world with a Butterfinger — a Butterfinger she really wanted.

Another teammate, Chrissy Spiezio, joined the fun. She grabbed the candy bar and ran out of the room. Soaking wet, Chrissy might tip the scale at 130 pounds. But, here she was, half-amused, half-terrified, running down the "do not run in the hallway" hallway of the Olympic Training Center with Krista thundering behind her. Like the women's Olympic basketball and volleyball teams who did each other's hair, or the Olympic swim team who got their nails done together, or veteran swimmer Janet Evans who did 14-year-old roommate Amanda Beard's laundry, here was a group of grown women truly enjoying each other's company, enjoying themselves — even acting like kids — and able to do so because of the unifying spirit of sports. That is what sports are all about: teamwork, camaraderie, friendship, confidence, and fun.

Let the reader beware! Because this is a women's sports book, there are female issues involved. Although we believe this book will benefit all who read it, there are bits of humor that are truly female. For example, the women's basketball team at Cal-Berkley was having a hard workout when everyone became aware of a maxi pad lying on the court. Everyone froze. Only the sound of a lone bouncing ball could be heard echoing off the gymnasium walls. As professional basketball player Trisha Stafford tells it, "We knew no one would claim it." But, suddenly, one of the team players broke from the pack, scooped it up, and ran to the locker room, leaving behind her the howls of her teammates, all rolling on the floor. Yeah, you probably had to be there, but for those women it was one of the funniest things they had ever seen. It is the kind of humor that perhaps only women can truly appreciate, but, in dealing with female athletes, we must deal with the issues that are part of us, too, even menstrual cycles, pregnancies, mood swings and tampons.

We do hope, however, that this book will appeal not only to women and to competitive athletes, but to men, recreational athletes, former athletes, and those who might have been but were not athletes. The message in the book is intended for athletes, coaches, parents, and fans. It is for women and men. We believe that the experiences of the women about whom we have written show that everyone wins — male and female — when girls and women reach their full capabilities in sport and when they learn to reach their full potentials in life.

Notes

1. Richard Zoglin, "The Girls of Summer," *Time* (August 12, 1996), 50.
2. Claudia Glenn Dowling, "The Other Dream Team," *TV Guide* (July 27- August 2, 1996), 17.
3. Bob Hunter, "Dream Team Couldn't Hold Candle To Women," *The Columbus Dispatch* (August 9,1996), 1Sports.
4. Cecil Harris, "Women Not Equal Yet At Olympics," *The Standard Star* (Westchester County, NY) (July 20,1996).
5. Gene Yasuda, "Olympics, pro teams give boost to girls' athletics," *The Columbus Dispatch* (August 9,1996), 3F.

Why Am I Doing This?

On assignment, freelance adventure writer Alex suddenly found herself at the bottom of a pile-on. At age 36 the mother of three small children had agreed to try out for a professional woman's football team and, assuming she made it, write about her experiences. She chose the Austin Rage football team and flew back and forth for several months between her home in Ohio to Austin, Texas.

With decent foot speed and strength, she was assigned the position of defensive end. It was there, playing at the right side, that Alex saw (and recognized) a reverse play in action and was able to recover a fumble. She heard an almost overly excited, "fummmbble!" and, realizing it to be her own voice, she dove on the ball. One body after another slammed against hers. She could feel fingers working away, trying to tear the ball from her grip. She grunted and struggled to keep the ball close to her chest, determined not to give it up.

Rolling around in the mud, fighting for the pigskin, a couple of questions came to mind. Had she lost her mind? What was she doing? Why was she doing this? For a story? She could be killed.

Gymnast Shannon Miller had been questioning her participation in sport for some time. "My back hurt, the pounding of practice was hard. I was bored. I mean, I had been in gymnastics for so long." She had already won five medals at the 1992 Barcelona Olympics (more than any other U.S. athlete) and three gold medals, including best all-around at Worlds. What more did she have to prove?

Nationally ranked cross-country athlete Rachael Scdoris received the bronze medal in the women's exhibition 400 meter at the USATF Olympic Track and Field Trials when she was 16 years old. Already a seasoned runner, this was to be a pivotal year for Scdoris. She was racking up the medals in running,

Rachael Scdoris, participating in the Olympic Torch Relay before the 2002 Winter Olympics (photo by Jerry Scdoris).

but it wasn't enough. She decided to enter a 500-mile International Pedigree Stage Stop Sled Dog race that would take her 11 days to complete in below-zero temperatures. It was a race that would carry her over the Rocky Mountains and across Wyoming armed with no more than a sled, her dogs, a sleeping bag, and a bivvy sack. In the middle of the grueling race Scdoris had her 16th birthday and she had to wonder why she was doing this. She was almost a decade younger than the next youngest competitor and this race was her first big race. She was, by all accounts, out of her league.

"I remember I just wanted to go to bed. I was so tired but the dogs needed to be fed, cared for, rubbed down. I was so tired and sore and I knew I had a 60-mile race the next day and I was thinking 'I want out of this race.'" And, she had other things running through her mind: the encouragement to try from her mentor-father Jerry Scdoris (see the 'Atta Boy chapter), the personal physical challenges she wanted to prove to herself (see The Athlete Within chapter), and the external pressures from others. "A lot of people were coming up with reasons I shouldn't race. I'm a teenager. I'm a girl. I'd tell them, 'Just watch me.'"

We all have different reasons for selecting and sticking with (or not) our sports of choice and the accompanying hard work. Long before that fateful pile-on with the Austin Rage, co-authors Alex and Michelle each had to ask themselves: "Why am I doing this?" While training for the U.S. Bobsled team we began at Accelerate Ohio, training home of professional football, baseball and hockey stars.

Then-31-year-old mother of two, Alex, was running on the giant treadmill while 33-year-old Michelle was bent over at the waist, trying hard not to think about throwing up. Alex, however, could think of little else. After an hour of running at 12 miles per hour on a 30-degree incline, we were exhausted. But our trainer was telling us to pick up our knees. "High knees. High knees." In our weary minds, our knees were very high. It was only a matter of time now before one or both of us threw up.

This training program may sound like a contradiction of our assertions about having fun. In truth, we complained and we moaned, but we loved every minute of it! Almost all the athletes we interviewed said the main reason they got into their sport was "because it seemed like fun." There were some exceptions. For example, baseball player Julie Croteau says she initially just wanted a high school varsity letter. Some athletes got into sports because an older brother said they couldn't. Some, such as 6'5" basketball star Lisa Leslie, took up a sport because someone assigned it to them. "You should play basketball!" Some, such as speed skater Pooch Harrington, even did it to meet boys. (To Pooch, Dutchie — skating around the frozen lake — was the cutest boy in the whole world.) Most, however, did it, and continue to do it, for fun.

The fun of sports, of course, is not limited to top athletes; all of the children we interviewed said they participate in sports for fun. While the parents may be signing kids up for exercise, social, and even baby-sitting purposes, the kids clearly play sports because they're having fun.

But as we get older, the fun becomes more complicated. Whatever the reasons we participate in sports, competitively or recreationally, whether for weight loss or rehabilitation or Olympic gold or just to get away from the kids (or parents), we've probably all wondered at some point, "Why am I doing this? Why do I bother?" Perhaps, despite running 15 miles a week, the weight is not coming off. Perhaps shin splints make every step painful. Perhaps the kids have started tagging along. Whatever the reasons to start, and whatever the reasons to continue or to stop, they are sure to be of a very personal nature.

But when these internal choices are reinforced by external pressure (such as sexual harassment or family discouragement), the resulting decision to quit or continue takes on much larger dimensions. Perhaps the kids are only tagging along because their father refuses to watch them. This is the usual sort of resistance women face. And females who try to participate in male-dominated sports face even greater adversity. The young woman sprinting the stadium stairs in 90-degree heat for football practice may find herself, at the very least, the victim of verbal sexual abuse. ("This isn't a girl's sport." "Do you want to be a boy?") She is questioned endlessly about her motives: "Why are you doing this?" "Do you just want to rock the boat?" And so she questions herself and the sanity of what she's doing. Is it worth all the criticism? Does anyone else think this is a good idea? Does anyone support her?

The same cannot be said of boys for whom participation and success in sports is not questioned. For females, however, resistance and self-doubt are normal. So why do some girls and women ride out the resistance and stick with their sports and convictions? There are as many reasons as there are female athletes.

Sue 'Suicide' Horton vividly remembers following her older brother to football practices and games. More than anything

Sue "Suicide" Horton being applauded after an amazing catch (photo by Alexandra Allred).

in the world, she wanted to be able to don those same pads and play. It looked challenging, exciting, fast-paced, and something she was sure she could do. Years later, still tagging along to her brother's games, a coach spied her throwing nice spirals on the sideline and told her in another year, he could use a player like her. It was a promise that took her breath away.

"For an entire year I waited to see that coach again and drove my family crazy talking about it," says Horton. "It was all I could talk about, think about." She practiced throwing the ball every chance she got. So, when the following season came, she could hardly wait to talk to the coach and show him how good, how improved, how ready she was. "He patted me on the shoulder and said, "Sorry, girls can't play." She was heartbroken. While the coach simply thought he was being nice to her the year prior, he set her up for her first real disappointment in life.

Horton continued a sports life, minus football, and is one of the best personal trainers in a prestigious fitness club in Dallas, Texas. "But all I really wanted was to play football. Even as an adult, it was all I thought about." It just so happened she was on hiatus from work, visiting her mother in upstate New York, when she heard there was a women's professional football league and one of the teams was to be in Austin, Texas.

"I called the coach and begged for a tryout. When I heard about the Rage tryouts, they had already started the mini-camps. Coach said that she didn't think so. I was too small, and she really wanted bigger players." At a generous 5'3", 115 pounds, "Suicide" (aka Horton) knew she would be one of the smaller players in the league, but there are some things that defy size. One is tenacity.

Horton couldn't stand it; she called back and began to barter with the coach. "What if I try out with the New York team here?" she reasoned. "If I make the cut here, will you give me a look?" By the end of that telephone conversation, Coach Dee Kennamer of the Austin Rage sensed there was more to Suicide Sue than her 5'3" stature and told her to come to Austin for a look. Normally a shy, reserved person, Horton was suddenly unwilling to take 'no' for an answer. Playing against six-foot Amazons with NFL-sized biceps, size means nothing to Horton, who plays with incredible speed and determination.

U.S. power lifter Carrie Boudreau also defies the impossible. After being diagnosed with severe asthma and scoliosis, Boudreau was told by her doctor that exercise would help strengthen her spine and her lungs. The doctor probably did not have power lifting in mind, yet Boudreau refused to let a medical condition slow her down. In fact, Boudreau — who "thrives on things stacked against" her — is the world record holder in her weight class and, according to *The Guinness Book of World Records*, the strongest woman in the world pound for pound. At 4'11", weighing in at 123 pounds, Carrie has deadlifted 500 pounds.

Jackie Joyner-Kersee, also an asthmatic, knew at age nine that either athletics or the corner liquor store would run her life. Living in a crime-ridden neighborhood in East St. Louis with a liquor store on every comer, Joyner-Kersee made the local YMCA her safehaven and never gave up her dream of being the best athlete she could be. When young Jackie told her teachers she wanted to go to UCLA on an athletic scholarship, she was told she couldn't — that her grades weren't good enough, that she didn't have enough money. Undaunted, Joyner-Kersee studied and trained harder than she ever had and received a basketball scholarship to UCLA (where she met track coach and future husband Bob Kersee). To those teachers who had not believed, Joyner-Kersee proved that anything is possible if you work hard enough. In 1994, she was named "The Best Female Athlete Ever" by *Sports Illustrated*.

Julie Croteau of Manassas, Virginia, also had a lot to prove to nonbelievers. The first woman to play men's college varsity baseball and later coach NCAA baseball, she was introduced to T-ball by her mother at the tender age of five. Mrs. Croteau had no visions of her daughter becoming a pioneer, but simply wanted little Julie out of her hair for the summer. But by age 17, Croteau had become an outstanding first basewoman — so outstanding, in fact, that the high school varsity baseball coach told her she was good enough to play varsity ball. But he also told her that she could not play because she was a girl.

This did not sit well with Croteau, whose parents had raised her to believe in herself, to be the best that she could be. So Croteau and her family sued the school for the right to play. While making national headlines, Croteau drew upon her family and a very close circle of friends for support. "We lost the suit," Croteau says. "At [age] 17, that was very hard to understand. The truth is, at first, all I wanted was that varsity letter. At the time, I didn't even know the meaning of feminism." But being denied the opportunity to play ball quickly became a challenge about principle. Like so many other female pioneers, Croteau started out quietly, letting the storm within her grow until she could not be contained.

The lawsuit, and subsequent ostracism at school, proved to be a hard lesson. Croteau had always believed she was equal to boys. It was difficult to discover that being better than most of the boys was not only not good enough, it wasn't acceptable. Doubly painful was hearing the coach at Osborn Park High School deny under oath that he had ever told Croteau she was good enough to play. This was particularly ridiculous because Croteau had been invited to play semipro ball. (And she would later go on to be the first woman to play on a men's collegiate baseball team — at St. Mary's College in Maryland). Still, the lesson was a hard one and Croteau was not the only one punished. To this day, Croteau believes that many of her good friends "ended their baseball careers and, for one, the chance to be homecoming queen," by supporting her. "But even at 17, we knew it was the right thing."

A reporter covering the case agreed. And he was more than just another reporter covering the court case. He was also the co-owner of the Fredericksburg Giants, an all-male semipro baseball team in Fredericksburg, Virginia — and he offered Crouteau the chance for a tryout. She took it and made the team. "Earning a spot," Croteau says, "surprised a lot of people and vindicated me a little."

Never again did she question herself. During her five years with the Giants, she says she was treated like just another player. Then she played with the Silver Bullets, an all-female professional baseball team. Unlike other women who had to request a tryout, Croteau was recruited by the Bullets' coaching staff.

A torn rotary cuff in the spring of 1994 led her to sports commentary for Liberty Sports. Then, in that same year, she was offered a coaching position for the University of Massachusetts's Division I baseball team. No woman had ever coached men's baseball before.

Again, Croteau found herself in the sports spotlight with people questioning her ability and motives. But this time she was not one of them. "What have I learned over the years?" Croteau asks. "To trust myself, be true to myself. People stared and there was some harassment," she acknowledges. "It was a hard job, but I reminded myself that men do this all the time. I could, too."

Such a radical idea — If men can do this, I can, too — has gotten plenty of us in trouble, but it also has opened worlds of opportunities. Alex and Michelle got involved in bobsledding because people told us we couldn't, that it was not a sport for women. That drove us. We did it because we were determined to see women's bobsledding become an Olympic event, if not for us, then, for the young women and girls who followed us. And we succeeded. In the 2002 Games, women's bobsledding debuted as an Olympic sport. Not only did the U.S. women take the gold, it was the first gold for the United States in over 50 years and only the women would strike it! We watched the Salt Lake City bobsledding events like proud parents because we knew that those young women sliding were reaping the fruits of our labor. Even better, golden driver Jill Bakken was the only remaining member of that first women's team. Watching her win the gold offered great closure for many who fought the fight. We know the answer now to the question we may have asked in frustration then. Why were we doing this? We did it to prove that women can; we did it to force open another door for women and girls.

Whatever reasons the athletes we have interviewed have had for getting into sports, all of the results were successful and the long-term benefits often phenomenal. The roads paved by all the pioneers mentioned in this book, by all pioneers everywhere, have made life's journeys smoother for the girls and women who have followed. And women who stick with their sports and convictions are pioneers. Every girl or woman who takes to the mound or tosses the old pigskin or pulls in a rebound is debunking stereotypes, breaking down barriers. In fact, every female who participates in any form of physical activity is special. As Olympic rhythmic gymnast Wendy Hilliard points out, all of us, "from tennis-great Billie Jean King to a mall-walking grandmother, we're all accomplished. We're strong, healthy, competent, confident, and empowered."'

When a girl or woman begins a new sport, any sport, she embarks upon that journey toward empowerment. She often must venture into uncharted territories, but when she succeeds she shows not only little boys that little girls can throw a ball as well as they, but she also shows little girls — proving to them that they can do anything, giving them the self-confidence to believe in themselves. And this is the ultimate reward.

During the first week at Accelerate Ohio, we pushed our bodies beyond any level we had ever dreamed possible because we had a goal. We wanted the thrills of the bobsled ride, and we wanted the respect of the other bobsledders. While our trainer screamed "high knees" at us and our 30-something-year-old bodies responded with creaks and groans, 11-year-

Olympians Jean Racine (front, middle) and Jill Bakken (front, right) with fellow teammate Alexandra (far back, left) next to her sister, Michelle (photo from the collection of Alexandra Powe Allred).

old Colleen Clark sat quietly waiting her turn. Barely sweating, barely breathing, she was in this sprint-training program because her brothers were; she thought it seemed like "fun."

Clark already understands that there is often a double standard for male and female athletes — that females are not supposed to be both tough and attractive. Yet she seems to have found the appropriate balance between who she is and what she wants. Yes, at the age of 11. "I want to play sports and be a girlie-girl," she says with a wry smile. Her brother Greg,13, teases her because she is always painting her nails and doing her hair. Still, she held her own on the treadmill at 10 miles per hour and a 20-degree incline. "I can be feminine and a great athlete at the same time," says Colleen. When asked to name female role models, Colleen chose Gabrielle Reece. Her brother Greg, for all his teasing, chose Colleen and Cindy Crawford. Sometimes we just don't see ourselves as others do.

Why Colleen? "She's a straight-A student, she plays select soccer," he shrugs. "She's really dedicated; she's just really good."

Girlie-girl or tomboy, the question remains why do most of us do this? The name-calling and stereotyping of "manly" female athletes can be difficult to tolerate, particularly for young athletes. As Alex stepped into the world of women's professional football, she found people were either incredibly pleased for her, thinking this a great opportunity for female athletes, or completely put off by it. "Why?" one man asked. There seems to be no middle ground with female athletes.

In her book, Pipher (quoting Simone de Beauvoir) points out that adolescent girls too often "stop being and start seeming."[1] They bend to social pressures, putting away their independent selves and adopting properly feminine personas.

This is why sports are so important. Sports give girls and women self-worth and confidence; they help them to be the persons they can and want to be. We need to start helping more girls and women stay in sports, so that they may be strong and happy and become role models for girls who follow them.

And what about Cindy Crawford, one of Greg's two female role models? We talked with her trainer Radu Teodorescu,

The WPFL in action (photo by Alexandra Allred).

who confirmed Greg's belief that Crawford serves as a definite role model. Cindy Crawford? Really? "Cindy became a person who explores," Radu says, "a doer, an athlete." When Crawford first went to Radu, she needed to get in shape for a calendar. Nothing more. What happened next is very common in athletics. Crawford got an attitude. "She developed an immense self-confidence, a feeling of power." As Crawford herself puts it, "The training transcended the physical. It taught me that I'm powerful — that I could conquer the world when I walked out of the gym."[2]

There is another edge to "why am I doing this?" As perverse as this may seem, it is the internal arguing — "I can't do this! This is too hard." — that becomes so rewarding when we can finally say, "I did it! I did it!"

Imagine the heat, the pain, the fatigue, the internal yearning to stop because everything hurts so much and the external pressure to give up because other people think what you are doing is foolish, dangerous and/or plain dumb. Welcome to the tryouts for the Austin Rage football team. You could see it in the eyes of so many of the women who were new to the sport and did not feel comfortable talking to the other rookies.

You could see people looking nervously around, wondering if they were more nervous than everyone else. The likelihood of getting severely injured was very real, and for what? At the time, the grassroots WPFL (Women's Professional Football League) was paying athletes $1 per game. One dollar!

Why go on then? Why do this to ourselves?

When we spoke to celebrity trainer and a celebrity in his own right, Billy Blanks (creator of TaeBo), he answered these questions. We do this because there is an athlete within wanting to get out. Whether training for the Olympics, preparing to do movie stunts (as some of his clients do), or just wanting to push yourself to the limits, there is an athlete wanting to get out. "They've done their time watching other people do things as they sit on the couch!" Trainer Radu agrees. The metamorphosis that comes over the trainees says it all. "They are different people," Radu says. "Stronger, healthier, happier, more productive. Exercise becomes a component of preparing for everything else in your life." And, he points out, the beautiful thing about female athletes is, "they are pure. They do sport for the love of it. You never hear about a woman athlete holding out on her team for more money." Well, almost never. This is certainly true of the players from the WPFL, who are willing to risk life and limb for the love of the game. In fact, it was after a great game (Austin Rage vs. New England Storm) when Alex was recounting the stats and athletic feats of the game to her husband, Robb, that he was struck with the thunderbolt. She was telling him how Dori Livingston made an amazing run, flying down the sidelines and right before her own teammates, did a pretty little stutter step, faking out two New England players and gaining another 10 yards before going down. Livingston was so agile, so light on her feet, so swift and clean it was like watching Jerry Rice in his prime and her teammates roared with appreciation as she moved. There was instant mimicking on the sidelines. "That's what you call a st-st-stutterstep," joked defensive end Sherron Day, pretending to throw a few fakes of her own. Cornerback Dawn Back joined in, walking toward other players, "How you doin'?" stutter stepping around people, drawing even more grins. It was just so pretty to watch.

"Yeah, but," Robb marveled for a moment, "you act like it's never been done before. People do that all the time in the NFL." So animated was Alex, a lifelong watcher of the NFL, that Robb misunderstood.

"But now it's our turn," Alex responded, patting her chest. It's our turn. The stutter steps, the fist pumping, showboating, slam-dunk, grand-slam hitting, touchdown-making plays are ours!

Imagine how Colleen Clark is going to feel when she finishes her program (the same program professional football players have struggled through), takes her speed test, and realizes what she can do! There'll be no stopping her! It's her turn. And, as it turns out, it was still Shannon Miller's turn. Now, looking back, she says she is so happy she continued on with the sport she loves. She would go on to the 1996 Atlanta Olympic Games to win two more golds, become part of the Magnificent Seven, and turn pro. "It's not about the medals," she insists. Instead, it is about living a dream, becoming a better person, and serving as a role model to other little girls.

Nancy Lieberman-Cline, former Olympian and WNBA player, and the first woman to be inducted into the Basketball Hall of Fame, believes so strongly in the importance of keeping girls in sports that she encourages communities to hold awards and grants banquets for their female athletes. "Three great things happen when those young athletes are honored," she says. "Girls and young women know their

Shannon Miller (photo by Sheryl Shade of Shade Global).

participation in sports is valued, encouraging the development of pride and confidence; people who learn of the sports achievements of girls and women are more likely to support them; and more girls will be encouraged to take part in sports."[3]

Encouraging the development of pride and confidence in females is so important. Nancy Woodhull, senior vice president of the Freedom Forum, co-founder of *USA Today*, and former president of Gannett News Services, had this advice for young females getting into sports today: "The important thing is to set realistic challenges and goals and work to realize those goals. Not every young soccer player will grow up to be a Mia Hamm. Not every young girl who dedicates herself to track and field will be Jackie Joyner-Kersee. If her goals are achievable, however, and she succeeds in reaching those goals, any young woman athlete has won something as important as a gold medal. The important part is realizing young women can succeed in a broad spectrum of activities and knowing what it takes to do it. You may not quite have the natural ability to be a star, but if you learn that discipline, conditioning and commitment will improve your game, no matter what level you are at or what game you compete in, you've gained valuable knowledge for the rest of your life."

Across the board, all the top high school female athletes we spoke to were on their school's honor rolls. Becoming disciplined and committed in sport has clearly carried over into their everyday lives. For many, it is a quiet confidence. They know they can succeed in their sports. They know they can handle their studies. But when we asked many of the athletes about their grades, they would shyly say, "I do OK." Always the parent would pipe up, "She's an honor student."

When Allie Sizler's parents were called into a parent/teacher conference with her second-grade teacher, they were told "not to expect too much" of their daughter. Allie had been labeled "slow" because of an undiagnosed hearing impairment. As an honor roll student, the 15-year-old all-state basketball player was receiving recruitment letters from colleges around the country. "The thing about Allie is she is an extremely dedicated and focused little kid," says father John SizIer. "She gives 150 percent effort in everything she does. At a very young age, she's very driven by athletics. That crosses over into her academics. Sports have really helped her with time management and to keep her priorities in line."

Rachael Scdoris is up before 6 a.m., feeding and exercising her dogs. With more than 100 dogs in her father's kennel, Scdoris has her hands full. She is at school by 7:30 a.m., running cross-country (sometimes up to seven miles a day), back home for homework and more sled training and kennel responsibilities. All while juggling her responsibilities as a Bend Winter Fest Snow Princess, 3.8 GPA student, high school chorus member, and spokesperson for a variety of sports products, including Atta Boy dog food (oh, the irony).

But, she's not the only Rachael to rock the sports world. Rachael Myllymaki turned pro in the Professional Rodeo Cowboy Association at the age of nine. Nine! She traveled the rodeo circuit; competed against some of the strongest adult rodeo riders in the country; hauled trailers, horses, and equipment and did her homework. She was an honor student all through school and was given a full scholarship to the University of Montana.

"I learned to just sit myself down and do what needed to be done," she says. Like mastering barrel racing, Myllymaki has also mastered her schoolwork. She is an example of Lieberman-Cline's point that sports build confidence on all levels in girls and young women.

This point is particularly critical at a time when the rates of obesity in children and the incidences of anorexia and bulimia in teens are on the rise in this country. Girls who exercise are far more likely to have positive body images and healthy relationships, are 92 percent less likely to use drugs, and 80 percent less likely to have unwanted pregnancies. They are three times more likely to graduate from high school and, by exercising as little as two hours a week, have lower incidences of breast cancer later in life. Pretty powerful plugs for sports.

The importance of young female athletes feeling significant and valued cannot be stressed enough. Particularly during adolescence, when so many girls are so unhappy and self-critical, imagine the glory of feeling special, needed, and important. And, these feelings and benefits of physical activity certainly are not limited to young females. Menopause, the gradual change women experience from the reproductive to the nonreproductive years of life, can bring on many physiological changes. Hot flashes, fatigue, depression, weight gain, and irritability often are experienced. Osteoporosis and arteriosclerosis, changes that often occur later in life, can be devastating to a woman. The answer?

You've got it, whether in midlife or later — exercise.

Cardiovascular exercise and weight maintenance can control mood swings and hot flashes, stimulate bones to retain the needed minerals to keep them strong and healthy, and reduce the risk of coronary artery disease through loss of abdominal fat, to name a few benefits.

At the age of 82, Mary Grace tested for her 2nd degree black belt. Just like the other black belt candidates testing, Ms. Grace was expected to break boards and one cinder block. As we watched in awe, this remarkable woman did all her required kicks, punches, sparring routines, and board breaking. When she came to the cinder block break requirement, she failed to break the brick on her first attempt. Then, Ms. Grace gave a loud *ki-yup* (yell) and broke the brick, and a thunderous cheer echoed throughout the gymnasium. Even the judges allowed themselves to smile and nod their heads. At the age of 82, Ms. Grace stood as a reminder to us how important it is to support all athletes. She was rightly proud; not only had she worked hard for this moment, she had given all the rest of us something to look forward to. The creed of the marital arts is, you don't get older, you get better and wiser!

Ms. Grace is committed to her exercise program because it is good for her health, keeping her bones stronger and circulation better, and it keeps her mind fresh. "I don't do this for anyone but myself. I have made amazing friends and have learned to love myself. I am an amazing woman!!" No arguments here.

Seventy-four-year-old Helen Klein of Rancho Cordova, California, another inspiration for younger women, has taken physical fitness to a higher plane and is educating women about the benefits of exercise along the way. "There's too much separation between the mind and the body in our culture. What's the sense of living to 100 if you can't move?" An "endurance athlete extraordinaire," she receives weekly fan mail. And she is taken

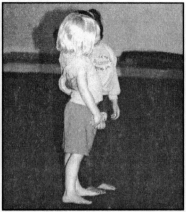

Some of the greatest friendships can develop from participation in sports (photos by Alexandra Allred).

quite seriously by her far younger competition. At the end of the 1995 Eco-Challenge, a 373-mile, 9-day race, a cameraman caught footage of a team that had passed Klein. "They were resting," Klein recalls, "when one of them looked up and saw me running down the hill. They were frantic. I heard one of them say, 'Oh my God! Here she comes! Get your packs! We gotta go!'"[4]

Klein, like so many of the athletes we talk about in this book, has bucked society's notion of "proper feminine behavior." Says the great-grandmother, "I was programmed to believe I'd be an old lady who couldn't walk a mile, who played bridge, and went to lunches." Instead, she demonstrates to women that there is no limit to what they can do.

In some regards, physical activity is even more important as we get older — as women and as athletes. Most athletes believe that the talents of female athletes have not fully begun to be tapped until the late 20s or early 30s. Trisha Stafford of the now-defunct American Basketball League's San Jose Lasers told us, "I don't think women blossom as athletes until after our college years. No one ever sees that. As we get older, we are more in sync with our capabilities. Everything is in harmony"

When we repeated this to gold medallist sprinter Gwen Torrence, she agreed wholeheartedly. "Exactly! We, as women, get better with age. We learn more about our bodies and get more confident as we age. Men come into sports thinking they're God's gift. Women don't. We build up to it. Women in their late 20s and early 30s are the medal winners. Gold medal winners are always older. In track and field, our peak years are 26 to 33 years." In fact, as we spoke to amazing athletes Mia Hamm, WNBA's newest hotshot Jackie Stiles, Marion Jones, and fitness pro Cynthia Bridges, we found that they all agree that the female athlete — if given the opportunity to prove herself — simply gets better with age.

For this reason, Torrence advises young athletes to take their time in training. Torrence says she hates to see high school athletes pushing themselves too hard, and worse, coaches pushing unrealistic goals. "What kids don't realize is it's more than just running fast in a straight line. It takes time to mature." When they push and train too hard too soon, she warns, they burn out before their peak. Her advice: enjoy yourself!

Beyond better health, better grades, and better relationships as reasons to join sports, there is another recurring theme: that special friendship, the bonding that female athletes share. Athletes have told us story after story about experiencing special "moments" with their teammates. During the Atlanta Games, swimmers Amanda Beard and Kristine Quance chased each other around their dorm with magic markers, coloring each other until they couldn't see their skin. *Sports Illustrated* reporter Alexander Wolff wrote of the 2000 Games gold-medal-winning women's basketball team: "In the Sunday's final, the American women parceled out 30 assists and mounted the medal stand holding hands, a gesture of togetherness that evidently hadn't crossed the minds of their male counterparts the night before. Gilt, you could say, by association."[5] In fact, reporter after reporter noted the closeness these women shared.

The U.S. women's soccer team was called "the team of sisters." And they were the team of aunts as well, sharing parental responsibilities for teammate Joy Fawcett's baby daughter.

Four-time Olympic champion speed skater Bonnie Blair confessed to us that perhaps more than anything else, she misses her teammates and the competitors from other countries who became her friends over the years. "I've gone from seeing these people every day to occasionally having lunch with them. I really miss them." U.S. luge veteran and four-time Olympian Cammy Myler agrees that after more than a decade of competitive sliding, she is going to deeply miss the friends she made all over the world. They are her second family.

Tennis superstar Monica Seles also has made many friends during her career. And she has learned that true friends are there for you during the bad times as well as the good. Indeed, she learned who her true friends were during a terrible crisis which began on April 30, 1993. During a break between sets of an important match, a deranged sports fan stunned the world when he stabbed Seles in the back. Although her wounds healed fairly quickly, the emotional scars of the attack kept her from competition for more than two years. As Seles tells it, "Night after night, I woke up in a sweat with my mother standing over me, frightened by my cries. I would ask her to sleep in my bed, to hold me like a baby."[6] Returning to tennis seemed terrifying to Seles. Slapping the ball back and forth with her brother, Zoltan, was one thing. To compete before thousands on an open court was something else.

Then, in February 1995, Martina Navratilova called Seles. Navratilova was flying to Florida for a tennis tournament and wondered if she could visit Seles. "Maybe we could hit a few balls for a while." They did. Navratilova asked Seles to return to the game, assuring her that everyone missed her. And as she stood to leave, Navratilova unclasped a diamond tennis bracelet from her wrist, telling Seles she wanted her to have it. Seles protested.

"When you come back, you can return it to me," Navratilova told her warmly. It was just the kind of encouragement Seles needed. In July 1995, Seles played in an exhibition game in Atlantic City against — who else? — Martina Navratilova. Whether it was the bracelet or, more likely, the support of a fellow athlete that gave Seles the courage, she was back. Seles won the match, and as Navratilova hugged and congratulated her, she told Seles, "You're back, girl!" Seles happily gave back the bracelet.

There are so many payoffs in sports — better health, strong bodies, strong minds, confidence, discipline, healthy relationships. And fellow bobsledder Courtney O'Neil told us about another payoff. At 36, O'Neil had never been an elite athlete. In fact, she had had a lifetime of abusing her body. Drugs and alcohol had nearly ended her life on several occasions. Ruined relationships, financial woes, rocky employment records, DUIs and, subsequently, arrests played a much larger part in her life than she had planned. There seemed to be no controlling her own life while drugs and alcohol were involved.

In 1985, O'Neil woke up in a motel in Lake Placid, New York. She was in room number 0. She had received a DUI, had no car, and only a few fleeting memories of the night before. She had to ask her mother to drive from Connecticut to get her. That was the turning point in her life.

In 1995, she returned to Lake Placid to make the U.S. women's bobsled team, having been sober for 10 years and in training. As each athlete met and discussed her workout regimen with Olympic weight trainer Jon Osbeck, O'Neil shared hers.

"What's your sport?" Osbeck asked. Most were soccer or track and field.

"Well," O'Neil smiled, "I smoked for 18 years."

Later in the week, O'Neil traveled alone back to the fateful motel. She found room number 0 and sat outside, watching the door for some time. Look at me now, she thought as she returned to her room at the Olympic Training Center. Talk about payoff!

Notes

1. Mary Pipher, *Reviving Ophelia*, 22.
2. Radu Teodorescu, with Maura Rhodes, *Radu's Simply Fit* (NY: Cader Books, 1996), 3.
3. Nancy Lieberman-Cline, "Communities should support, honor girls in sports," *The Dallas Morning News* (July 11, 1996), 2B.
4. Jane Gottesman, "Your Grandma Wears Hiking Boots," *Women's Sports & Fitness* (May 1997), 51.

5. Alexander Wolff, "Power Grab," *Sports Illustrated* (August 12, 1996), 59.

6. Monica Seles with Nancy Ann Richardson, "Advantage: Courage," *Reader's Digest* (September 1996, 130-31

There's No Crying in Football, Ladies!

As bobsledders, we endured the bumps and bruises of the sport. We could handle that. More difficult were the negative responses we got from fellow male athletes. When we made the U.S. women's bobsled team, there had never been an official U.S. team before us. There were many who felt women should not be in such a brutal and demanding sport. Jill Bakken was once told by a coach that she would never be in the Olympics in his lifetime. But when she stood on the Olympic medal podium in Salt Lake City ready to receive her gold medal with teammate Vonetta Flowers, in his lifetime, Jill demonstrated the power of perseverance. She lived and fought the battle and was on hand to declare victory ... in her lifetime. How glorious.

It was a beautiful image that Alex took with her as she stepped up to her next challenge: women's professional football. However different the sport, many of the rules (or stigmas) were the same. In women's football, she faced an old dichotomy: If you try to please everyone, you end up pleasing no one. As women football players, if you are too nice, you'll get stuffed by a fellow player. If you are too macho, you risk negative stereotyping by outsiders. One could say, 'who cares,' but in a world where sponsorship and media perception can equal critical support, image is everything.

After the official Austin Rage roster was announced, the team came together early one Saturday morning for its first WPFL practice, complete with our introduction to team leader Jennifer Monsevais.

"Look," she eyed her team, "we had some problems last year with people getting their feelings hurt. I don't want to have to deal with that again. I can be hard on people. I can yell and curse." As she spoke, Rosemary Satterwhite, a tough-looking defensive tackle nodded behind Monsevais. "If you screw up a play, I'm going to tell you about it. If anyone has a problem about being yelled at or can't handle it, speak now." Everyone shuffled her feet.

A very tall, striking woman, Monsevais looks more like a teenage model (although she's actually 25) than the fierce football player she is known to be. "I like being a girl," she feels the need to explain. "I like dressing up and

Before the pre-adolescent girl 'hears' all the negative societal messages, there is nothing she can't accomplish (photo by Alexandra Allred).

putting on makeup. But not here. Here there is no whining or crying. This is football, ladies. So, leave your panties at the gate!"

Welcome to the real deal.

While image plays a big role in women athletes' lives, there is a time when girls can be themselves — a time we need to consider and to preserve. The average preadolescent girl is oblivious to negative societal messages. She is busy climbing trees, challenging boys to arm wrestling matches, and usually winning. She challenges boys verbally as well. She is happy and confident and assertive.

So what happens? Why, so often, does that assertive child grow into a passive adolescent? In a brief span of time, as she crosses the line separating preadolescence and adolescence, childhood and womanhood, that young girl completely changes her demeanor. Gone is the tough-talking, tree-climbing tomboy; enter the "prom queen."

Schools play a major role in promoting this prom queen image of the quiet and pretty girl. While much has improved since that 1992 study conducted by the American Association of University Women (AAUW) entitled "How Schools Short-change Girls," girls still report feeling somewhat displaced in the classroom and school hallways — the social runway for the geeks, jocks, beauties, and freaks. Ahhh, some things seem never to change. In its study, the AAUW showed that boys are twice as likely to be viewed as role models, five times more likely to be called on by the teacher, and 12 times more likely to speak up in class than girls. Classroom material is slanted to appeal to boys rather than girls, having three times as many boy-oriented stories. The study also found that boys are given more detailed instruction by their teachers and praised for academic work, while girls are praised for appearance and behavior.

And the bias is not only gender-focused; it has racial overtones as well. While studies have shown black girls to be more assertive in the classroom and to have better self-images than white girls, they are seen as boisterous and unruly for speaking out, and — as a result — are ignored more by teachers. In a study of first-graders, black girls were praised for social maturity, while white girls were praised for academic success. When compared with white boys, the black girls were praised for their accomplishments, while the white boys were reprimanded for not reaching their full potential.

While great efforts have been made to rectify this in public schools since the release of this study, some girls and their parents still complain that more work needs to be done to make the classroom an even playing field. Boys continue to receive more one-on-one attention in school. While white boys still receive more positive reinforcement than black or Hispanic boys, boys on the whole receive more encouragement than girls.

The statistics tell us discrimination is a very real problem, but somebody forgot to tell that to Jenna Brader.

Week two at Accelerate Ohio found Alex and Michelle not only still thinking about throwing up, but also wondering how exhausted a person had to be to actually die. Both the speed and incline of the treadmill had increased as had the intensity level of the workouts. While we huddled near the water fountain, wondering why the trainers were trying to kill us, then

11-year-old Jenna stood by the treadmill, cool and confident, daring the trainers to make her workout too hard.

"Harder?" Michelle wheezed to Alex. "Did she say harder?" We looked suspiciously at this newcomer. "Who is she?" Alex asked a kid who had sauntered over for a drink of water.

"She's my sister," he told us proudly. "She plays all-state basketball."

Basketball? At age 11, Jenna stood four feet, six inches and weighed in at about 70 pounds.

She may have been small in stature, but basketball and speaking out have never been problems for Jenna. She certainly fits the typical female jock profile: honor student, healthy, articulate, confident. So confident, in fact, that at one point during an interview we asked her mother if she was sure Jenna was only 11. Jenna's not afraid to speak out in class or shine on the court.

"I wish you could see her when she plays," her older brother, Joshua, said of Jenna. "When she plays three-on-three, Jenna is up against girls twice her size and she gets the ball almost every time. I'll take her to the 'Y' to play, and she'll start dribbling the ball, passing it between her legs. She'll be all decked out in her Nike stuff, the wristbands and everything. Grown men will stop and watch her play. She'll be shooting three-pointers and guys will come up to me and say, 'Is that your sister?'"

She looked like a little doll: creamy skin that only a Campbells soup kid could have, big brown puppy eyes, a perfect little nose. But on the court, she was — as her brother describes her — "an animal." "Jenna," he said with understatement, "is real aggressive."

Not much intimidated Jenna. Not even adolescence. She understood that it is a time of physical change and was ready for the challenge. Not all girls are so confident. In fact, most girls have some trouble during this time. For just as their bodies are beginning to metamorphose, hips rounding, fat-cells increasing, and breasts developing, girls are bombarded with the media female image. Rail-thin models and actresses with big breasts push anything and everything from potato chips to toilet cleaners. It is impossible for any female to escape this self-image sabotage. Girls focus on what is everywhere before them: the perfect female image. Perfect body. Perfect face. Perfect hair. Perfect clothes. Adolescent girls fixate on material things and obsess about their bodies. While boys in puberty think, "I'm getting strong," girls think, "I'm getting fat."

Feeling fat, especially in comparison to their male peers, is very often understandable. Dr. Wayne Westcott, fitness consultant and researcher for the YMCA, conducted a body composition analysis on second-, fifth-, eighth-, and eleventh-grade students in the Hanover, Massachusetts, public schools. Of 630 students studied, the average percentage of body fat for boys in all four grades was below the recommended level for males (15 percent). The girls' average percent of body fat increased from 21 percent in grade two to 24 percent in grade eleven.[1] While Westcott explains this as a normal pubescent change in female body composition, girls still think, "I'm fat." As unbelievable as this sounds, the National Eating Disorders Association has reported that by the fourth grade as many as 40 percent of girls have dieted.

So it's easy to see why so many girls give up on sports. It's pretty tough to muster up confidence when one is obsessed and mortified about changing body parts. It is a confusing time.

This book's co-authors serve as examples of the confusing female images we see in the media. While a preadolescent Michelle wore mini-dresses (it was the 70s, after all) and ran with limp wrists, the younger Alexandra was the terror of the neighborhood. While Michelle collected butterflies and dog statues and constantly fussed with her hair, Alex played war and saved her stitches (acquired from jumping off low buildings) so she could throw them in her sister's hair.

While Michelle spent hours in front of the mirror perfecting her curling iron skills and trying to look like Charlie's Angels' Farrah Fawcett, Alex was doing things like walking the narrow banister of her family apartment's eighth-story balcony on a dare.

Our flower and football player roles were set at an early age. But, then, a strange thing happened. While Michelle was a late bloomer (devastating by prom queen standards), Alex developed early (devastating by tomboy standards).

Every night Alex would beat her chest, hoping this would stunt her breasts' growth. And she would stand on her desk chair and jump off, landing on her bottom in the hope of keeping her hips from changing. Her thinking was it really hurt to do that, so surely it had to stop the growth process. While Michelle (along with millions of other girls) was performing her ritualistic "I must, I must, I must increase my bust" exercise, Alex was beating her chest like Tarzan gone wild. For her, development was robbing her of her power. In fact, development became so devastating that Alex actually dropped out of sports because she was embarrassed about the size of her breasts. She was so embarrassed by comments boys made when she ran that she stopped running altogether and began playing with her hair and makeup.

For Michelle, developing late was equally devastating. She endured cruel comments by neighborhood boys about her undeveloped physique every day of the eighth and ninth grades. The damage to her self-esteem took years to undo. But she began playing sports and, slowly over the years, became an athlete. Eventually Alex, too, reattained her athlete status.

Anyone who remembers suffering through adolescence is sympathetic to the low-esteem of so many teenagers today. Becoming an athlete, or holding onto that jock power, is a state of mind. It means mastering your emotions rather than letting your emotions master you. It is believing in yourself, loving yourself, and knowing you are worth all things. But these are not common feelings among adolescents whose self-images are generally at an all-time low.

Tori Allen serves as an excellent example of how important good self-image can be. At the tender age of eight, Allen knew she wanted to be an Olympian. But, as it happened, her newly discovered passion was a sport that did not allow females. While attending a state fair with her family, she watched a pole-vaulter and fell in love. "I loved the speed and the height. It just looked so exciting. I begged my parents to let me do it." But for Allen, there was no future in it. Instead of conceding defeat, Allen found a new outlet. While Christmas shopping in a Gaylan's Sporting Goods store, Allen saw people climbing a wall and begged her mother to let her try.

"When we go back to the store," says Allen's mother, Shawn Allen, "the employees still fight over who was the first to spot her. I guess she did really well," she says with a laugh. So well, in fact, that the young Allen mastered all four walls in just two weeks. "The people who worked there kept telling me I had to get her into this," so the Allens took their daughter to a regulation climbing gym and Tori Allen took off. In no time, she was going to competitions and within three months of that time, she was winning everything. Her mother remembers, "After three months, we decided to put her in an adult division because it just wasn't fair to the other kids."

It should be noted that at the time Tori Allen was less than 70 pounds and not even a teenager. She was becoming known in the rock-climbing world as a phenomenon. She was unbeatable. She had her own website, was featured in various magazines and newspapers. Then, an amazing turn of events changed the life of this straight-A honor student: She was watching the 2000 Sydney Games when a woman named Stacey Dragula won an Olympic Gold for the U.S. in women's pole vaulting. Women's pole vaulting!

The Allens spoke to a high school coach who was more than happy to train Allen. Although she was only 12 years old, she was two years ahead academically. She was in. "We had no problems letting her do it," says her mother. "The sport is relatively cheap. We had to invest in shoes and her pole. The hard stuff is up to Tori."

Clearly, Tori is up for the hard stuff. She is juggling the title of World Champion Rock Climber, training for two sports with the hopes of making the U.S. Olympic team in pole vaulting for the 2004 Games, and holding on to a 4.0 GPA in high school. One has to wonder, how does she rise above peer pressure about how she should behave? Simple. She ignores it. She redefines femininity to fit her. She recognizes that her future doesn't depend on boys; it depends on her and her willingness to work hard.

Allen's stand on boyfriends also is simple: She doesn't have time for them right now. She is serious only about her school and sports. These, she says, are the things that are going to take her places. "I don't understand it when people say, 'We're going out.' What does that mean? You're not going anywhere. Boys don't know what they want at this age," she explains. "I like to hang out with them, with all my friends, but I don't have time for them [as boyfriends]."

Allen has made time for sports, family, her studies, and setting lofty goals for herself, i.e., making sports history as the youngest pole-vaulting Olympic champion ever. That's plenty for right now.

For years, Karla Keck tried to make sports history. Once ranked second in the world in Nordic ski jumping for women, Keck had her eye on the world record and one day being an Olympian. Keck overcame tremendous pressure to quit (no coach, no training facilities, no sponsors) and she pressed the International Olympic Committee to include women's Nordic ski jumping as an Olympic event.

Keck began jumping when she was 5 years old and continued until well into her 20s. She was always one of the best, beating the boys — despite the ramifications. "I lost of couple of my best

Karla Keck, captain of the U.S. Women's Ski Jumping Team, competing against men from 11 nations, soared 100M (328') during the Longest Standing Round on the Large Olympic Hill (photo provided by Karla Keck).

[male] friends after I beat them," she says. When she turned 18, the guys were all looking to the Olympics, and she was supposed to go away. Instead, she is one of the leading pioneers for women's Nordic ski jumping and, certainly, the best known. On the international circuit, Keck became the unofficial spokesperson for women's jumping.

Keck became the first female international jumper to be invited to an exclusive school in Austria for competitive jumpers. Keck, still a senior in high school, was starstruck to attend classes with Olympic medallists and various national teams. But she was causing a stir of her own. Her presence had been an experiment. Could female athletes go head to head with male athletes if given the proper instruction? Only Keck and one other Austrian woman were invited to the school. The pressure was on.

"When we first entered the scene, a lot of guys were saying, 'What's this?' But some thought it was really cool. There were definitely mixed opinions about us being there. There was a lot of pressure because you didn't want to fall." Although even the best in the world fell from time to time, the young women felt the sport was riding on their shoulders.

Since that time, Keck has become a popular competitor on the circuit, well known and liked by coaches and athletes around the world. Her constant presence (despite major funding problems) has been most powerful. As she battled to make women's Nordic ski jumping — the last of the winter events to exclude women — an Olympic event, she has paved the way for a new breed of fast, powerful jumpers.

Participation in athletics, however, is certainly not the only way to further the cause of female sports. Tamara St. Germain's own dreams of Olympic glory in skiing ended abruptly with a broken femur in 1992. Despite her personal loss, she still wanted to be able to give back to women's sports some of what she felt she had gained. She wanted to encourage young girls to give themselves a chance.

Appalled by the amount of drug and alcohol use by local teenage girls in Lake Placid, New York (site of the Olympic Training Center for winter sports), and the fact that "nearly half of the high school's senior girls were pregnant," St. Germain resolved to do something. She founded the Winter Sports Foundation (formerly the Winter Sports for Girls), now based in Boulder, Colorado, a nonprofit organization that introduces inner-city kids to the world of sports. "Being able to share what I love to do most and seeing the expressions and reactions of the girls [have been] the most rewarding experiences of my whole life," she says.

St. Germain stresses that girls need athletic role models, just as they need academic or professional role models. They need the confidence and self-esteem to know that they can do whatever they choose to do. More and more posters are going up on walls with female soccer and basketball stars, more and more actresses are taking on roles as heroines rather than damsels in distress. But we are still inadvertently teaching girls what their limitations are. We still question women in aggressive sports, we still feature the damsel in distress, never the lad in distress.

Too few teachers and parents are challenging girls as much as boys. One teacher, however, who does challenge girls is Greg Williams, a fifth-grade math teacher in an inner-city Columbus, Ohio, school. Williams believes education, exercise, and self-esteem are all interconnected. And he has created the concept of "mathercise" to further that notion, combining mathematics and exercise.

Fitness, Williams says, is too often presented in a negative sense. In boot camp, soldiers are ordered to "drop and do 20" push-ups for disciplinary reasons. "I switched that," Williams laughs. When one of his kids answers a math question correctly on the board, Williams booms, "Right! Now, give me 15 push-ups." Kids, he says, love the challenge. Learning and exercise become fun. More importantly, at this age, his female students see that not only can they do the push-ups (and the math), but many times they can do more push-ups than the boys.

A little girl approached Williams after class one day. "Not athletic at all," he remembers, she confided in him that she had been doing exercises at home. "She was very smart, but never believed in herself." It was no surprise to Williams, then, that as the girl became more physically fit, she also became more confident and more vocal in school.

"Catching that fourth- or fifth-grader at that age and instilling in [him or her] the importance of health, self-esteem and fitness is so important. They can think, 'OK, not only am I capable, but I can do things — all kinds of things.'"

I can do all kinds of things. If men can do this, I can, too. This is what we need to be teaching girls. And sports are a means to that end.

In fact, self-esteem and confidence (or the lack thereof) are actually the reason TaeBo was created. Billy Blanks used to be a karate instructor who tried to motivate more women to come to the sport because he believed they could excel and benefit from martial arts. But, he says, too many women believe the lie that aggressive sports are for men and that to be feminine one must not be too tough. So, he developed a kickboxing routine and "put it to music; a simple concept, but it worked." Indeed it did. Now, scores of women are lining up to give testimonials about how their lives have changed since taking Blanks' TaeBo classes.

These women are strong, confident, self-assured and very comfortable with their own femininity. Over the years, as we have spoken with athletes from all disciplines, we have noticed that once a girl or woman becomes an athlete, she becomes very comfortable with who she is.

Sports allow girls to act out, speak up, become notable through their actions, giving them the confidence to be assertive. Sports give them more positive self-images, stronger self-esteems, and allow them to focus on internal rather than external characteristics. Sports teach them teamwork and the ability to be competitive on (and off) the field/court, but still walk away as friends.

As beach volleyball star Gabrielle Reece says, sports force girls "to work as a team with other girls, to work together under every possible condition — winning, losing, tired, grumpy, happy. It forces them to deal with unpleasant, ungracious emotions and get over it. It forces girls to rely on each other. It gives them confidence in other girls,"[2] which ultimately gives them confidence in themselves.

But self-confidence is still one of the biggest problems for girls. It plays a role in how they approach everything they do and in how they perform. Girls, for example, apologize far more than boys, saying sorry if they miss shots or bump into other players. During our sprint-training regimen at Accelerate Ohio, one of the trainers told us she preferred girls on the treadmill over boys any time. "Girls are so easy," explained Shanda Eickelberger. "They do whatever you tell them. The guys always complain, try to argue their way out. On the whole, the girls work harder. Because they have been told by people they can't do something, they have something more to prove."

Other trainers also have told us they think the females are more prone to put forth a greater effort because they have something to prove. But they also concede that lack of self-esteem and confidence play a key role in the performance of females, something we saw demonstrated at Accelerate Ohio. For many girls, the intensity of the training program is new to them, and so is handling the stress and fatigue. "Most girls don't play sports or really get into something until they're in fifth to sixth grade," trainer Mike Neff theorized. "By that time guys are already trying to touch the ceiling or the basketball rim. They're always testing everything." Girls don't question their program on the treadmill because most girls aren't experienced in testing their boundaries. It is socially ingrained in us to stay within the established bounds. When we step outside, we are labeled. So, very often, we stay safely inside and our self-confidence diminishes.

Neff laughs and says, "The entire time I've been here, I've never seen a girl try to touch that exit sign," pointing to the fingerprint-smeared exit sign hanging 10 feet above the ground. It is a challenge too tempting to resist for the boys.

But Coach Pat Diulus laughs at the thought of Sameka Randall passing up such a challenge. The Associated Press' Ms. Basketball in 1996 and member of the 1996 Junior National basketball team became part of what *Sports Illustrated* dubbed the "Fabulous Four" during the 2000 NCAA Finals. Randall loves a challenge. "Are you kidding me?" Diulus asks. "No doorway is safe from Sameka. I'm always yelling at her for hitting the basketball rim. She's not that tall (5'10"), but she has incredible jumping power. I'm afraid she's going to hurt

her hand on the rim one of these days, but I can't stop her."
The temptation is too strong for her to resist.

Randall is unusual. When her mother urged her to play
with Barbie dolls, Randall chose the basketball court. While
her mother was worried she would get hurt, Randall looked
for pickup games with the guys. The rougher, the better. Either
someone forgot to tell Randall the "rules" about little girls, or
she wasn't listening.

Sports teach kids that kind of confidence and self-esteem
— the ability to see their own inner beauty and worth, to believe in themselves. And sports teach girls how to set and obtain goals, how to deal with defeat and go on, learning from
these experiences and becoming stronger because of them.

As adult athletes, we remember the anger and the pain of
being told, essentially, to go away in the early years of bobsledding. It took a lot of confidence and strong feelings of self-worth
to continue in the face of rejection. Imagine facing that kind of
pressure when you are only a child.

Sarah Fisher had scads of self-belief and she would need it
in her sport, the male-dominated arena of driving racecars.
Fortunately, Fisher is the epitome of an athlete: focused, determined, self-assured, and driven. Since her driving debut at the
age of 5 in the quarter-midget race, Fisher has known that she
loved racing.

"I was never doing this for anyone but me," she says, "but
now, if I can help other girls along the way, maybe be a role
model or help someone else face challenges, I'm proud to do
it." By standing her ground, doing what she loves and letting
her talent speak for itself, even her most ardent foes have had
to give her credit. As you will later read, Fisher's credit goes
beyond breaking racing records ... she broke into one of the
biggest good ol' boy clubs and is gaining popularity with the
boys.

If you who have never tried to break into the boys' club,
never strayed too far from the norm, it may be hard to understand the hurt, the feeling of betrayal by people you thought
would or should have known better, and the personal toll it
takes on you. But, there's no crying in the boys' club.

Ironman athlete Julie Moss says that the strength — physical and emotional — acquired through sports is particularly important for women. "You have physical strength, but you also have inner strength to attack the other things you want to do in your life," she says. "When women become empowered physically, it helps them to become empowered in all other aspects of their life."

Sports, in short, teach girls how to be part of and succeed in society and the world of work. After all, says St. Germain, the goal setting and strategizing they learn in sports are the very characteristics necessary to succeed in the business world. "That's what business is. Ninety-nine percent of women never get the chance to feel these benefits, which is why men run most businesses."

In *Games Mother Never Taught You*, Betty Lehan Harragan argues that to become a "player" in the business world, one must learn sports terminology. Learning about game plans and strategies (not to mention coaches and officials) is the key to success, because games (traditionally male games) are the training ground, the preparation for life and business. As children we understand that some kids can run faster than others, throw better or jump higher. As teenagers, we understand that it is nothing personal when the coach puts in the better players; but we also know in many instances we can control our own fate by lots of practice and dedication.

Playing team sports teaches us about human nature and relationships; it teaches us general on-the-job rules. Harragan says in real life, in the business world, women tend to cling to the notion of fair play and take turns, while men apply their "football" rules and forge ahead. In fact, while working on a business book, Alex had an opportunity to talk to mega-CEOs Debbi Fields of Mrs. Fields Cookies and Jenny Craig of Jenny Craig International. As both of these women talked about success in business they used sport analogies to illustrate their points.

Freedom Forum's Nancy Woodhull agreed with the sports analogy. "The experience of dealing with adversity, defining solutions, and believing in their ability to achieve," Woodhull said, "is an advantage men [have] brought to the business world for decades.

"My advice to young women entering the business world is plan to succeed. By that I don't mean you should figure out how to become CEO before you even leave the personnel office. I do mean that, like the athlete, you should set achievable goals and then be willing to do what it takes to reach them. Realize that only you can really define success, and it won't always be at the top of that mythical pyramid. Set goals you can reach — like sports. [When you reach those goals] set new ones, if that's really what you want. Don't allow society to set your goals. Make your life YOUR LIFE."

The benefits of participation in sports speak for themselves, some of which we've already mentioned: girls who learn sports have stronger family relations, are better connected to their parents, have better self-images, do better in school, and stay away from drugs and alcohol more than non-active girls. They also do better in business, learning networking and essential skills that foster success with organizations. As Wendy Hilliard says, "It's no accident that 80 percent of the female executives at Fortune 500 companies characterize themselves as having been 'tomboys' in their early years."[3]

Senator Hillary Rodham Clinton's father use to throw footballs to her in the front yard; her mother played tennis with her. And both parents cooked. Clinton explains the importance of this equity in her book, *It Takes A Village*: "Children learn what they see. When they see their fathers cooking dinner or changing the baby's diaper, they'll grow up knowing that care-giving is a human trait, rather than a female one. When they see their mothers changing tires or changing fuses, they'll accept troubleshooting as a human quality, rather than a male one."[4]

Breaking down barriers and leading the way is part of who a female athlete is. She is powerful, amazing, graceful, beautiful, demanding, expecting, daring, and motivating. These words so completely describe Babe Didrikson-Zaharias, Amelia Earhart, young Tori Allen, Sarah Fisher, and scores of other up-and-coming athletes who ask: Is it unreasonable to want to be the best? To push the envelope to do more, jump higher, go faster? When a male athlete tries to perform a stunt we think is particularly stupid (because he's likely to break his neck), no one asks him if this is proper male or social behavior. There is still no equivalent to "boys will be boys" for girls. And, for this reason, there will always be barriers to push for girls and women in athletics. It is often those barriers that make the accomplishments of female athletes all the more exciting.

There will be those who roll their eyes at such notions. They simply don't understand. They have not stood in our shoes, watched women athletes grow, seen the sports pages detail the statistics of more and more women's events, and talked to countless athletes about the changes in sports competitions. We feel the shift, we see the results of women engaged in all sports, and it is exciting. It is cause for celebration.

To keep the momentum going, lots of encouragement is needed and role models are critical. That's one reason the Women's National Basketball Association (WNBA) is so important (and why the loss of the now-defunct American Basketball League so distressing). U.S. female basketball players have been playing in Europe for years, making well over $200,000 a year. But now many of these athletes have decided to take a chance and stay home to play the game here, taking salary cuts of more than half in some cases, because as former Dream Teamer and gold medallist Dawn Staley says, someone has to make the sacrifices. Someone has to show this country's kids that women can be athletes, role models, leaders — anything they want to be.

Next year Alexandra will pen another children's book entitled *My Mother Is A Football Player*. The book features typically male-dominated jobs such as truck driver, police officer, judge, construction worker, auto mechanic, firefighter, and, yes, football player to children, reminding us all how versatile and vibrant women can be. For some people, this is a tiresome topic. Just another feminist crying foul, they might say. But there is a need. Mind you, Alex is not one for donning makeup and wearing dresses. (Point in case: Alex was shopping for back-to-school clothes for her girls when both Kerri and Katie saw a dress and begged Alex to buy it and wear it. "You need one dress, Mommy," Katie

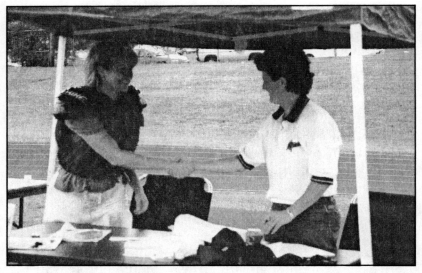

General Manager Donna Roebuck officially welcomes Alex to the WPFL, after contracts are signed (photo provided by Alexandra Powe Allred).

pleaded.) Still, these very girls informed their pony-tail -sporting, jeans-and-T-shirt-wearing mom that girls don't play football. When Alex first made the team, her girls were a little uncertain about their mother's new role. Even though they had been raised by a sports-loving, strong, active mother, they still have their own societal ideas about what is and isn't appropriate behavior for women. Not only must we continue to remind ourselves and our daughters of our abilities, we must also show our boys. In a recent study conducted by Girls, Inc., over 2,000 students between the grades three through twelve were asked whether girls and boys have the same abilities and strengths. Only 47 percent of the girls answered 'yes' and just 27 percent of the boys thought girls were equal. [5]

No one wants the success of the WPFL more than Coach Dee Kennamer and her Austin players because they feel very strongly about showing little girls they do, in fact, have something to dream about. One tough, hard-hitting, fast player, known both for her agility and graciousness, put it this way: "It's an honor to be out here. Someone had to sacrifice a lot so we can do this, too."

Cornerback Bobbie James is eager to work with her sisters on the field and act as role model to young girls. "Every day we've got people — kids — watching us. I want to make this happen. There's no reason for it not to." Certainly, not for lack of talent. These women bring skill and determination to the field and they do so, in part, so little girls can dream. And little boys can watch the ever-expanding talents, growth, and dreams of their sisters, mothers, aunts, and grandmothers.

That skill and commitment come at a price, as Anna Lee knows. After long, hard practices in the heat, Lee can feel the scrutiny from the stands. Tall, lean, and very pretty, she defies the stereotype of female football player. Acting as tight end for the Austin Rage, she's fast, powerful, and good with her hands. In particular, the coaches enjoy working with her because, as Coach Melvin says, "She's a quick study," and determined to make every play her best one yet. But, for her critic in the stands, it was hard to do anything right. When, at last, the torture was over and the team was released from practice, Lee had to face her real test. It would be a long drive home. It always was.

"See, Mom, this is what you did wrong ... " her 12-year-old son, Tramaine, would say. Also playing football for his school, Tramaine was eager to come to Lee's practices and games and critique his mom. "He's hard on me," Lee laughs, "but I love it. He really thinks it's cool that his mom is a football player. I still can't believe I'm a football player. It's like a dream ... "

Dreams can and do come true. Keep knocking down walls and breaking down barriers, giving a good victory whoop each time. These are our days to celebrate!!

Notes

1. Wayne Westcott, Joyce Tolken and Brian Wessner, "School-Based Conditioning Programs for Physically Unfit Children," *Strength and Conditioning* (April 1995), 5.

2. Gabrielle Reece and Karen Karbo, *Big Girl in the Middle* (NY: Crown Publishing, 1997), 83.

3. Wendy Hilliard, "The Trickle-Down Effect," *Women's Sports & Fitness* (October 1996), 55.

4. Hillary Rodham Clinton, "It Takes a Village," *Working Woman* (May 1996), 30.

5. Helen Cordes, "Raising Confident Girls," *Child* (September 2001), 75.

The Goddess Within

The Year of the Women certainly had an impact on young girls everywhere. Everywhere there were reminders of women's Olympic successes — magazine covers with smiling female medallists, television interviews, best-selling autobiographies. Young girls began signing up in droves for gymnastics, swimming, track and field, basketball, soccer, softball. Our girls had caught the fever. But the Year of the Women also was gratifying for older athletes. As we watched women from all sports, women of all shapes and sizes, all skin and eye and hair colors, all different kinds of backgrounds win the hearts of Americans and the world, there was a certain feeling of coming into our own.

Most importantly, we finally saw that it is time to rechannel the anger and let go of the insecurities. While writing this book, we were repeatedly asked by male interviewees: "Is this a male-bashing book?" Anger was assumed. And certainly women have been held down long enough to have cause for anger. But anger no longer serves us. We've proven time and time again what we are capable of. Now we must remain focused and positive.

Still, as far as we have come, the persistent power of this beauty thing has us at a loss — even now. Everywhere we feel its pressing influence. Marathon runner Patty Driscoll, for example, was preparing for the Boston Marathon in the mountains of Vermont. Alone with her thoughts, pushing herself along the isolated highway, she suddenly found that she had company. An 18-wheeler barreled down behind her. She edged over, making room. The driver leaned out and shouted, "Wide load!" "Oh, yeah?" she shouted back. "Up yours, asshole!"

The truck disappeared around the bend of the mountain, but not before Driscoll made sure the driver saw — in his side-view mirror — her obscene hand gesture. Then, as she came around the corner, she saw the driver had pulled his truck over to the side of the road. Panicked, she slowed her pace.

Is he going to kill me? Beat me? I shouldn't have yelled that at him. I shouldn't have flipped him off. Now, he's mad.

Cautiously, she neared him, still unsure of what she should do. He climbed out of the cab and said, "Ma'am, I yelled 'wide load' because I was coming by with a wide truck and didn't want you to get hurt." He tipped his baseball cap, crawled back into the cab and drove away. It was a long run home, Driscoll says, especially since she felt only 3 inches tall. The anger from past hurts had kept her from focusing on the tangible and the positive in the present.

Another, more well-known marathoner, Joan Benoit Samuelson, was so embarrassed when she first began running that she would stop and pretend to look at flowers every time a car passed. She went on to become the first woman to win Olympic gold in the marathon in the 1984 Olympics, but she had to struggle to overcome her insecurities about others' perceptions of her as an athlete and as a woman.

Indeed, a problem for women in sports is that females are judged by harsher standards of appearance than are males. Even the world's best female distance swimmer fell victim to the harmful scrutiny so often applied to girls and women. During the 1988 Seoul Olympics, a 17-year-old, 90-pound Janet Evans took the pool by storm, earning three gold medals. When we next saw her during the 1996 Atlanta Olympics, Janet was no longer a girl, but a young woman, two inches taller and 20 pounds heavier.

"Wow," people said, "look at Janet. She's ballooned." But she had not. She had become a woman. Now, there were hips, more rounded thighs, a bust line. Her body mass had changed from waiflike to slim. Evans says she had to stop reading newspapers because of all the references to her size. "The media," she says, "can develop ... your image of yourself."

The harsh expectations that a waiflike body is the ideal still exist, particularly for young females. But the real pressure exists mostly within ourselves. The top athletes we interviewed all were comfortable with their bodies, quietly confident. While they work at their sports to become the best, they discover and rediscover themselves. They know exactly who they are. They know exactly what they are capable of. They know and appreciate their bodies. They know that strong is beautiful.

Case-in-point: a teammate recently visited Alex's house and saw a picture of her with longer hair standing next to the Mediterranean Sea. The teammate said, "Alex, you look like a downhill skier!" Ah, the ultimate compliment for an athlete: to be compared not to a model or movie star, but to another powerful athlete.

As gold-medalist swimmer Angel Martino says: "A muscular woman is a beautiful woman. It was hard for me in high school. There were a lot of guys who wouldn't go out with me because I was too muscular. I think muscles are beautiful ... If I have a little girl, I hope I will be able to make her feel like being an athlete is beautiful." Even better, Martino had a little boy. Now, he can grow up appreciating the athleticism and power of female jocks.

But for young girls only beginning sports, or not involved in sports at all, thinking of a strong muscular female body as beautiful may be a foreign concept. As they gain weight during puberty (typically 35 pounds), female adolescents are

While the wait seemed endless, Martino finally got to celebrate gold with her son, Michael (photo provided by Angel Martino) .

continually bombarded with airbrushed images of "emaciated models and actresses with breast implants." Around the time of puberty, the female hormone estrogen turns on fat production for, well, reproduction. Breasts develop, hips widen, and body fat increases. It's normal. The average body-mass index (BMI) for a healthy woman is 25.1 but the average BMI of a model is 17. It should be noted that a BMI below 17.5 is considered anorectic.[1]

Weight — or rather, weightlessness — has become equated with beauty in our society. "Society's standard of beauty is an image that is literally just short of starvation for most women."

Since 1979, "Miss America contestants have become so skinny that the majority are now at least 15 percent below recommended body weight for their height."[2] The average height and weight of a model is 5'9", 110 pounds. The height and weight of the average American woman: 5'4", 142 pounds. According to Hollywood director Joel Schumacher: "Sophia Loren and Marilyn Monroe could not get a job today. Their agents would tell them, 'Go on a diet, get a trainer.'"

In fact, when we spoke with actress/model Courtney Thorne Smith, she spoke rather candidly about her failing health as she starred in the hit series Ally McBeal. "I had lost so much weight, it affected my hair, my teeth, and my skin. I was so tired." Because so much emphasis had been placed on the weight of the actress and show's namesake Calista Flockhart, the other actresses on the show felt the pressure to stay thin and not be compared to (or contrasted with) Flockhart. While Thorne-Smith is careful not to point an accusing finger, she does concede that a kind of unhealthy competition developed. Thorne-Smith left the series soon after.

And, then, everyone began to notice that while the male characters of the popular television show Friends were gaining weight, their female co-stars were fading away. It became the hot topic of talk shows, magazine stories, and newspaper articles. Why, everyone wanted to know, were Chandler and Joey allowed to be chubby and Monica and Rachel looked like concentration camp survivors? No answer was ever provided; the issue just seemed to, dare we say it, melt away.

Karen Rothmann, an elementary school teacher for 18 years in Washburn, North Dakota, has seen the perception of body image change over the years she has taught. Many of her students are very insecure because their self-worth is wrapped up in their bodies. "They want to be stick-thin, they want to be beautiful, they want to be popular, and they want a boyfriend," she says. These are their priorities. "For a lot of my little girls," she says, "that's what beautiful is — stick-thin."

Rothmann told us about one of her students who had stopped eating lunch. Melanie would go all day without eating. When Rothmann questioned her about it, Melanie said "the only thing she could control was her weight. She was trying to keep up with her older sisters, to measure up to them." By the spring, Melanie had lost so much weight that she was having to belt her pants to keep them up. Rothmann spoke with Melanie's mother, noting the significant weight loss, but was told not to worry about the little girl. Her mother said that she was very proud of the 9-year-old for using self-control.

So strong is the pressure of how to look, walk, and dress that gymnast Shannon Miller says she is thankful for sport and her coach for shielding her from it. It's a funny statement since gymnastics is about how you move and look. "But there are guidelines," Miller points out. "They are moves designed for sport and the look is about attitude. 'I can do this' attitude. 'I am strong' attitude. Not, 'I want to get a boy' attitude. There is a big difference." Thank goodness for sports. As more and more girls and women are getting into competitive sports, they are learning how absolutely necessary food is and how weight can sometimes help. We give you football. "This is the one time in your life you will be insulted for not weighing enough," General Manager Donna Roebuck of the Austin Rage yells at her players. How wonderfully liberating it is to see women happily telling their weight to each other. At 5'7" and 175 pounds, a defensive tackle for the New England Storm says with a proud chuckle, "It's cool to be a big girl!"

Sports allow, even encourage, that process of self-discovery, of learning who you are and what you can do. Now acting as unofficial spokesperson for healthy living, actress Thorne-Smith talks about the importance about healthy diet and exercise. No longer starving herself, "I am happier now than I have been in a long time. I look in the mirror and like what I see. That is so incredibly important."

While boys are busily judging their female classmates on a point system, girls are desperately trying to measure up to the "standard." And they put pressure on one another to conform to this unrealistic and unfair picture of "femininity," making those in sports more reluctant than ever to strip down to athletic shorts to "act like boys," and to risk social criticism or ostracism.

In fact, few teenage girls discover their true bodies. A staggering 75 percent of them diet rather than exercise, but even more disturbing, younger girls are dieting, too. According to some studies, as many as 50 percent of 9-year-olds have dieted, and 80 percent of 10-year-olds already do not like their bodies. Reported cases of anorexia and bulimia have doubled since 1970. But cases of obesity are up as well because kids do not exercise. Dr. Wayne Westcott, who is on the President's Council on Physical Fitness and Sports, says, "In the last 15 years we've seen 50 percent of children fit into the obese category. There has been a 100 percent increase in super-obesity with these kids. It's very sad."

But with teen bare-midriff role models like Britney Spears who, these days, barely wears pants above the middle of her hip bone, Christine Aguilera, Pink, and Lil' Kim (egads!), it's no wonder girls are suffering from identity crisis. And what's with the idea of having former senator and presidential candidate Bob Dole tell his dog, "Easy, boy," while watching Britney Spears dance in that Pepsi commercial?? Wasn't he just pitching Viagra — a sexual stimulant for men? The message being sent to youngsters can only exacerbate feelings of confusion in already perplexed teenagers.

Still, for every caffeine-induced, half-dressed princess of pop, there is hope! In the last decade men, women, boys, and girls alike have been exposed to fun, strong, independent female warriors both on the playing field and in the media. Even little girls are benefiting from this new era. Alex's daughters (and, let's face it, Alex) watch Powerpuff Girls, Sailor Moon, and Rocket Power in which the older sister, Reggie, is a rockin', awesome surfer and skateboarder.

There was a time when it was difficult to name strong female role models. Now, the list is long and getting longer. Publication of women's and girls' sport and health magazines is growing. *Muscle & Fitness Hers*, *Fitness*, and *Shape* all highlight everyday fitness buffs and athletes, motivating and enlightening their readers. *Jane* and *Jump!* are hip new magazines for older teens and 20-somethings. But even that isn't enough for some.

Like us, Karen Bokram felt that girls between the ages of 9 and 14 were being left out. Because this is such a critical age, it is important that they not look at the more racy topics included in many of the better known teen magazines. "What does a 9-year-old need to know about dating, kissing, and 'going out'? That's too young," says Bokram. We couldn't agree more. So, in 1999 Bokram launched the magazine *Girls Life*. The magazine touches on young role models such as Tori Allen and other young Olympians, healthy living, suitable yet fashionable clothing, and fun facts.

Karen Bokram (photo provided by Karen Bokram)

Girls Life builds on a trend: that is, steadily, females are moving toward better self-image and confidence as sports play a bigger role in young girls' lives. Models are changing, becoming more and more fit. Look how many models are creating their own workout videos. Muscle is in. Still, high school track athlete Tia Trent told us that one day, as she was walking down the street, a schoolmate told her, "Girl, you got good-lookin' legs. Comin' up behind, you look fine. But in front, you got no chest." Trent reports, "I said 'OK, my family isn't breeding for big breasts!' ... Like I'm gonna be able to sprint with big boobs."

Enter Florence Griffith Joyner. Known to the world as Flo Jo, she crashed onto the world scene at the 1988 Seoul Games. Like no other female athlete before her, she wore one-legged spandex running pants, and her long, painted nails glittered. She wore makeup and had long hair that flowed behind her as she blazed down the track. She was beautiful and flamboyant. And it was a package that everyone bought into. Her family didn't breed for large breasts, either.

But what the Griffith family did produce was a woman who could run 23.5 miles per hour in the 100 meter. They produced a woman who broke track records in the 100 and 200 meters that still stand today, and they produced a woman who stressed again and again that "believing in yourself" is the key to all things. Hers is a story particularly bittersweet. Two weeks before we were to talk to Ms. Joyner, she died in her sleep — a shock to everyone in the sporting community. In our hearts, our minds, and our history books, Flo Jo is legendary.

Another legend is Mildred "Babe" Didrikson-Zaharias, labeled by the Associated Press (in 1950) the "Greatest Athlete of her Era" and the "Outstanding Woman Athlete of the Century." While she never wore one-legged tights, she also battled society's perceptions of proper feminine behavior. At the qualifying event for the 1932 Olympic Games, Didrikson-Zaharias entered, as a one-woman team, eight events and won five — the shotput, 80-meter hurdles, javelin throw, broad jump and baseball throw — outscoring the entire 22-member second-place team of the University of Illinois (Urbana).

She qualified for six individual events for the 1932 Games in Los Angeles, but rules at the time forced her to choose only three. She won gold medals in the javelin and 80-meter hurdles and a silver in the high jump, setting new world records with almost every effort. She would have won the gold, rather than silver, in the high jump but the judges ruled her jumping style illegal; her head preceded her body and legs over the bar — which is how athletes jump today. She was ahead of her time.

Babe Didrikson-Zaharias (photo by AP/Wide World Photos)

After the Olympics, Didrikson-Zaharias toured the country pitching for an all-male baseball team, shooting with an all-male basketball team, and boxing against men. In April 1935, she won the Texas

Women's Golf Association Amateur championship, but the United States Golf Association (USGA) declared her a professional athlete because of her years of exhibition touring. She was heavily ridiculed for her tomboyish manners and style, for her short-cropped hair, lack of makeup, and flamboyant showmanship. And it was made very clear to her that she was not welcome at such socially elite functions as golf tournaments.

While awaiting reinstatement of her amateur status, Didrikson-Zaharias took up sewing, gardening, and housewifely duties. Not until she grew her hair out and began curling it, wore makeup, and polished her nails did she gain the kind of acclaim she deserved for her athletic abilities. After three years of waiting, she finally was awarded her new status. In 1946 she won the National Women's Amateur title, and in 1947 she went on to win 17 straight amateur victories — a feat still unequaled, even by Tiger Woods. She turned pro in 1948 and won 33 professional tournaments, including three U.S. Opens.

Didrikson-Zaharias went on to be the driving force behind the creation of the Ladies Professional Golf Association. In her career she won, over a 40-year period, more medals and tournaments and set more records in more sports than any other 20th-century athlete — of either sex.[3] But the lesson for all women athletes was clear: you won't be allowed to succeed unless you look and act the way a woman should. For Babe, this was something she had to contend with until the day she died. And female athletes remain caught between those two still contradictory roles: Settle for "you throw like a girl" comments, which mean you're a lesser athlete but appropriately female, or risk "you throw like a boy" compliments, which mean you're a superior athlete but a lesser female.

Such classification of female athletes by their physical attributes rather than their athletic abilities discredits all female athletes. We are not seen as powerful, strong, determined, competent, but as sexy, graceful, lithe (that is, if we're lucky).

And such classifications are certainly not limited to national sports magazines or sponsors. In a review of high school girls' basketball, sports editor Eric Davis of a local newspaper, the *Marion Star* (Marion, Ohio) wrote: "And, at the risk of sounding sexist, I've got to say that Carrie Carr is just about the prettiest girl I've ever seen on a basketball court. I honestly don't watch for such things when I attend girls ball games but I ain't blind, either, don't you know?"[4] Those who played with or against the pretty Carr were devastated. While girls making layups, rebounds and three-pointers got no credit at all, Carrie Carr got a full paragraph based on her looks.

Today, the same thing is happening with tennis sensation Anna Kournikova. Although she owns no major win, no title, Anna is the most downloaded athlete in the world. More than 20,000 Web pages are devoted to Kournikova with sites like "Annamaniacs," "Anna at the Temple of Babes," and "Annaholics Anonymous." One professional tennis player who asked not to be identified said this of the Anna-hoopla: "She's more interested in being a diva than a tennis player. She plays decent tennis now, but she could be really great if she could just walk away from the cameras." Never has one athlete become so well-known just for being beautiful.

The high visibility of athletes sometimes leads to false images. Rachael Scdoris is an example. Her racing peers, in an

Rachael Scdoris (photo by Ty Downing, www.downingphoto.com)

attempt to describe Scdoris as determined and unrelenting, dubbed her the Anna Kournikova of the dog world. It is the wrong image. Scdoris is no diva and she holds several titles in her sport. She is down-to-earth, hard-working, and almost embarrassingly sweet. At the age of 16, she has already made the record books and continues to get stronger, faster, better. So, why the tennis reference? Like Kournikova, Scdoris is a leggy, blonde bombshell. For Scdoris, it is a label she is determined to shake.

But many athletes feel that any kind of publicity is good publicity because it puts the athletes and their sport out in the public eye. Perhaps this is why some have been willing to pose nude for men's magazines. Even before the much touted battle between Laila Ali (daughter of Mohammed Ali) and Jacqui Frazier (daughter of Smokin' Joe Frazier) took place, they had primped and posed for so many glam shots that many of their fellow female boxers were seeing red. And some of their fans were unhappy, as well. A frequent complaint has been that Ali and Frazier are being disrespectful of the sport by using the names of their fathers to sell tickets to a fight of, at best, average fighters.

Ann Wolfe readies her "rocket right" (photo by Alexandra Allred).

Having personally seen Ann Wolfe fight and knowing how hard she trains and how very dedicated to the sport she is, we understand the frustration that many women boxers must feel. Just as it must be mind-boggling to title-winning players such as Martina Hingis to watch Anna Kournikova be dubbed the It Girl of women's tennis.

Responding to all the media hype, professional boxing coach Lori Steinhorst chortled, "What? To see them get all the money? Actually, I think Laila Ali has real potential but, let's face it, she got in the door because of her father. But she has real potential. It is sad, however, for me to see the women who have worked so hard like Sumya Anani and Kathy Collins get such little recognition."

When boxer Mia St. John posed in the nude, she claimed that exposure of any kind was good for the sport. But Steinhorst says, "When one of my [boxing] kids asks me why we don't have a picture of Mia, I tell them it's because I can't seem to find a picture of her wearing anything appropriate. I can't look at a little girl and say, 'Yes, it's OK for you to take your clothes off.' The role models I chose for my kids are role models in and out of the ring."

Steinhorst, who runs her own gym where she teaches boxing, has her walls covered with boxers she has met through the years. Larry Holmes; Joe Frazier; Hector Comacho Jr.; Evander Holyfield as well as Diana Lewis, Delia Chaquita Gonzales, Jane Couch, Kathy Collins, Valerie Mahfood, and Sumya Anani. Surrounded by these outstanding athletes, Steinhorst recounts a favorite story: "The other day one of my boys, my big 15-year-old, was looking at the wall and said, 'My favorite is Kathy Collins.' I asked why and he said, 'Cause she's got class. She just looks like she's got it goin' on.' He's talking about her boxing, not her body. That's the kind of exposure you want."

In the boxing ring or on the field, beauty is in the eye of the beholder. Fortunately, there has been a notable shift in our conception of beauty, embracing the emergence of female athletes. There was a time when our notion of beauty was embodied in white females in their early 20s. "Unfortunately, African-American women will never get as much spotlight as white women," said Wyomia Tyus, who returned from the 1964 Mexico City Olympics as the first person ever to win a gold medal in the 100 meters in two consecutive Olympic Games (a feat not repeated until Carl Lewis did it two decades later). But an African-American woman, she was a product of her time; there were no endorsements awaiting her.

In more recent years Marion Jones, the Williams sisters, and scores of other remarkable black female athletes have graced the covers of fashion and news magazines, been named in *People* magazine's annual "Most Beautiful People" list, and hold major corporate sponsors. Happily, although rather slowly, Asian and Latino athletes are getting more and more coverage. [Authors note: Our perception of beauty is that graceful, muscular athletes who are dedicated to their sport, family, and fans are the most beautiful of all.]

We've come such a long way since the days when Wyomia Tyus was pressured to stay away from sports. She was always asked why she was running, training so hard, and moving into a then-male-dominated arena. She was warned that if she kept it up she would "get muscles and never be able to get a husband."

Now, everyone is pumping iron, including actresses and models who want to have toned, defined bodies. As more and more women enter the field of sports — either as executives, commentators, coaches, fans or athletes, the issues of self-esteem, self-worth, better body images, and healthier lifestyles will continue to capture our interest. The growing number of women in positions of influence and authority is helping to redefine perceptions of femininity and acceptable feminine behavior. Happily, our female athletes are beginning to feel able to present themselves to the sports world and the media just as they are. As Nancy Woodhull pointed out, "The important thing in sports' Year of the Women is that it's very obvious that women have choices they can make. You can succeed on the playing field, on the sidelines, or in the classroom. You can be noticed because you scored in double figures for the basketball team or because you wear short skirts."

Billie Jean King, Micki King, Donna de Varona, Wyomia Tyus, Nancy Lieberman-Cline, Martina Navratilova, and their many colleagues opened the door for those of us who follow. Many people cite Dorothy Hamill, Chris Evert, and Peggy Fleming as important mediators. At a time when the media and public alike were redefining what was acceptable feminine behavior, these women were soft and pretty, but also serious athletes. Now enter the Tori Allens of the world — determined, focused, anything they want to be, redefining femininity and opening a new door.

There was a time when we asked how we could get the message to all girls that sports can, and should, be an important part of their development. There was a time when we wondered how we could override the images of Pamela Anderson Lee and Kate Moss, the super-busted and the super-starved. But Pamela Anderson had her breast implants removed, citing they were too large and awkward. (Although she still has implants, she opted for a smaller size.) And Kate Moss put on a healthy 15 pounds, looks more beautiful than ever and is leaving behind the unhealthy starvation lifestyle she once led.

Certainly, we would be the first to agree that body image and the weight issue are still very much alive in Hollywood and beauty magazines. But, for the first time, fitness is becoming the number one priority for celebrities and politicians —

The beautiful Kim Mott is the essence of the female athlete – powerful and fierce on the field, loyal and kind off (photo by Alexandra Allred).

those in the public eye and those who can most influence young girls. When we spoke to celebrity trainers Billy Blanks, Kathy Kaehler, Radu, and Kathy Smith (trainers who collectively 'own' most of Hollywood and New York), they all agreed that their clients want rock hard-abs, sculpted arms, shoulders, and backs, and well-toned tushies, and they are willing to work as hard as they have to get them.

There are those who love to say, 'Yeah, well, I'd look like that too if I could afford a trainer.' Maybe. Maybe not. The fact is, the celebrities still put in the time to get those bodies, and little girls are seeing the muscles. Helping girls and women find their way into the sports and fitness world may be the most important thing public figures can do. Sports psychologist Pat Bach says that finding themselves allows females to find their "inner-athlete" — the long-suppressed, competitive, resilient, strong-minded being. And when females find that inner athlete, they find their inner beauty. Better yet, they feel comfortable in their own skin, willing to risk public scrutiny to do what they love. We give you race car driver Sarah Fisher, the first members of the U.S. women's bobsled team, and professional women football players and boxers.

Enter Cory Everson, the blonde bombshell of the bodybuilding world. Initially, she was criticized for stepping into the male-dominated sport, but Everson confused the old guard by being sexy and intelligent and athletically gifted. As Everson continued to train and to shine on the posing stage, it was hard to ignore her. Fans loved her. She has been a positive role model for young women. (In fact, Everson is one of several sports celebrities who agreed to talk to us even though she has her own book to promote — simply because she believes in the message we are sending.)

Now with her own workout show on ESPN, a book, and a staff writer position for *Muscle & Fitness*, Everson has dispelled many stereotypes about female athletes. "Fitness," she says, "is sexy for everyone."

Sexy, indeed. While training in the Olympic Training Center weight room, we spied a Cory Everson poster. Actually, it wasn't hard to spy since two speed skaters, a luger, and a trainer were holding it up and evaluating every inch of Cory's well-toned and muscled body.

"You like that?" we asked, feeling out our audience. "She's hot!" was the quick response.

"Yeah," we said, playing devil's advocate, "but she's got all those muscles."

"Yeah, and she looks gooooood."

When we asked Everson about this, she laughed and said the image of women with muscles is a healthy one for men to see. Everson is a solid, muscular woman who could easily bench press most of the young men who ogle her picture. "Girls can learn from us that having a fit body and fit mind are attractive and feminine," Everson added.

Recently, a women's sports magazine has been running a feature called, 'What's My Sport?' in which only the name, body stats, and pictures of the athlete are provided. Her pictures are shown to other athletes, coaches, personal trainers, and/or sports fans. It is so fun to read as the unknown athlete is complimented on her various muscles. "She must be a pole-vaulter." " ... her upper abs. She does some kind of pulling motion. The first thing I thought of was windsurfing." "I think she's a soccer player because she has strong thighs. She looks like she runs a lot." She's scrutinized by men and women, called strong, beautiful, and fresh-faced.

Alrighty, then. Chalk another one up for the athletes. But it's not just women athletes who are demanding equal billing any-more. Female movie and television stars, so powerful in influenc-ing youngsters, boys and girls, have come into their own.

When the movie *Cagney and Lacey* aired on CBS in the 1980s, very little promotion had been done and, in fact, there were no plans for a series. CBS decision makers concluded that there was not much of a demand for a female cop show. But when feminist Gloria Steinem and actress Loretta Swit appeared on the *Phil Donahue Show* urging viewers to write to CBS, net-work executives sat up and took notice. Thousands of letters poured in to CBS demanding a series depicting two women as co-workers and friends.

For decades, women and men have accepted the notion that women cannot work together. And if a woman did ven-ture into a male role in television land, she had to be flanked by men. *Police Woman* and *Mod Squad* starred pretty women who worked side-by-side with men.

Olympic beach volleyball player Angela Rock says this no-tion about women is a consequence of the perception that the only time women compete against one another is over men. And Rock may be on to something. For so long, women were deprived of the right to play sports. Women who were "catty" about who was prettier, who had the nicer hair or figure, were simply expressing a natural human instinct — competitiveness — in one of the few avenues allowed to them by society. When other avenues, such as sports, are allowed, we see that women can and do work and play together well.

In that regard, the show *Charlie's Angels* was actually a step forward for women. Hard to believe with as much fluff and cheesecake as appeared in the series. Fred Silverman, former president of ABC Studio, has said that *Charlie's Angels* was the forefront to feminism. It was a show that, for the first time, allowed women to be friends, co-workers, and professionals at the same time. The three women never fought; there were no stereotypical cat fights in a pool, no hair pulling, no mud wrestling. The characters of *Charlie's Angels* respected and loved each other. They were professional, independent, and doing dangerous work. OK, the plots left a lot to be desired, and the women were gorgeous, but the scripts allowed women to have healthy, strong relationships without being a pretext for merely fulfilling male sexual fantasies. It was, in that healthy way, real life.

That was the beginning. Today, while our children watch cartoons with super-powered heroines like the *Powerpuff Girls* (who are made of sugar, spice and everything nice, plus something called Chemical X that allows them to fly and beat up evil-doers), adults are watching *Buffy the Vampire Slayer*, *Alias*, *Dark Angel*, *Witchblade*, and *Charmed*. As an aside, in 1993 when *Witchblade* actress Yancy Butler got her first break in film, she played the damsel in distress. (Oh, sweet justice.) All these hits are shows with strong, smart women who fight evil in one form or another, save the world, and serve as great role models.

Women and men are ready for images of strong, smart women. Perhaps that is why the syndicated action-adventure series *Xena* was such a success. Running for six seasons, it was one of the most talked about, popular syndications around. In it the heroine, who possessed superhuman strength, battled warriors in the "golden age of myth." In real life, the nearly 6-foot tall actress Lucy Lawless said of the show while it was still airing, "It just seems to have hit the world at the right time. The world is ready for a woman hero who is smarter and stronger than she is good looking. People somehow find her empowering."[5]

Of course, Lawless/Xena is very good-looking and men love her character. (In fact, the show regularly topped *Baywatch* and *Star Trek: Deep Space Nine* in the ratings.) But it was women who loved her character most, who gave her the greatest support. Fan letters, Internet forums, and, impressively enough, *Ms.* magazine honored Lawless for her portrayal of a superhero. Xena-fests, Xena trading cards, action figures, CD-ROMs, and more than 60 Web sites reflected her tremendous popularity. And not only did Xena battle evil, often taking down scores of evil warriors, but her best friend and sidekick was also a woman — Gabrielle. Together they kicked some serious, evil butt. We liked that.

We like the fact that CBS, the very network that was uncertain about *Cagney and Lacey*, specifically looked for buffed babes for their *Survivor II* reality show series. We like the fact that, for the first time in motion picture history, women are top-selling openers. *Erin Brokovich*; *Josie and the Pussycats*; *Bridget Jones' Diary* (for which actress Renee Zellweger had to gain weight and the public loved her!); *Save the Last Dance*; *Miss Congeniality*; *Angel Eyes*; *Charlie's Angels*; *Lara Croft: Tomb Raider*; and *Crouching Tiger, Hidden Dragon* in which the two lead female characters outfight all the men combined on screen; were all hits. Just as there was the Year of the Women in sport, this must be the Year of the Women on screen and the fallout can only mean good things for everyone.

In fact, when Drew Barrymore first approached movie executives about a remake of *Charlie's Angels*, they were skeptical. Not because jiggle wouldn't sell but because Barrymore proposed this would be a movie where the leading ladies didn't carry guns, there would be no nudity (except one hilarious stunt that leaves Barrymore herself wearing little boy clothes and riding a scooter), no sex scenes, only three strong women using brain and brawn! It was a mega-hit.

But what is more exciting is a good many of these women are now insisting on doing some of their own stunt work and buffing up for choice parts. When Cameron Diaz, Drew Barrymore, and Lucy Lui took on their perspective roles as Angels, all agreed to intense workouts with Kung Fu masters that required months of training. "They really wanted to learn stunts. It helps them get into character," says Hollywood stuntwoman Lisa Hoyle, who doubled for both Drew Barrymore

Lisa Hoyle (photo provided by Lisa Hoyle).

and Cameron Diaz. So committed to their roles as Angels, the actresses were sometimes so sore they could not move the following day. "At some point, however," says Hoyle, "the stunt coordinator would have to say, 'Look if you sprain an ankle or break something, it will shut down production and I'll be responsible.' That's when I step in, but most actresses really want to do a lot of their own stunts today."

In fact, for the action-packed *Buffy the Vampire Slayer*, actress Clare Kramer (she played the delightfully villainous Glory), stunt work was seen as a reward. "As a special reward at the end of the season, I got to do the ratchet stunt." In the final scene when a wrecking ball comes crashing into the character of Glory with the hopes of killing her off, actress Clare Kramer wore a harness that jerked her back, making it look like she was smashed into a wall. What would have been perceived as a punishment to most artists was pure pleasure for Kramer. As a high school and college athlete, this mega-stunt beckoned the athlete within! I can do this!!

Yes, the shift is there. Chris Lee, producer and former head of Columbia TriStar Pictures, readily agrees. "A real shift is taking place. Women are refusing to be easily categorized. They're out there kicking butt, both literally and figuratively."[6]

However, let's be careful not to sugarcoat this. There are still unhealthy goddesses out there in the media. Too much hair, too much makeup, too much silicon. As many kick-ass heroines as there are, there are an equal number of lingerie catalogue models who are rail thin with implants. Not surprisingly, there are growing numbers of teenage girls who are getting implants.

In doing research for another book, we discovered no one is disputing that all implants leak. The question is really, is the level of residue that is absorbed into the human body acceptable? Unfortunately, our government has answered yes. We believe this is a social issue that is going to have very real, very serious, and very costly ramifications as these children become adults and think about childbirth and breast feeding and begin raising little healthy (we hope) girls of their own.

We wish that this book could come with a small tape recording so that everyone could hear the words of trainer Radu as he practically yelled at us when asked about women's images and cosmetic surgery.

"We have forgotten what is important," exclaims Radu, his voice rising. "Don't ever be proud of something you can buy! Be proud of the things you do. Be proud of the things you can accomplish. Make people respect you. For people who have cosmetic surgery, they don't even understand it's not them. Women's liberation fought so hard. For what? It is up to you to convince society what you are. You must do! Let us judge on what people do. Create! Do! Make things happen! Dream! This is living. But you must work for everything. Don't ever be proud of the things you can buy."

It is no wonder that Radu's star pupil echoes his philosophy of physical honesty. How many times have we heard Cindy Crawford say, "I don't look like Cindy Crawford when I wake up in the morning." She admonishes teenage girls not to be fooled by media images of beauty — citing the hours spent before photo shoots applying dark make-up to her outer thighs and backs of her arms where women normally have fat, and taping her breasts and applying more dark makeup to her cleavage to make her breasts appear larger. She is an outspoken beauty, not afraid to disclose her weight — well over 130 pounds — or imperfections.

Supermodel Tyra Banks also acknowledges that modeling is about deception. "We wear hairpieces and all this makeup. And the oil on our bodies reflects muscles that aren't even there. I don't have muscle tone," she says, "but it looks like I do on the cover because of the oil."[7]

In contrast, so many celebrities deny their beauty enhancements and plastic surgery, refusing to be responsible about what is real and realistic beauty and failing as role models. This is why we are proud of Tyra Banks who takes her role as mentor so seriously.

And, then, there is *Playboy*, still peddling the Stepford Wives image. For example, in 1997, Farrah Fawcett celebrated turning 50 with a Playboy Home Video in which she, one of the biggest sex symbols of the '70s and '80s, is remade by the *Playboy* folks to be taller and more buxom than she actually is. As if she isn't sexy enough.

According to a casting notice which was circulated in Hollywood, in search of a Farrah Fawcett look-alike, the producers were looking for a 5'6", 110-pound model with 34-36 D bust, 25-inch waist, and 36-inch hips. Hello? Does anyone besides us remember Fawcett's scantily clothed body on *Charlie's Angels* or in her big-selling posters? 110 pounds and a 36 D bust?! How would she walk?

The women on the U.S. women's bobsled team teased Michelle constantly about her size 6 svelte body. At 5'6", Michelle has 36-inch hips and weighs in at 135 pounds. So we must ask ourselves, if Michelle is teased by elite athletes for being "stick woman" at 135 pounds, what would a woman of the same height, but weighing 110 pounds with two watermelons stuck to her chest look like? A chiropractor's dream? An avid *Playboy* reader's fantasy? Or yet another destructive and unrealistic image for young girls?

We all need to look at our real accomplishments. We need to rally around all our female athletes and be proud of their successes. We need to embrace our Tori Allens, Marion Joneses, and Brandi Chastains. And we need to put an end to preconceived notions of what athletes should look like. Was Babe Didrikson-Zaharias less of an athlete or a woman because she didn't wear makeup? Of course not.

We also need to be aware that prejudice can work two ways. We don't want to imply that beauty and athletics can't go together. We accept that in the world of the media, in the corporate marketing strategy, beauty is frequently as important as athletic ability.

Woodhull asks, "Is Lisa Leslie any less of a basketball player because she also can have a career as a model?"

Um, no. The Leslie we saw was grunting, sweating, and hustling the ball like nobody's business. The Leslie we know can dunk, pass, and shoot like a champion. "Is a beach volleyball player less of an athlete because she plays in a bikini?" Um, no. Nancy Reno is an animal on the beach. She grunts, sweats, spikes, drives, rallies, and bullies with incredible force and determination. And about Gabrielle Reece, Woodhull said, "In my opinion, Gabrielle Reece has done a lot for the self-esteem of countless young women simply because she has been able to parlay athletic ability and a 6-foot-2-inch, 180-pound body into a role as sex symbol for Generation Xers. As long as marketing firms are convinced sex sells — and they are — I don't think we can get away from good-looking men and women dominating the commercial endorsement field."

OK, but we can and must expand what (and who) is considered beautiful as we define our own images. We need more women with the confidence and inner beauty of Sky, Nancy Reno, and basketball star Sheryl Swoopes. Once, while traveling to a game, Swoopes was asked by a flight attendant if she was a model. "No," Swoopes replied, "I'm a basketball player."

Surprised, the attendant said, "Oh, you don't look like a basketball player." Swoopes asked, "What does a basketball player look like?" Exactly.

Notes:

1. Beth Sonnenburg, "The Female Athletic Mystique," *Muscle & Fitness Hers* (August/September 2001), 79.

2. "Mission Impossible: Deluged by images from TV, movies, and magazines, teenage girls do battle with an increasingly unrealistic standard of beauty - and pay a price," *People* (June 3, 1996), 66-68.

3. "Heroine Worship: Most Valuable Player," *The New York Times Magazine* (November 24, 1996), 62.

4. Eric Davis, "Some Thoughts on Local Girls' Cage Season," *The Marion Star* (March 31, 1996), 3B.

5. Eileen Glanton, "Mighty 'Xena' heroically battles for justice, ratings in syndication," *The Columbus Dispatch* (October 27-November 2, 1996), Teleview Plus 26.

6. Shawna Malcom, "They've Got Power!" *TV Guide* (June 2001), 17.

7. Chuck Arnold, "Chatter," *People* (March 10, 1997), 128.

The Athlete Within

Nancy Hogshead is on top of the world. At 14, she was the number one swimmer in the world, and she later graduated from Duke University and won three gold medals and a silver medal at the 1984 Olympic games. She is in six Halls of Fame, including the International Swimming Hall of Fame and the International Scholar-Athlete Hall of Fame. She served as president of the Women's Sports Foundation and on several boards of trustees for various women's sports organizations. She went to Georgetown Law, specialized in Title IX cases with a private practice, had a baby boy, then left her practice to accept a position as a professor at the Florida Coastal School of Law. But it's no fairy tale. While at Duke University, she was raped for 2½ hours by a stranger she would later say "clearly hated women." She believes she was picked because she was a well-known and respected world-class athlete and was being punished. For her, it would be that athlete within who would save her life.

"Of course, sports are so important to us all. It teaches how to win, learn to be part of a team, how to postpone short-term gratification and to achieve longer-term goals but, for me personally, it was a wonderful way to recover from being raped. It helped me reclaim my body.

"It [swimming] allowed me to become the author of my body again. I could set sports goals and meet them. This is a very common feeling among rape victims, women feel very out of control of their own bodies. I was taking it back. Every day I trained, every day I swam I got a little back. And, it gave me a socially acceptable way to vent anger. I could scream under the water. I could channel anger. I could be very mad at the East Germans for using steroids," she laughs now.

The athlete within is so incredibly powerful.

Every successful athlete, success being measured individually by goals set and results attained, has been in the "zone," the point at which her mind and body work together and everything else falls into place. An athlete is more than a person with a special ability and a strong body; she is also a person with a strong mind. Being the strongest or the fastest is not enough — a successful athlete must have the will to prevail, the will to succeed.

There is something we did not mention before about the amazing Rachael Scdoris. Her resume reads like this: nationally recognized runner, nationally recognized racer. Already having made sports history in her debut of the 500-mile International Pedigree Stage Stop Sled Dog Race, Scdoris is vying for her chance at the Iditarod (the most grueling and harsh race on earth). This honor student-beauty queen-spokesperson-model-motivational speaker is up before dawn, caring for more than 100 dogs, training up to 30 miles per day, and running another seven that same day. And, oh yeah, she is also legally blind.

Rachael Scdoris (photo courtesy of Pinnacle Marketing Communications).

Born with a rare condition called achromatopsia that gives her a 20/200 vision, the images before her blend together. She can see images, but with any change of light Scdoris is completely blinded. Imagine racing along on ice and snow up to speeds of 20 miles per hour and suddenly seeing nothing but white.

Turning directly into the sun also spells trouble for Scdoris. Having watched video footage of Scdoris wiping out at a hard turn during a race, it is hard to imagine competing in this gruiling sport without sight. But Scdoris looks at it this way, "Sighted racers wipe out just as much as I do. I know it's not just me." In fact, in some instances, it has saved her. While other racing teams have wiped out on a hard, icy turn, Scdoris is able to use her intuition and athletic grace, working on her own balance to save the sled. After one such race, a downed racer asked, "How did you make that corner?" Simple, she says. "I didn't see it coming."

But Scdoris is very insightful about what lies ahead for her, and she acknowledges it is only going to come with hard, hard, hard, work. "I decided a long time ago that I wasn't going to be a cute, litte blind girl. I have so much I want to do and I know I can do it."

Will is what carries athletes through pain and disappointment. It is what picks us up when we have fallen, what carries us toward our goals. It is will that drives us to be dedicated and successful athletes, students, businesswomen, and mothers.

Sometimes women are already accomplished athletes when injuries occur and they must will their bodies to fight weakness and vulnerability. Sometimes the injuries come before great accomplishments. In this chapter, the reader meets women who have overcome terrific odds, often defying disease, debilitating injuries or trauma to become athletes or to remain athletes.

Wilma Rudolph overcame severe childhood illnesses that threatened to paralyze her. At age 4, Rudolph was struck with polio, scarlet fever, double pneumonia, and lost the use of her left leg. For two years, her mother drove her 60 miles for physical therapy, and every night Rudolph's 10 brothers and sisters took turns massaging her leg until she was able to walk with a brace. At age 8, she was fitted with an orthopedic shoe to help her walk more normally. She wore this shoe until she was 11, when she finally discarded the shoe to play basketball with her brothers.

She played basketball and ran track through high school and college. While still a high school student, she won a bronze medal at the 1956 Olympic Games as a member of the U.S. 4x100 relay team. In 1960 at the Rome Olympics, Rudolph became the first American woman to win three gold medals in track and field (the 100-meter, the 200-meter, and the 4x100 relay), and she did it with a severely sprained ankle. Labeled "The Gazelle," "The Black Pearl," and "beauty in motion," Rudolph's amazing accomplishments popularized women's track and opened the door for the female athletes who followed.

Venus Lacey, a member of the gold medal women's basketball team at the 1996 Atlanta Games, also overcame childhood disabilities and prognoses that she would never walk without a limp. As a small child, Lacey's brother carried her everywhere because she could not walk unassisted. But Lacey was determined that she would not only walk, she would run and jump. And, indeed, she soared.

In 1988, Gail Devers, fighting Graves' disease, came within one week of having her feet amputated; a change in medication turned things around and saved Devers' athletic career. She says, "Deep within, I was scared to death that I was finished as an athlete."[1] Instead of giving in, she fought back to become the Olympic champion in the 100-meter race in 1992 and 1996.

Recognized as the greatest female athlete of the second half of the 20th century, Jackie Joyner-Kersee battled injuries (particularly a recurring hamstring injury) and asthma throughout her career as she set world records in the long jump and grueling seven-event heptathlon; obtained four Olympic gold medals, one silver medal, and one bronze; and participated in four Olympic Games.

Two years after being diagnosed with thyroid cancer, triathlete Karen Smyers, mother of a three-year-old girl, placed fifth in Ironman Europe, won the Rock & Rock Triathlon in Cleveland, and went on to win the Inaugural

Jackie Joyner-Kersee (photo by AP/ Worldwide Photos).

New York City Triathlon all in the summer of 2001. Next stop: the mother of them all, the Hawaii Ironman.

U.S. soccer player Michelle Akers battled debilitating chronic fatigue syndrome during her career with the U.S. team, which won gold at the Atlanta Games and silver at the Sydney Games. She underwent 12 knee surgeries in her career and is now playing with the first U.S. women's professional soccer league, which kicked off in 2001.

Mary Ellen Clark overcame bouts of terrifying vertigo to continue diving from a three-story platform and, consequently, win back-to-back bronze medals in platform diving (Barcelona and Atlanta). She refused to walk away when the vertigo seemed insurmountable. "No regrets," she said at the Atlanta Games. "I want to be able to say that in the end. And I can't if I'm walking away because that's quitting. And I'm not a quitter."

In retrospect, she says, "In a strange way vertigo, I think, has made me a better diver, a calmer and more focused athlete. It's given me a greater appreciation for the blessings I've had in my sport and helped me see that life is more than competition and diving."[2] Clark is now giving motivational speeches, hoping other women can learn from her. "If people I know get discouraged, I tell them to look at me," she says. "I'm a living example that the impossible is possible. I've been down so many times, but I've been able to get back up. And so can they."[3]

Six-time Ms. Olympia Cory Everson entered a terrifying world of paralysis due to a blood clot. Everson suffered from what could be compared to a stroke, losing the ability to walk, talk, and even feed herself. While we spoke with Everson, we found her incredibly inspiring as she spoke candidly about relearning to feed herself. Always determined she could do it and return to athletics, Everson persisted. "Physical fitness and sport are so important for taking control of your own life and never giving up again," she says. While Everson quietly serves as a role model for so many breaking into the world of weightlifting and bodybuilding, few can imagine her personal struggle to simply stand again.

The world of sport is filled with stories of athletes who have overcome handicaps and dealt with pain. Co-author and former bobsledder Michelle Powe is another one of those athletes. Literally incapacitated by head and neck injuries suffered in a car accident in 1993, Michelle — already an asthmatic — spent a year bed-ridden, suffering tremendous pain, unable to work, or even function well from day to day. Since the accident, she has undergone a series of surgeries and countless treatments, seen countless doctors, and become an expert on the subject of chronic pain management.

Despite her constant, severe pain, Michelle decided in 1994 that she had to "get back in the game." And the national try-outs for the first U.S. women's bobsled team was the event she chose for her sports debut. She joined that special group of women who comprised the first-ever American women's team in the sport of bobsled.

Michelle's constant pain is still with her and will always be with her. But instead of letting it defeat her, Michelle excels in spite of her pain. She was the first U.S. women's national champion (1995), and one of the first two U.S. women bobsled drivers to compete internationally. Without a coach, the proper equipment or, really, an idea of what they were doing, four U.S. women competed in St. Moritz, Switzerland — the first time U.S. women had ever competed in international competition. Alex likes to say that Michelle and driver Jill Bakken literally paved the way for the U.S. team. They were the first international drivers the United States ever produced!

In 1991, Valerie Still, a professional basketball player, was involved in a near-fatal automobile accident. While driving, Still was cut off by a speeding car, causing her to lose control of her own car. Still confesses that she, too, was driving at a high speed and, as a result, lost control. Her car swerved off the road and into a tree, crushing Still. Her face was broken, her nose virtually torn from her face. She suffered a broken wrist and cuts and gashes all over her body, but these injuries were the least of her problems. Her pelvis was shattered, broken in six places. Her first vertebra was fractured, causing doctors to believe she would never walk again, much less play basketball.

Like so many of the women who grace these pages, Still defied medicine. Today she walks and plays with, literally, the best of them. In fact, she was the ABL championship series'

Most Valuable Player in the Columbus Quest's victory over the Richmond Rage in 1997.

Canadian rower Silken Laumann is another striking example of an athlete who has overcome pain to succeed, to mount an inspirational comeback from injury. In 1992, Laumann was preparing for a competition in Germany when another boat unexpectedly cut across her path. The boat's bow ripped into Laumann's right calf, mangling her leg. Nerves were shredded, muscles badly torn, and her fibula fractured. Her leg required nearly constant attention, with six changes of dressings every day for the next five weeks.

Less than a month after the disastrous accident, Laumann was back in training. She pointed out to those who tried to stop her that there were only 78 days left before the Olympic trials. Daily training meant rolling her wheelchair to her shell and crawling into the scull; but she did it, and she made it through the trials. Then, Laumann showed everyone her athlete within; she pulled on everything she had and won the bronze medal in Barcelona.

Laumann's leg had not regained its original shape and strength, her ankle was still swollen, her balance was unreliable, and the pain was always with her. And what was this great athlete's response? She took a silver medal at the 1996 Olympic Games in Atlanta and was one of the stronger contenders in the Sydney 2000 Games, just missing a medal.

Joan Benoit Samuelson had arthroscopic surgery on her knee 17 days before the 1984 Olympic trials for the first women's marathon in Olympic history. She began training five days after surgery, but because she was compensating for her injured right leg, she pulled her left hamstring. It seemed too much to overcome, yet she would not quit. On the morning of the Olympic trials, Benoit Samuelson decided to start the race and run as far as she could. She won the trials, and went on to win the Olympic marathon itself.

Samuelson realized many women before her had laid the groundwork for this day — women such Roberta Gibb Bingay, who in 1966 was the first woman to run in the Boston Marathon (she wore a hooded sweatshirt to disguise her appearance since women were not allowed), and Kathrine Switzer, who ran in the 1967 Boston Marathon (she used her initials when signing up) and was accosted by a race official trying to prevent her from running. "To see a woman run [the Olympic marathon] with such courage and brilliance showed the world that women, too, can be heroes," Switzer says of Samuelson.[4]

Such women demonstrate that sport actively gives health, channels energies in positive ways, and allows people a means for overcoming handicaps that might otherwise overcome them.

The power of the will to persevere, the will that makes a winner, is demonstrated by Ana Fidelia Quirot, Cuban 800-meter runner. Quirot became a runner in an unusual way. She was incorrectly identified as a child with learning disabilities and sent to a special school. It was there that a coach saw her racing barefoot and recognized the athlete within.

And what an athlete she is: two gold medals at the 1987 Pan Am Games; a bronze at the 1992 Barcelona Olympics (in spite of a leg injury, being pregnant, and mourning the recent death of her friend and trainer); and silver medals at the 1994 Central American Games, the 1996 World Championships, and the Atlanta Games. The last three victories were won following a disastrous kitchen fire that engulfed the upper half of Quirot's body, leaving her with third-degree burns and resulting in the premature birth and subsequent death of her baby. The doctors did not tell Quirot of her baby's death for many days. As Quirot herself clung to life, they were sure the news would kill her. Despite months of surgery, Quirot has restricted head and arm movement, a handicap that she is determined to defeat just as she has beaten lesser injuries and overcome poverty and the trauma of her child's death.

In the races that followed the tragedy, Quirot shocked the medical community by running. Each time she ran, she cracked and split healing skin. Many of the medical staff who treated Quirot burst into tears when they watched her racing on television, not because they were happy for her, but because they knew the new level of pain she had reached by splitting the healing skin. It was extraordinarily painful, but Quirot persisted to win a silver at the Atlanta Games.

"What helped me rehabilitate quickly," she says, "was going back to sports. Many people believed that was impossible. But if I had not started running again, I believe I would have died. It was what kept me alive."[5]

Perhaps of all the athletes we had the pleasure of meeting, we were most touched by Barbara Underhill, a Canadian pairs figure skater. Anyone who loves ice dancing knows Underhill. She and skating partner Paul Martini perform fast-paced, steamy, on-the-edge-of-your-seat dance routines that wow their audiences. Happily married, mother of beautiful twin girls, Canada's sweetheart, she was on top of her game. But on May 29, 1994, tragedy struck. Her 2-year-old twin Stephanie Gaetz drowned. "Our whole lives were turned upside down," says Underhill. "I didn't think I would be able to skate again. I just thought, 'How could I ever feel joy again? Smile again? How could I do anything?'"

Slowly, Barbara found her way back to the ice. "It felt strange at first. Then, it began to be a release. When you are grieving constantly and it is the constant thought in your head

Canadian Olympic pair skaters Barbara Underhill and Paul Martini (photo provided by Barbara Underhill).

and it surrounds you, you need an outlet. That's what skating was for me. I would be on the ice and just cry and scream and get out all of my emotions. Other days, I would find myself actually smiling, and I would suddenly realize what was happening to me. Skating was a big help. It became my therapy. Skating at that point in my life was what I needed most. Paul and I skated through that season. I think back on it now, but I can't really remember it very well. But it was there for me."

Paralympian runner Sara Reinertsen, born without a left leg and told she could not run, is a world record holder in the women's 100-meter dash for above-the-knee amputees. Reinertsen is also responsible for introducing a leg-over-leg method of running that has become popular with the best amputee athletes. (The leg-over-leg running style is faster, but requires extraordinary strength and coordination.)

Wheelchair racer Linda Mastandrea has triumphed on the track and in the law, simultaneously setting world records and graduating from law school. She is currently a practicing attorney with world records in the 100-meter, 200-meter, and 400-meter races. Participating in the Atlanta Games was particularly sweet for Mastandrea, who had gone to the Barcelona Games and learned upon arrival in Spain that she would not be racing because her events did not have enough participants to be included in the Games.

In the 1996 Atlanta Paralympic Games, Mastandrea won the gold in the 200-meter race, again showing the world her tremendous will to win (in all ways). She continues to train today.

In 1990, Karen Gardner was a competitive gymnast and track and field athlete (and a recreational skier) with a history of orthopedic knee problems. When she began complaining of pain in her left knee, her doctor blamed the pain on scar tissue from multiple surgeries and disregarded her concerns. But, after finally insisting on a diagnosis from another doctor, it was discovered that, in fact, Gardner had bone cancer and had to have her left leg amputated to save her life.

As she left the hospital, just having been informed of the large, malignant mass behind her knee, Gardner kicked her bad leg with the good and said to her mother, "Well, at least I can ski again." And ski she did. Six months after the surgery, she learned again how to ski, and is now the world champion in the disabled super giant slalom.

We have met so many brave and persevering athletes and have heard about countless more. We never cease to marvel at the remarkable strength of the human spirit. One of our favorite sources of motivation is champion bodybuilder and former member of the first all-women America's Cup crew, Shelley Beattie (aka "Siren" of the "American Gladiators"). Beattie has overcome numerous obstacles — from uncaring foster parents and the special disability of a hearing loss to physical injuries and mental depression.

Beattie's severe hearing loss made her an unusual crew member for America 3 and set up new challenges for her and her teammates. But Beattie has frequently been in first-ever circumstances and has paid the price. She was, therefore, not afraid of this challenge. She talks about being the first and only girl in her school to go near the weight room. At 14 years of age, Beattie wanted to do some lifting to help her gain weight for the track season. She says, "People thought I was weird for [weightlifting]. And especially when I quit track after my junior year to become a bodybuilder!

"A few years later, I became a pro. Then, 1992 was my first year with the 'American Gladiators.' In 1995, I made the first all-woman America's Cup sailing team. [Have I been] criticized? [Have I been] ridiculed? That's like asking if the Pope's Catholic."

Beattie is unusual in another way: She has accomplished most of her goals alone. Now she has the strong support of her husband, John, who encouraged her to try out for the women's America's Cup crew. But John was not there when Beattie was growing up the hard way, in a series of foster families who didn't have time for or interest in the ambitions of a developing athlete. By the time Beattie was 17, she was on her own, supporting herself and finishing high school. She kept right on working for the next four years while going to college and training as a body builder. She says that throughout the years, there were always one or two people who were friends, people "who accepted me and tried to understand me, no matter how closed I was at the time." Those are the people she credits with helping her by believing in her just enough to let her believe in herself. As Bonnie Blair says, "One person believing in you can give you great power, even if that one person is yourself."[6]

In 1990, Beattie won the USA bodybuilding championship and a contract with a major vitamin supplement company. She was in the limelight more and more, not an easy thing for a woman who is naturally withdrawn. For Beattie, the bright side to her growing fame has been the children who are her fans. She hopes she is helping them by being a good role model. "I love the letters I get from children and parents of deaf kids. I always send them free photos and a reply of thanks. I love to go to deaf and hearing schools to 'talk' with the kids. I can't explain how good that makes me feel. I think it helps me more than it helps them," she says.

Prior to making the America 3 crew, Beattie had never been a team member. Combined with her hearing loss, that made for some uneasy times in the beginning. "At first, being on a team with all hearing women, I was very frustrated and angry with myself. Teamwork requires good communication and keeping up. I had to confront many issues — especially those relating to my hearing loss — for the first time in years.

"In college, I had a sign language interpreter for meetings, social functions, and TV interviews, but on the boat it was just me and my teammates. I taught them some basic signs for 'grind' and 'stop,' and also ways to get my attention, like tap me on the shoulder, wave to me, or stomp on the floor. The grinders asked me to teach them more sign language, so we all could talk to each other from a distance and in social settings.

"In the end, this was the best experience I've ever had — belonging to a group. My deafness forced me to confront and deal with real life without hiding it or pretending it's not important."

Beattie has had to confront other issues during her athletic career. Being a female bodybuilder, especially one of national note, makes her a person who stands out, who looks different.

When we asked Beattie about the feminine models that society promotes to young women, she responded, "I don't pay attention to what other people define as 'feminine' or 'masculine' because I've always felt everyone has both. And nobody I've met has a perfect balance of the two. I've never been one to follow what the media defines as feminine."

What does a football player look like? What does a female athlete look like? One and the same (photo provided by Alexandra Allred).

Because of her personal independence and her athletic choices, Beattie says she has never been perceived as "normal" in lifestyle or in physical appearance. "When I made the all-women sailing team, some of the women just stood and stared at me in the locker room. My best friend, Amy, told me once that it's because no one has ever seen a body like mine. I asked her if that was bad. She said no, but they still don't know what to think of it. As a professional bodybuilder, I have always been stared at and [had] comments [made] behind my back, some positive and some negative. Ignorant people are everywhere. I try not to interpret how others see me, or I may become the idea of what they think I am. I don't let others define who I am or label me. I am only concerned [about] my image for the children's sake."

For the children's sake. That statement is a sure sign of a female role model. And Beattie's role models? They are Jackie Joyner-Kersee and Cory Everson. Beattie considers herself fortunate to have one of her role models, Everson, as a good friend.

When we asked Beattie about the benefits of athletics, she knew exactly what she wanted to say: "Through athletics, I have gained self-esteem and value in myself. I would not be here today if I [hadn't had] sports to turn to. The older and more experienced I've gotten, [the more] my 'shell' has softened, and it has helped me be less fearful of failure and making mistakes — like the time I froze on stage in the middle of my routine because I looked at the audience and lost the beat.

"[Athletics has] continually challenged me to push past my mental and physical limits, having to go past my pain threshold over and over again, recovering from mental [defeats and physical] injuries. ... Trying to prove to myself that I have worth, that I have inner strength to overcome any obstacle.

"As my hearing worsened, I became more hard on myself and, several times, I pushed myself to the edge. Athletics has always been a way for me to release buried anger and frustration. That may sound negative, but what I mean to say is sports benefit women in so many ways. ... Women learn to communicate emotions and learn leadership skills. ... Team sports help women to make quick decisions and learn self-control and discipline. ... Sports will help an introverted and withdrawn person to be more aggressive and outgoing. All women should feel in control of their destiny and empowered [to act]."

The benefits of sports are so varied; they can help us overcome so many obstacles life throws before us. Will. Determination. Courage. Empowerment. The women in this chapter show us that pain and injuries often go beyond the physical, but that women have the strength and fortitude to endure and achieve and become even stronger. They show us that there is hope for those who suffer all types of pain and that winning comes in different forms. High jumper Louise Ritter expressed best the feelings of the athlete within: "It's about the challenge, the journey — all the stuff we learn about the sport, ourselves, and the confidence-building that goes along with it. Even if you never reach your dream, you still learn something from the process."

No one knows this better than Michelle. She never made the Olympic team for bobsledding. But she was able to do two things — two monumentus things — that few people would ever be able to fully recognize. One, she was instrumental in getting women's bobsledding on the docket of the International Olympic Committee just to be considered as an Olympic event.

She was willing to fight the big boys and be less than popular while other sliders hid behind her, allowing themselves to remain in good standing with the federation yet benefit from Michelle's hard stance. Even Alex sometimes played the role of 'good cop' to her sister's 'bad.'

Secondly, Michelle was an accomplished athlete. She was one of the first international (one of four) sliders, the first of international drivers (one of two) and the United States' first driving champion. But she did all of this managing — or trying to manage — extreme pain that would land in her in the hospital time and time again. In a time and place where most people would have given in to the pain and hid in a little cocoon, Michelle drew up the strength of the athlete within. Like Ritter, Michelle just saw this all as part of the challenge, part of the journey ...

Notes

1. "Naked Power, Amazing Grace," *Life* (July 1996), 57.
2. Mary Ellen Clark "Dizzying Heights," *Guideposts* (January 1997), 4-7.
3. Christine Vaccaro Lawson, "Mary Ellen Clark's New Platform," *Women's Sports & Fitness* (June 1997), 65.
4. Kathrine V. Switzer, "From 'K.V. Switzer' to Girl to Woman in the Span of 4 1/2 Hours," *The New York Times* (April 13, 1996), p 9, sec 8.
5. Alan Baldwin, "Quirot Ran to Stay Alive," *Reuters* (July 29, 1996).
6. Bonnie Blair, *A Winning Edge* (Dallas: Taylor Publishing, 1996).

Are You a Mother or an Athlete?

In front of some 600 fans and while the New England Storm was making its drive against the Austin Rage on the 6-yard-line on a second down, a dog wandered onto the field. A whistle was blown, play was stopped, and a slightly aggravated ref sauntered over to the confused pooch and patted his side, trying to coax the dog off the field. The dog sat down. The ref looked to the other officials who only smiled and shook their heads. The fans were laughing and the dog was going nowhere. Coaches used this opportunity to run in more plays from both sides.

Then, the dog sprawled out on the field and for reasons no one is quite sure about, a flag was thrown making the scene all the more amusing. The head official bent at the waist, enthusiastically patted the tops of his thighs and made kissy noises to the pup. The stray crawled forward a little and the crowd cheered. Ears pulled back, tail tucked, the pup edged toward the sidelines while more plays were run in. The cheers escalated as the dog neared the sidelines and the official became more and more animated as he realized this incredibly embarrassing moment was nearing an end. Then, the dog stopped.

"Well, for hell sakes," a coach yelled. The general manager for the Austin Rage trotted over to the other side of the field in hopes of speeding things along. Now, all the players have heard all the new play options and there is a growing concern among coaches that too much time has elapsed and linesmen are going to forget their plays. Then, a voice: "She's gonna have puppies!!"

Slowly the dog rolled over to her side and a startled looking ref began calling to the dog. "Come onnnnnnn!" The EMS crew was called out, complete with a stretcher, and that age-old question of 'how many people does it take to remove a pregnant dog from a football field' was finally answered. It

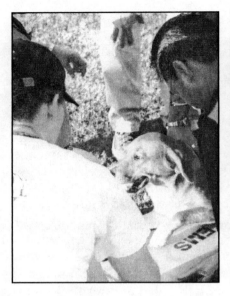

The WPFL is a family affair — even with our canine fans (photos by Alexandra Allred).

takes a general manager, a team trainer, and three EMS guys to strap a pregnant pooch down and trot off the field. The Rage went on to shut the Storm down and win the game 32-16, but not before new puppies are introduced to women's professional football. Only in women's sports, in the midst of an intense drive, could the prevailing question from the sidelines be asked: 'How's the momma?' Intensity and aggression levels never wavered and the desire to win raged on. But, as a local reporter noted, these female players were able to give a sideways glance to the other things happening around them. "Football and family," laughed player/mom Sheri Dillard-Davis. "It's what it's all about."

No one knows this better than Demetra Logan. When she heard there would be tryouts for a women's professional football team in Austin, Texas, she didn't hesitate. Never mind that she weighs only 115 pounds or that she was still breast-feeding her 20-month-old son. She packed her baby and belongings into her compact car, waved good-bye to her fiancé, and left L.A., headed southeast. Motherhood, she said, wasn't going to stop her from being a football player. It was going to make her a better one!

When Mary Rust, 1999 Ms. Olympia, announced to her sponsor that she was pregnant, she had big hopes. "I was sure the company I had an endorsement with would want to work with me. I thought they would want to follow my pregnancy and even do a post-pregnancy feature. This would be neat for the fitness industry because there are so many women who are afraid to get pregnant for fear of what it will do to their bodies." In a recent photo shoot for *Muscle & Fitness Hers*, Rust looked drop-dead gorgeous. Even the magazine's editor commented that Rust never looked better — even post-Olympia. But not 10 minutes after Rust made her announcement to her sponsor, her contract was terminated.

In 1994, at the first tryouts for a U.S. women's bobsled team, the culmination of the competition was the push championship. The competitors pushed a 325-pound sled on a rubberized track (the equivalent of a 450-pound sled on ice) for 50 meters, going as fast as they could go. The top eight finishers made the team.

At the time, Alex was 29 years old and four months pregnant with her second child. She won the championship. The woman who placed second, Liz Parr-Smestad, was 32 years old and three months pregnant with her first child. Both women had planned their pregnancies so that they would sit out the first season, but have their babies in plenty of time to get back into shape and return for the following year's nationals and subsequent season.

Despite the fact that Alex and Liz proved themselves worthy athletes, despite the fact that they trained as hard (or harder) than their teammates, they were informed by a major player in the bobsled federation that they would have to choose between the roles of motherhood and athlete. "Are you a mother or an athlete?" he asked. Two years later, the new team director told Alex and Liz that he was counting them out as competitive team members because they were mothers.

There was a time when we were quite miffed about what was happening, but the reality is this is our burden to bear as mothers. As we spoke with Mary Rust and Demetra Logan, as well as countless others, we heard how the constraints of motherhood make for a very difficult path in sports and business.

You will read about how these women have managed (or are trying) to make it work while going for the gold, figuratively speaking. For most, pregnancy, labor, and delivery were the easy part. We know that our bodies not only come back from pregnancy but look better than ever. As Mary Rust says, "We have muscle memory," meaning that our bodies come back and come back stronger. The hard part is adjusting to our new lives, making our significant others understand and help, and overcoming all the guilt and fears we face as new moms. (Guess what? That never goes away!)

The U.S. women's soccer team, which is widely funded, could afford to have a traveling nanny for the growing number of team babies. But for the bobsledding team, struggling for each penny, this was not an option. When Alex and Liz were told they would not be competing in 1996, it was a simple matter of money. Neither woman could afford to leave her baby to travel Europe for two months and there was no sponsorship to help them.

For a long time, we placed a burden of confusion on mothers in society-at-large and particularly on mother-athletes. The message is to be nurturing, caring, loving, and all-giving; just don't bother having outside dreams or aspirations. But, just as we have seen a shift in the public perception of the ideal female body, athlete-moms are beginning to see a shift in sports. We are just now realizing that mothers without dreams and aspirations cannot possibly inspire and encourage their children.

In 1997, we discovered there were more than 100 athletes listed with the USOC as parents, with just over a dozen mothers. Today, that list has nearly doubled. Many of the national governing sports federations help or provide child care and, as it becomes more socially acceptable to be an athlete-mom, more and more families are pitching in to help. Because child care alone is a logistical and financial nightmare, it is the number one reason for female athletes failing to be all they can be. We have come such a very, very long way. But when we hear about Mary Rust, one of the top names in the fitness industry, a woman known for her athleticism, grace, and professionalism, being dropped like a hot potato when she announced her impending motherhood ... well, that progress seems pretty slow. For those who struggle every day with body images, weight, and diet, it seems inconceivable that Mary Rust wasn't hoisted up on to the corporate shoulders of the sports world for showing would-be moms how awesome you can look by working out.

Over the years society asked female athletes, "How can you neglect your baby to train?" and "How can a woman whose body has endured pregnancy and childbirth still be strong enough to compete?" But anyone who has experienced childbirth knows just how strong you have to be. In fact, during the filming of *Courage Under Fire*, Meg Ryan proved the point to a reporter. During a break, crew members and actors were swapping war stories, showing off scars and wounds. Ryan piped in, "'I had an 11-pound baby.' After that," she says, "everyone shut up."

There are some amazing athlete-mothers who began to quiet disbelievers early on. For example, Fanny Blankers-Koen, a Dutch sprinter, became the first mother to compete in the Olympics and win — winning four gold medals at the 1948 Olympic Games. She was 30 years old, already the mother of two daughters, and three months pregnant at the time of the Olympics.

In 1958, (two years before she would win three gold medals at the Rome Games), Wilma Ruldolph became pregnant. Tennessee State University had a strict policy against allowing anyone with children to participate in the school's athletic program. Rudolph had no college degree, no husband, no job, and a child on the way. And the 1950s were a tough time for a single African-American woman. But Tennessee State track coach Ed Temple took a chance. Rather than ostracize her, the team and coach rallied to help her. The results, of course, were phenomenal, leading to prestigious athletic and business careers and, eventually, the Wilma Rudolph Foundation (established in 1981).

There are so many great mom-athletes, so many stories of overcoming training/family conflicts, so many issues and concerns that have to do with training and dieting while pregnant, and so many athletes eager to share their experiences that Alexandra ended up writing a book entitled, *Entering the Mother Zone: Balancing Self, Health and Family*. (For your autographed copy, visit www. alexandra.com.) As a perfect illustration of how many moms were eager to share or ask questions, celebrities and models joined in, asking questions, talking about the challenges of motherhood, and passing on advice. The end result was a great book and proof positive of the amazing, scary, ever-changing, and ultraimportant topic of athlete-moms. So many elite mom-athletes have said motherhood helped them improve as athletes. In fact, all of these women became credible mother-athletes and championed the notion that pregnancy and motherhood actually improved their performances.

This was not news to us, particularly since Alex had learned a lot about being a mother and an athlete through her own study with Dr. James Clapp, a renowned obstetric researcher at MetroHealth Hospital in Cleveland, Ohio, who studies the correlation between athletics and healthy pregnancies. He has examined the intensity of many types of exercise, monitoring pregnant athletes from aerobic dancers to marathon runners. What he has learned is encouraging.

Clapp has conducted thousands of case studies on training injuries during pregnancies. While pregnant women's equilibriums do tend to be off (the new shift in weight tends to make women more clumsy), Clapp's research shows that injury rates do not increase during exercise. One reason: Clapp believes that "pregnant women exercise more control and pay more attention to factors that contribute to injury."

Concerns about preterm labor induced by extreme exercise also have been reduced greatly. Clapp's studies show that exercise does not initiate preterm labor, and neither does it affect the length of labor. The incidence of fetal distress is actually reduced, he reports, for women who continue to exercise throughout their pregnancies. His studies have yet to uncover a single case of unexplained demise, fetal trauma, cord accident, or clinical utero-placenta insufficiency in the fetuses of exercising women. And women who remain active throughout their pregnancies have more than an 85 percent chance of having a normal vaginal delivery.

Clapp is particularly interested in placentas — more specifically, the growth of the placenta as a result of exercise. The placenta is a membranous organ that lines the uterine wall and helps protect and cradle the baby. Clapp believes that the largest placentas have been produced due to vigorous workout programs during the critical period of placenta growth. This theory, as Clapp

This is how Dr. Clapp measured how hard I was working (photo provided by Alexandra Allred).

explains, has been confirmed by "using ultrasoundography to estimate changes in placental volume." Simply put, Clapp believes that exercise produces larger placentas, which offer healthier, stronger wombs and, thus, healthier babies. He also believes exercise results in easier deliveries.

Case-in-point: As Liz went into the hospital to have her baby (she was already in labor), she stopped in front of the hospital sign to pose for a picture so that her first-born, later to be named Austin, would see where he was born. Two hours later, mama and baby were fine.

Like Liz, Alex also had her (second) baby in record time. Both women firmly believe their exercise regimens made for easier deliveries. After only five pushes, Laura Katherine was born to Alex and Robb and, while the doctor sewed her up from her episiotomy, Alex was sitting up telling jokes. Her physician, Dr. Ann Wurst, would later call this the gold-medal push plan.

As encouraging as all of this is for pregnant women who wish to exercise, it is equally important for pregnant women to confer with their physicians first. Education, training, monitoring fetal development, and safety are extremely important for pregnant athletes. In fact, Clapp prefers to see a woman and discuss these issues before she becomes pregnant so that both doctor and patient understand what to expect. Because all patients and athletes are different, each woman may respond differently to exercise during pregnancy.

Like Clapp, Dr. Kevin Hackett points out that no matter what level of exercise the pregnant woman is performing, whether she is just beginning an exercise program or continuing intense training, she must understand how her pregnancy will change her body and abilities. Low self-esteem can attack when she least expects it. And despite the glow of her pregnancy, the now-rounding woman periodically finds herself becoming depressed over her body's changes. Both Clapp and Hackett lecture on the importance of mothers-to-be having positive mental attitudes about their bodies and accepting that there will be physical changes during pregnancy.

As we said, the easy part is being pregnant and going through labor. If you are pregnant, now is the time to have fun, work out with a fitness routine your body is adjusted to, and get as much sleep as you can. You're going to need it. Fortunately, pregnant women are now able to go to the gym without scrutiny. We are finally understanding that a fit mom (this includes pregnancy) is a happy mom.

When we spoke to celebrity trainers Radu and Billy Blanks, both confirmed that they don't recall another time when so many pregnant athletes were working out in their studios. But because there are still so many outside pressures for women — elite athletes or not — to have a certain weight or shape, we can sometimes lose sight of what is important.

No one knows this better than All-American record holder and two-time Olympian Michelle Rohl. We were particularly impressed with her candor about her weight, the fear of missing out, and the anticipation about meeting her new baby. We wanted to share her story.

An athlete most of her life, Rohl was determined she was not going to let her pregnancy slow her down. As a race walker, her speed and weight were essential to her success in the sport. "Some people can continue for several months into their pregnancies without seeing a difference in their training and racing, but I am not one of those people. I tend to slow down significantly in the first two months, and then level off."

Remember while reading this story that all women are different. Alex was a hormonally raging lunatic while pregnant in her first trimester, beating everyone else's times when running sprints, the stairs, and lifting weights. Demetra Logan really didn't work out, and Mary Rust reduced weight lifting and did light cardio workouts. Everyone is different. But for Rohl, new to the mommy game, worry began to set in. If she was this slow in the beginning, what would she be like in three more months? Rohl feared she would never get back into shape.

She became obsessed with the notion that she could and would still train with her team. In reality, this was one of the most destructive things she could have done. She began comparing her times with everyone else and beating herself up for her own slowing pace. "My coach stopped giving me goal paces. He didn't want to be party to my obsession, but I was still obsessed with the stopwatch, and my position in races and even workouts. I also began to have an unhealthy attitude toward my diet. I never really worried about diet or weight loss before I was pregnant; I ate whatever I wanted to eat."

Rohl put on an instant 10 pounds and panicked. "Since my body fat is normally very low, my body knows it needs to store enough fat to support my pregnancy as quickly as possible. Of course, this being my first pregnancy, I didn't understand what was happening. I thought, "If I keep gaining 10 pounds a month, I will gain 90 pounds by the end of this pregnancy."

This initial weight gain is what experts call "Mother Fuel." It is because of the mother fuel that some women put on most of their weight in the first month. It is the necessary loading of needed fat for both baby and mother. But, it is something that can be controlled during the second and third trimester. Not knowing this, Rohl fixated on her weight. She weighed herself constantly and refused to give on her workout routines — no matter how hard it was.

She remembers, "My due date was July 18th, but I didn't believe this. I gained so much weight so early that I was sure I had to have conceived earlier. Therefore, I decided that the Fourth of July would be a good day to have the baby. This was a particularly hot day for Wisconsin, I remember. I went to the track. 'Eight hard quarters should put me in labor,' I thought. Ninety-second quarters were never so hard. Luckily, I came to my senses after four." With a pulse rate of 200 beats per minute, her face bright red, and calves so cramped that she was on her knees as she gasped for breath, Rohl decided the baby wasn't coming and limped back to the car.

She took it easy for the next few days, running light one- or two-mile jogs. Molly arrived July 7th. "I felt so sorry and guilty when I saw her. The doctor had decided she was wrong about the due date, in the other direction. Instead of being one to one and a half weeks early, she was three weeks early. She looked like she'd rather crawl back inside and bake a little longer, and I wished I could accommodate her. While she was inside of me sometimes she seemed to be little more than a growing tumor that made me fat and slowed down my workouts. Now she was a tiny, fragile, precious little girl. Being the best athlete suddenly plummeted on my list of priorities in life. I just wanted to be Molly's mother."

Rohl is Molly's mother and a great one, but she was a victim of what so many moms have felt. Besides the fact that it was unhealthy for both mom and baby, how could she have enjoyed her pregnancy? (Rohl has had two more happy pregnancies since Molly.) Ms. Olympia has an answer: "That's why I want to be able to talk to women," says Mary Rust. "I can't tell you how many people have told me they are afraid to have a baby because they don't think they will look the same. They're afraid of losing their body and it makes me kind of sad. Part of the reason I want to get more exposure is to show people that having a baby is such a positive thing. Your body will come back and your life will be so much better. It is just amazing how much stronger you become, not just physically but emotionally."

Challenging? Yes. But, as one athlete put it, "The fun things are difficult."

Athlete after athlete has talked about the fact that they had less bonding time with teammates, there was less time to socialize once they had children. Another challenge, says Rohl, "is finding the time to do everything. I lack the recovery period." Unlike her European competitors, Rohl does not have the luxury of properly cooling down with massage treatments or whirlpools. "I can't do nearly what they do," she says. "I skip cooldowns to be with my kids."

Unfortunately, there is no guideline on how to manage family and sport/work. There is no magical potion to make everything work out. As a new mom, that is just one of many personal challenges you must face. But, interestingly, all the mother/athletes agreed that by being moms they became better managers of time, training, and commitments. Because they were moms, all spoke about prioritizing what was really important and that, most often, everything else fell into place.

Demetra Logan is a young 24-year-old with a megawatt smile, looking more like a high school cheerleader than a mother football player. She heard the call to try out and went. Boom. Just like that. But, because she is a mom, there were a few guidelines she had to follow.

Starting out from Los Angeles, Logan says, "I gave myself five days to find a job and an apartment if I made the team. And, it had to be a job where I could be near my son." Had she not had to worry about her baby, she might have

Demetra Logan signs on, foiling the images of a football player (photo by Alexandra Allred).

floated around. Who knows? Instead, she found a job with Kinder Care and a home in four days.

The question we began to ask was not 'Are you a mother or an athlete?' It has no place here. Rather, we began to ask, 'Are you a better athlete because you are a mom?' and the response was overwhelming. Professional and Olympic athletes alike agreed that because they learned to prioritize their lives everything, including their athletic skills, got better. When we spoke to mothers from the U.S. women's soccer team, professional basketball players and fitness pros, all said they have found more balance. "And as you know," says gold medallist and professional soccer player Carla Overbeck, "that is key to being a good athlete."

Mary Rust agrees. "Being a mom has made me a better person because it has put balance in my life which can only strengthen everything else around me."

When we spoke to the always gracious 'Queen of the Ice' Peggy Fleming, she laughed at this question. "Well, of course, I had children after the Olympics but, yes, since having children, I am much calmer as a performer. Children are so calming." We had a good chuckle over that statement while Alex's son Tommy was busily tearing up her desk and his older sisters were arguing (loudly) over a horse statue. There were moments when children are anything but calming. "It's the training we receive from those moments," Fleming said in good humor, "that makes us who we are."

Both Carla Overbeck and Joy Fawcett have cited that because of their children, they tend to get less stressed out than other players when the unexpected occurs. And WNBA standout Sheryl Swoopes agrees. "You learn not to stress out over the little things. You just say, 'Hey, whatever,' and go about your business cause you've got more important things to worry about."

Fitness model Cynthia Bridges finds motherhood empowering (photos provided by Cynthia Bridges).

"Fitness comes second," says fitness pro Cynthia Bridges. "And, strangely enough, that actually makes you a better athlete. There's no messing around when you need to work out. You learn to become time efficient and make the most of your work outs. ... Get in there and get it done!" Like so many of the Olympians we talked to, Bridges said she is always working around taking one of her kids to his/her own athletic, after-school activities.

American Gladiator Shirley "Sky" Eason, Mary Rust, and Cynthia Bridges all spoke about 'Muscle Maturity' — more dense muscle that allows for speedier recovery and stronger muscles. In fact, when we spoke to legendary track star Gwen Torrence and to six-time U.S. swimming medallist Angel Martino, they insisted that motherhood has made them stronger. It is a belief that the Europeans have held for years. Ollan Cassell, former executive director for USA Track and Field, discovered that the Russians hold a philosophy that childbirth makes women stronger. "Women who had babies came back better, stronger athletes," Cassell reports, "because they had trained as long as they could while pregnant, carried the baby nine months, and endured childbirth. They believed this made women stronger."

"Mother-athletes are the ones to beat," laughs Eason. We have muscle maturity and memory, the patience of Job when we need it, but with pent-up frustrations just waiting to be unleashed on some unsuspecting competitor or stopwatch.

Alex was standing on the sidelines (thank goodness) when Chenell "SoHo" Brooks put a hit on a running back so hard, so fast, so fierce, the sound of the

A force of her own, Chenell "Soho" Brooks is known for her hard hits (photo by Alexandra Allred).

impact could be heard clear across the field. "Sweet mother of mercy," someone uttered under her breath. "There's no mercy from that mother," said another.

There is no mercy from SoHo on the field. But she is two people. She's a mom. She's an athlete. As an athlete, you want her on your team. You don't want to face her. She's hard-hitting, powerful, mean. As a mother/teammate, she is one of the first people to greet you with a hug, always with a warm smile and strong words of encouragement that make you believe you are where you are supposed to be, that you are the best, that you can be all things! She is the kind of super mom/super athlete who has developed through sport. And, she was one of the first players to ask about that dog on the field. Such a mother...

And what a feeling it must be to have a mom like that. There is a funny scene in an old sitcom, *Hanging With Mr. Cooper*, in which one of the [female] character's daughters is being bullied at school. Enough is enough and the mother storms onto the school grounds. Suddenly, her voice booms across the playground. "Who's been messin' with my baby?!?" A sea of kids parts to reveal a lone, slightly terrified boy. As we watch SoHo lay on take-me-away-in-an-ambulance hits on other football players, one can rest assured no one ever messed with her baby!

On the flip side, there are days when it feels like the baby is messin' with us. Constant complaining, whining, and crying. As professional volleyball player Linda Handley once said, there are times when you just can't believe two little people (her sons) could drive you to such madness. A statement to which every mom in the history of humankind can relate. And, all the more reason to work out and release some of that anxiety, which led us to our second question: 'Are you a better mom because you are an athlete?' Again, the answer was a resounding "yes!"

Peggy Fleming says that being an athlete carries over into all aspects of your life and makes you a better mom. Speaking about her much-publicized breast cancer scare several years ago, she is convinced she was able to handle the stress and the fear that might have overwhelmed her family because she is an athlete. She knows how to manage stress better, face challenges, and fight back.

"I'm a role model for my kids," says fitness pro Cynthia Bridges. At 39, she is at that! "My kids have seen firsthand the health benefits of how I eat, work out, and, because I am happier with myself, I have more ... no, I make more time for them."

As a mother of a 10-month-old baby, Rust is just stepping into the world Bridges knows all about. While Bridges' children are 8 years and 15 years old, Rust is experiencing the sleep deprivation that is so common for

Peggy Fleming (photo by Harry Langdon).

new moms. She says, "Before you have a baby, you have an idea of who you are and where you're going. But until you have a baby, you have no idea about the emotions and changes that will go through your life. Your hormones are changing, your body is changing, you're exhausted ... working out gives you a little balance, helps energize you, and makes everything a little more tolerable. If you can exercise, it lifts your energy level and that right there makes you a better mom."

The benefits of women in sport go beyond feeling better about ourselves. It really is about the children. The children of female athletes not only benefit from team bonding, they promote it. New York Senator and former First Lady Hillary Clinton's book, *It Takes A Village*, is based on the African proverb, "It takes a village to raise a child." It also takes a village to support a mother-athlete. And, as we have seen time and time again, female athletes truly come together as villages to care for their young ones.

We have shared the wonderment of "It takes a village." When Alex and Michelle worked out at Accelerate Ohio, the trainers allowed Alex's younger daughter, Katie, to come to the gym while Kerri was in school. Always content with her

Alex's daughters Katie and Kerri had front-row seats to the WPFL — often sharing their hotdogs with the players (photo by Alexandra Allred).

bottle and her beloved "Donna" doll, Katie would sit and watch people running on the treadmill, lifting weights, or doing plyometrics. While we were working out, she would wander from trainer to trainer, sit in on office meetings, and even "work out" with other athletes. Barely weighing over 20 pounds herself, she proudly learned to lift the 5-, 10-, and then 15-pound barbells and even ran on a treadmill (with a little help). Welcomed and wanted, Katie became part of the Accelerate Ohio family and part of the village.

Because Kerri grew up watching her mommy on the track, she would often ask, "Can we go to the track? I want to exercise," as though it was the greatest reward she could think of. It beat out Disney. It was her excuse to run. She loves to run. She was the fastest kid in preschool, according to her teachers who couldn't catch her. And she's been the fastest kid in her class and on her soccer team every year since. While Alex WAS training for bobsled nationals, Kerri literally grew up running the track with her mama. One day, when she was 3 years old, Kerri ran four 100-meter dashes with Alex. On the last sprint, Kerri's little fists were drawn up tight, her little face pushed up toward the sky, as she ran as fast as she could to catch up with us. As she was cheered on, her pants fell down, but she kept running. With another 40 meters to go, Kerri never lost her stride. Already focused and determined, she is just like her little sister — a champion.

The sidelines of an Austin Rage practice are reminiscent of training with our bobsledding babies. While more than a dozen moms duke it out on the gridiron, a mob of little cute people race up and down the field, on the stadium stairs, and around the concession stand.

But, there is a big difference with Coach Kennamer. Unlike many coaches who discourage mothers, the Rage's coach says, "We're a family team." Her goal is to be able to one day emulate the U.S. women's soccer team and employ a traveling nanny.

For us, the epitome of the village mentality is the story of that gold (and silver) medal-winning soccer team. Just three weeks after having a baby girl, soccer player Joy Fawcett was planning to return to the 1994 World Cup tour with her teammates. Next stop, Beijing. But as she surveyed the baby formula and food, diapers, portable crib, stroller, high chair, car seat, clothing, and toys piled in the middle of her living room, she tearfully realized she could not do this alone. Then came the village.

One by one, without her asking, Fawcett's teammates called, each offering to carry a baby item. They had all limited themselves to one bag so that they could also carry a baby item. It was the beginning of an amazing relationship between then three-week-old Katlyn and the entire U.S. women's soccer team.

Fawcett told us that as Katlyn got older and was sleeping though the nights, she actually had a waiting list of teammates who wanted to sleep with Katlyn. They took turns playing with, watching, carrying, reading to, and sitting with the baby. As the months passed, there were times when Fawcett found herself alone in the middle of the field doing warm-ups because the rest of the team was on the sidelines watching Katlyn take her first steps, say her first words, clap her hands, or just do something cute. Fawcett would say, "You guys, you're gonna get me in trouble."

But she never did get in trouble, probably because the coaches were also watching Katlyn do her "firsts."

As the 1996 Olympic Games rolled around, Katlyn was turning 2 years old. Much of her life on the road had been missed by her father, Michael Fawcett. During the Olympic Games, teammate Julie Foudy gave Joy Fawcett a video and asked her to watch it. "I thought, 'OK, I'll watch it later,'" Fawcett says. "There were a lot of other things going on. I knew that Julie had been taping a lot of things — all our trips in different countries and stuff." But Foudy kept after Fawcett until she finally sat down to view the tape. What Foudy had handed her was not a tape of all their soccer experiences, but a documentary on Katlyn as she had grown up from three weeks old to 2 years old with her 21 aunts.

Sitting there, watching her daughter, Fawcett realized that every "first" Michael had missed, every smile or giggle, was being played before her eyes. As she repeated this story to us, we couldn't help but tear up, and we suspect Michael has rarely, if ever, had a finer gift.

It is a wonderful thing how our children and sport mix. One helps the other. Happy moms make happy babies and vice versa. But there was a time when Hollywood stuntwoman Lisa Hoyle didn't know how she was going to manage. "I was married before and when we separated, I was left with $75 to my name and I thought, 'How am I going to do this? How can I be a single mom and leave to go to work, raise my daughter, pay the mortgage?' Everything was building." But somehow, as all moms do, Hoyle struggled through. One of only 33 members inducted into the Stuntwomen's Association and at the top of her profession stunting for over 70 actresses, she says her daughter couldn't be more proud.

"But not because I do stunt work. When my daughter started going to school she told everyone I was a stamp lady and all the kids thought that was really cool that I put stamps on everything. See, it really doesn't matter to our kids what we do ... just if we are happy." Joining a team, playing a sport, expressing yourself, living a dream despite the odds, she says, is what makes us happier, healthier people and better moms.

As for her daughter, she did eventually figure out that stunts, not stamps, drove her mother. "One day we were driving under an overpass and she said, 'Oh, now I get it. If there was a movie and someone was supposed to jump off of that, you would do it!'" Although, Hoyle says it did take her daughter a while to understand that not every kid's mom flung herself out windows or allowed herself to be hit by a car.

Lisa Hoyle (photo provided by Lisa Hoyle).

"The most important thing is when I come home from work I am very happy. That carries over to my daughter. She sees a very happy and fulfilled mother."

For professional boxer Sumya Anani, boxing is a family affair. "Matthew is my training buddy. We do abs together, work out at the park, and I always tell him, 'When you get into sports I'll be right there for you,' because he's helped me so much." In fact Anani notes that Matthew, 11, has made her a stronger fighter, more dedicated to her training and more spiritual. *Because* she is a mother, *because* she is a role model, the way in which she conducts herself in and out of the ring is very important. "Besides," she teases, "I want him to think I'm cool." While all of Matthew's friends think it very cool that his mother is a three-time world champion, Matthew likes to play coy with his super mom. "I always say, 'They think I'm cool! Don't you think I'm cool, too?!' "

When her fights are within driving distance, Anani and son will travel together, but many times Matthew is forced to watch her fights on television or tape so that he doesn't miss school and family activities. Always, training and travel are juggled around her son.

One thing is clear: no matter what our sports or professional backgrounds, we will always struggle with the demands

Mary Lou and kids – lots of work but worth it! (Photo provided by Mary Lou Retton.)

of child care, household duties, and travel. Travel, for example, is an issue for every competitive mother-athlete. As we concluded an interview with basketball player Valerie Still, she asked what Alex did about child care while competing on the World Cup circuit. Learning to be a juggler is just part of the motherhood gig. As Mary Lou Retton was quick to point out, "Let's face it. Ultimately, the responsibility rests on the woman."

And that's fine by American Gladiator Sky. "If women could learn that we have it all, just think how great we all would be!? We can be the greatest athletes and the greatest moms. It's totally up to us." However you do it, like that great sports ad goes ... just do it.

Journeywomen

We first learned of U.S. high jumper Louise Ritter during an ESPN segment entitled "Women of Gold." That was also the first time we had heard the term "journeyman" applied to sports. During the Seoul Games in 1996, Ritter was labeled a journeyman by the media — something that in sports jargon (outside this chapter) is not considered a compliment. The term literally means someone who has successfully completed an apprenticeship in a craft or trade, a competent worker. But given to an athlete, the term refers to someone who is technically competent, but who is unable to excel, unable to win gold medals, or set new records.

Before Ritter even stepped onto the Seoul track, many observers had written her off — so we were thrilled to watch the footage as Ritter continued to beat out her opponents, jumping to new heights and, ultimately, taking the gold.

Ritter is a living example of the position taken by Coach Dee Kennamer and the Rage's General Manager Donna Roebuck. Just by creating a professional women's football team (an avenue for women flag-football and rugby players who always dreamed of playing professional football), they became journeywomen. But, more of that later. Once the team was created, they tried to instill some of that never-say-never spirit in their players. After the first preseason game against the Houston Energy, there were some frustrated players in the locker room who complained about not getting enough playing time.

Kennamer made no apologies. "If you didn't get the kind of play time you wanted, this is something we can all work on. If you are a second-stringer, it is your job to make the starters work harder. Keep working, improve your game to make them better. It is your job to try to take their job." It is a work principle that can only improve the entire team.

Coach Dee gives personal attention to her coaches (photo by Alexandra Allred).

Ritter was that second-stringer once upon a time. But she never gave up, took her Olympic gold, and became, for us, the epitome of what the term "journeywoman" means here: someone who has been counted out, told that she is wasting her time, told that she should cut her losses and move on to something more practical (and, often, more traditional); someone who has heard all the nay-sayers, then, headed toward her goal and, through her determination, proved her worth and taken her prize.

Ritter never gave up. She couldn't believe that this was it, that this was all she had. She was unwilling to step back, to step away from competition until she had nothing left to give. And because of that Louise Ritter is a true journeywoman!

Often athletes have shared stories with us that illustrated how, when they dug down deep, they found something more to give of themselves to their sport. Like Ritter, those athletes believed in themselves. They could not be stopped by commentators who said they had already been all they could be.

"Suicide" Sue Horton is a journeywoman. She was told over and over to give up on her dream of becoming a football player, that she was wasting her time. Then, when the WPFL came into existence and Horton thought she had found her chance, she was turned away by Coach Kennamer. Too small. But she refused to quit. It was her dream and her passion. She called back, she begged, she offered to try out with another team just to see if she could measure up to Coach Kennamer's standards. She turned out to be an incredibly dedicated, reliable player with great speed and agility. And the practices she attended three times a week? A three-and-a-half-hour drive one way! Horton was making all the practices that some players who lived just across town were missing. Nothing was going to stop Horton from living her dream. Not size, not geographical location.

The heart and spirit of the female football player is amazing. It seems funny that we would discuss the ramifications of stereotyping women and defining female athletes through their sports but, as open-minded as we all like to think we are, we still had to wonder what a team of female football players was going to be like. We found our answer: Football players are no different from the soccer and basketball players, no different from swimmers, bobsledders, skiers, or track athletes.

Some might disagree with that, however; especially the guests and employees of Holiday Inn in downtown Austin, Texas, when Alex returned from practice after a particularly muddy, hard practice. Still sporting her puddle-soaked, grass-stained football pants and her soaked, muddy cleats and shoulder pads, she drew lots of attention and comments about the strange things women do these days. She sniffed, punched the button to the elevator, and pretended not to notice the sensation she was causing.

"We're just awesome," says Andra Douglas, head coach and quarterback for the New York Sharks. "Last year one of our players got in trouble for wearing the wrong uniform and had to crab walk the entire field. She was two-thirds of the way and she gave out. Another came out to help her and, then, about 20 seconds later the rest of the team was out there "crabbing" with her. These women make me cry. I just have such a love for them."

When Douglas understood that Alex was playing the dual role of defensive end for the Austin Rage, she was elated. "It takes guts, Alex. I want to thank you because it takes guts to do what you are doing. The hurdles you are going over for other women will mean so much one day." Then, she imparted some words that would stay with us for the remainder of this book and, really, the rest of our lives. We lived it through bobsledding and see it in our children. She said: "We have to be termed different so others can be normal."

We have to be different to be normal. No one knows this better than the women of the now-defunct ABL (American Basketball League) and the WNBA. It is particularly true for the players in the ABL, which did not have the huge support from the NBA, network television, and major commercial sponsors that the WNBA has. These women continued to play basketball, to press for a women's professional league, despite lack of media or financial support. While these determined women vary greatly in size, backgrounds, and personalities, they all became blurred together in our minds. Believe it or not, this is meant as a compliment. As we went over notes and compared stories, one thing was clear: we were dealing with a group of happy, outgoing, enthusiastic, caring women who truly want to see their sport grow for the sake of little girls following in their footsteps.

Across the board, all said that children are our most valuable asset. We were swept away by their huge smiles, easy manners and hearty handshakes. The Columbus Quest, the Philadelphia Rage, the San Jose Lasers ... all these women were so eager to talk not about themselves, but about what this sport, what this league can do for little girls and boys everywhere. They even had T-shirts printed up with the league's motto: "Little Girls Can Dream." (We were tickled recently to see a teenage boy wearing an ABL "Little Girls Can Dream" T-shirt. Oh, yeah!)

The women of the WNBA (sister to the NBA) have the same reputation. While many of the overpaid stars of the NBA are known to slight their fans, dodging autograph seekers and even eye contact, the women are just the opposite. Take Teresa Weatherspoon of the New York Liberty, for example. She spies a little girl wearing her number 11 jersey. "Hey, baby! You my girl! You got my shirt!" While children and adults line up for autographs, Weatherspoon practically accosts her fans. She kisses one little girl and tells her, "Be sweet, tweety bird!" The flustered child can only utter, "Oh, my God!" Can anyone imagine Charles Barkley doing this?

Weatherspoon, like all the women basketball players, is reflective about her new station in life. It is not just an athletic opportunity or a job. It is the beginning of something much bigger. It is the beginning of all little girls being able to dream and fulfill those dreams. And she is part of helping those dreams become reality.

There are plenty of stories of individual journeywomen in all sports. Women who overcame personal injury, family problems, or their own insecurities to give it their all in sport and, most importantly, give back to little girls. Professional football player Bobbi James is that kind of player. Not only is it her dream to play but that

Valerie Still of the defunct ABL sports a shirt that will never go out of style (photo by Alexandra Allred).

others will play behind her, only better. Whatever your sport, it is hard not to be enchanted with the way these players have dedicated themselves not only to their sport, but also to their communities.

"It's just great to see the kids benefit," says Sonja Tate of the Quest. "Are we really pioneers?" asks Trisha Stafford of the San Jose Lasers. "We're founders of this league (the ABL), but we're not the pioneers. True pioneers set the stage, like Cheryl Miller, when it wasn't written about or talked about."

As though there had been a requirement of poise, graciousness and journeywoman-ism for induction into the leagues, these women have set a new standard for athletics. Perhaps it is one of the reasons WNBA player Jackie Stiles is so incredibly popular with players, coaches, media, and sports fans. Although she's made the pros, she still insists on the same hard training regiment she had in high school and makes herself do an extra hour of shooting six days a week. She is said to be one of the most compassionate, considerate players, always more eager to credit teammates than herself, and a dream player for coaches. Daily, she pays homage to her pioneering hero, Cynthia Cooper, and she refuses to give up her signature (Cynthia Cooper) NIKE shoes, model year 1997.

Perhaps it is the stories of these committed and unselfish athletes that makes it all the more depressing when a sister athlete forgets this unwritten rule of journeywoman-ism. We expect more from female athletes. We really do.

Recently, bobsledding buddy and still-reigning queen of the powerlifting world Krista Ford called us to air her frustrations. A former athlete-turned-bobsledder, an athlete who came on board in 1999, was making noises about being the pioneer for women's bobsledding. This was hard for our friend who had made the U.S. team (and shattered push-track records from the previous year) in 1995. But like Jackie Stiles, Ford was wanting to pay proper homage to those of us who made the first-ever team, struggled with no money, no sleds, no coaches. Perhaps that was what was most frustrating for those who were sliding in 1994 and '95. We had to make something out of nothing. We had to be different so that the female sliders of the later years could be normal.

It is the little regard for what has gone before and the lack of loyalty to team that is so disheartening. We, in turn, commiserated with our friend Radu about the "me" instead of "us" that we see in some athletes' behaviors, both in and outside the sports arena. When Radu turned the subject to "positive attitudes," we asked him if he had seen a shirt a lot of kids wear today. It reads in large letters: "Second Sucks."

"What?" his voice rose. We guessed that he had not seen the shirt before, but he had a reaction and he made his views clear. "Once the creator of the Olympics said this, and I quote, 'The most important thing in the Olympic Games is not to win but to take part, just as the most important thing in life is not the triumph but the struggle. The essential thing is not to have conquered but to have fought well!' To say that second sucks, it is very bad. We should not even discuss this. I think ... I think the man who created that shirt should be shot! You cannot always win, but does this mean it was not worthwhile? Look at the Muhammad Ali-Joe Frazier fight. Someone had to lose, but it was spectacular. Always, we will remember that fight, the courage they showed."

Florence Griffith Joyner once said she lost many more races than she ever won. She will be remembered for her victories, but losing was part of her growth. Who would have told Flo Jo she sucks?

During the 1994 Lillehammer Games, speedskater Bonnie Blair missed winning the bronze medal in the 1500-meter relay (which was not her best event) by three-one-hundredths of a second. She had already won gold in the 500 and 1000 meters, becoming the first American woman to win five gold medals in Olympic history, the first American to win a gold medal in the same Winter event in three Olympic Games, and the most decorated U.S. athlete in Winter Olympic history. "The media and everybody got carried away with the medals I won," she says, "but what I remember most was that the time I got for the 1,500 was my personal best." Blair tries to achieve her personal best in daily life. Who's going to tell Bonnie Blair she sucks for just missing the bronze?

Before the 1992 Barcelona Games, Shannon Miller watched quietly from the sidelines as everyone predicted glory for world champion Kim Zmeskal. Miller went on to win two silver and three bronze medals at the Games and then two world championships, and become this country's most decorated gymnast. Before the 1996 Atlanta Games, Miller again watched quietly all the hoopla about teammate Dominique Moceanu, then went on to lead the team to a team gold (the first for an American gymnastics team) and to win an individual gold on the balance beam. Miller did not let publicity (or lack thereof) or injuries or age sway her from her goal of an Olympic gold medal. Who's going to tell Shannon Miller she sucks for winning silver in Barcelona?

Ironman athlete Julie Moss gained fame in 1982 when she collapsed while leading the Ironman Triathlon World Championship with just a few hundred yards to the finish line. ABC's *Wide World of Sports* captured the heart-wrenching moment on film, as Moss crawled to the finish line, being passed by Kathleen McCartney with just yards to go. But her heroics resulted in an explosion of triathlon participation. "Julie Moss gave the world the definition 'Ironman Spirit' in 1982; she set out to finish what she started and she persevered until she reached the finish line," says David Yates, president of the World Triathlon Corporation. Who's going to tell Julie Moss that she sucks for finishing second?

Radu was still chewing on the T-shirt business. "I hate this 'second sucks.'" We played it safe and did not mention that No Fear has a T-shirt that reads: "If you can't win, don't play!"

Radu continued: "Perhaps you are on a team that works very hard, you train hard together, but just because you work together, another team might work a little better. Teams are like watches. Every piece is vital to the watch, each piece has its function, just like the team. There are leaders, supporters, followers. Maybe you lose one time because the other team has one better part, but it does not mean you suck! I do not like this shirt!"

Radu is not the only one who feels this way. In fact, most serious athletes do not buy into the philosophy that winning is all that counts. Just one week before Alex was to make her professional debut as a football player, she broke two fingers in one hand and displaced the bones in her forearms in the other. It was painful for a variety of obvious reasons but she was on hand (however disfigured) for the season opener. While she acted as ice and water girl, ran errands and did whatever she could to be useful to the team, the Rage put up a valiant fight against the Houston Energy.

Last year's champions, the Energy had a history of soundly pounding the Rage into the ground. But on this game day, the Rage gave the Energy a run for its money. A rookie quarterback was finding her legs and some rookie mistakes were made, but the Rage was an obvious threat in the WPFL. When the game was over, the coaches all made a point of stating that very thing. We lost because of some rookie mistakes, not for lack of talent. It was our first loss, certainly not a failure. And, it was only the preseason.

U.S. softball player Lisa Fernandez was told by a coach at the tender age of 12 that she would never be a champion pitcher because her arms were too short. "He said I wouldn't be able to really compete past the age of 16," Fernandez says. For Fernandez, softball was her life. This could have been potentially devastating news, but Fernandez did not let it be so. With the journeywoman spirit, Fernandez continued her training and dreaming. Then, at the 1995 Pan American Games qualifier tournament, the 24-year-old Fernandez devastated the competition by pitching a no-hitter, enabling the U.S. to win the gold medal.

U.S. soccer stud Brandi Chastain had her own battles. Chastain was told by a coach after playing a lifetime as forward that she would never cut it on a national level. Imagine how idiotic that guy must feel now. Whether his assessment was fair or not, Chastain refused to walk away.

Swimmer Angel Martino was banned from the 1988 Olympics after her birth control pills caused her to test positive in a controversial drug test (a testing method that is no longer used because it is so unreliable). "I did get to two more Olympics, but it was really hard" to get past the 1988 ban. "I took a year off; I quit! I just couldn't do it. I thought, 'Why am I doing this?' But after a while I realized this was my dream, so why should I let someone take it from me?"

She didn't, swimming to one gold and one bronze in the 1992 Barcelona Games and two golds and two bronze medals in the 1996 Atlanta Games. And while she never received a formal apology about the ban, she says many people have privately apologized to her, telling her, "We know you didn't do anything wrong."

By the early 1980s, Mary Decker Slaney had become the best female runner in the world in the mile, the 5,000 meters and the 10,000 meters. But a combination of bad luck and injuries have kept her from an Olympic medal although she has made four Olympic teams. She has undergone at least 20 operations on her legs, endured the U.S. boycott of the 1980 Moscow Olympics, and been injured (accidentally) by a fellow competitor (knocking her out of the race and out of medal contention) the following Olympics. Tests following the Atlanta Games where she had failed to reach the 5,000-meter final revealed she has exercise-induced asthma.

Finally, properly medicated, she was running like her old self, winning important races handily. But just as she had begun talking about competing in the Sydney Olympics at the age of 42 — she was hit with her newest, and perhaps toughest, challenge. She was banned from competition by USA Track and Field and the International Amateur Athletic Federation (IAAF) because of a drug test during the Olympic trials that showed high ratios of the male sex hormone testosterone.

The problem is this test has been shown to be highly unreliable for women, since menstruation, birth control pills, alcohol, and bacteria in the urine can affect its outcome. Slaney has tested clean for drugs for 24 years. After the Olympic trials, she was tested six times and all six tests were negative. She was finally cleared by USA Track and Field and the IAAF, but not before she lost most of the 1997 season.

Today, she still runs. "People I run against no longer tell me they had my poster on their wall," she says. "Now they thank me for showing them that they have 10 more years of running.

Even athletes who would never have been considered journeywomen — women like Bonnie Blair, who was never counted out — struggled with their own very private accomplishments. While we all only saw Blair's great speedskating triumphs, we never thought of everyday workouts as something she wrestled with. But for Blair, loop training was a challenge. While training, she and her teammates would run up a hill, on a straight, down a hill, on a straight, and start all over again. Blair did 10 loops to the guys' 12. Her goal was to finish before the men finished their twelfth loop. "I was ahead of them on the hill. I could call it ahead because I was so far behind."

While the guys focused on Blair, trying to pass her, Blair was determined to finish her set before they finished theirs. Unlike Fernandez or Ritter, this great feat was not performed before millions of spectators. In fact, few might even consider this a feat, but to Blair this determination carried over into her races, giving her that extra push.

Few also would consider super-model Cindy Crawford or singer/actress Vanessa Williams athletes, but Crawford proved something to herself she never imagined she could do. And she did it, of course, through sport and the journeywoman's perseverance.

Crawford was headed for the big screen, landing a part in the film *Fair Game* with William Baldwin. It was her big break. Together, Radu and Crawford looked over the script. It called for her character to run, jump onto a moving train, and punch out a bad guy. When Radu approached the stunt coordinator on the set about Crawford's training he was told, "Just keep her strong and toned. Don't worry about it."

The stunt coordinators and director were not even considering having Crawford do any of her own stunts. In truth, it had not occurred to anyone she could. Besides, they didn't want her getting hurt. Radu had other plans. While he didn't intend for her to actually make the jump onto the train, he did want the scenes to look as real as possible. Crawford trained as though she really were punching someone out, as though she were running for her life, and as though she were trying to jump on a moving train. In reality, all Crawford was expected to do was the lead-up to the stunts.

Finally, the time for the big scene came. Crawford was supposed to run hard to a certain point alongside the train, then drop off. A stunt double would take her place to catch the train. Crawford would later tell Radu, as she was running along she realized that all her training with him in preparation for that very scene had actually been a lot more difficult than the actual stunt.

Imagine the fallen expressions, the gaping mouths, and pounding hearts of the entire film crew when Crawford did not stop at her mark. As the train roared on by so, too, did Crawford. The cameras kept rolling as Crawford strained, dug down deep and chased that train, jumping on at the last moment, making a spectacular stunt for the movie.

Radu praises Crawford, saying, "I had given her the tools to achieve, and she used those tools to accomplish more than was expected of her, and more than she expected of herself."

Crawford is not alone. There is a new wave, a new shift in Hollywood where actresses are not only being given parts in action-packed chick flicks, but they are doing some of their own stunts! "It's an exciting time for everyone," concurs stuntwoman Lisa Hoyle. "There was a time when we [stuntwomen] would get a few falls or the occasional slap in the face. Now, we are doing free falls, motorcycle chase scenes, and hand-to-hand combat." In fact, on the set of *Charlie's Angels* where Hoyle did a 93-foot free-fall stunt, actresses Drew Barrymore, Lucy Liu, and Cameron Diaz did many, many of their own stunts. They trained in martial arts, with harnesses (hanging for hours) and weight-bearing exercises. There were no prima donnas on that set!

Another one of Radu's clients was chosen for a movie part. This time it was Vanessa Williams, who would star in *Eraser* with Arnold Schwarzenegger. Williams initially went to Radu for her casting as Spider Woman, and found herself climbing the thick rope that hangs from Radu's gym ceiling. Hers was the same story as Crawford's: Williams only needed to look good.

Very rapidly, though, the training carried over into new challenges, causing her to push herself beyond her own limits. "That seed I put in her built her confidence to new heights," Radu says of Williams. "There is nothing she can't do now. Her discovery of her own strength has empowered her. I wish all people could learn the feeling of such triumph. She may not go 600 miles per hour like bobsledding, but she can go 60 miles per hour!"

And what about bobsledding? It's true, we like to think of ourselves as journeywomen and many of the women we have met in bobsledding (Canadians, Brits, Swiss, Germans, and Latvians) share our feelings. We have all been told that this isn't a sport for women, that we're too small, too old ... you name it, we've heard it. We were counted out almost before we began, but we have refused to go away — despite the lumps. And there have been many.

There is no greater story of perseverance than that of Jill Bakken. From the beginning, the odds were stacked against her. In the eight years Bakken was with the bobsled team, she was told point blank she was wasting her time, her parents divorced, money was always a problem, she suffered numerous injuries and personal setbacks. She was lied to by other teammates jockeying for her position in the number one sled, promised corporate dollars that would never come, and dropped by a sports agent because she "didn't have the right image." The irony, of course, is that she is the girl next door. But those were a tough eight years in which she repeatedly asked "Why am I doing this?" In fact, Bakken lived most of the chapters from this book. While struggling to stay one of the best sliders in the world, she endured the athlete-within, goddess-within, journeywoman, and, as you will soon read, toting-the-chain struggles for a sport she loved. There was a time when she told us she was crying herself to sleep almost every night. The politics, constant money constraints and in-house fighting were exhausting.

"All I wanted to do was slide. It's all I wanted to do," Bakken says.

All any of us wanted to do was slide. Little did we know.

When the authors made the first women's bobsled team, we thought we would run, push the sled, hop in the back, and go for that exhilarating ride. Of course, we soon learned there was much more. We had to learn how to walk the track before a run, how to visualize our runs, how to handle the turns, the speed, the pressure, how to sit; how to always look 6 feet ahead while driving, how to crash. And much of this we had to learn on our own.

Laurie Millett, one of the first four American women to compete internationally, climbed into the back of a bobsled behind Michelle in Calgary, Alberta, although Michelle had never actually touched a bobsled before. She climbed in behind Michelle again in St. Moritz, Switzerland (one of the most difficult tracks in the world), although they only had about 10 hours ice time, so they could compete in the first international race including American women.

Persistence is the hallmark of the journeywoman. And there is not much glamour at this stage in one's career. Take the brake position in a bobsled. The brakewoman, crouched over in the back of the sled, holding on to the side bars, head down, counting out the turns in her mind, is part of the sled and track.

Michelle Powe and Laurie Millett make U.S. history in St. Moritz, Switzerland (photos by Alexandra Allred).

Sitting just inches above the ice in a cold, steel sled, there is no cushioning to pad against "tags" on the walls. (A "tag" is the understated way we describe how our bodies are slammed against the icy wall and only our required kidney belts can help hold our organs in place.)

The brakewoman can hear the blades (runners) cutting the ice, hear the rattle of the heavy sled, feel the turns. Then, just before there is a crash, there is the worst sound imaginable in the sport of bobsledding — momentary silence. (The sound bobsledders love to hear is that of the announcer saying, "Through and down," meaning the race is completed and the team finished the run right side up, on its blades.) The silence means the blades have left the ice.

Then, CRASH! Airborne only briefly, the sound that follows — directly after the driver and brakewoman mutter "oh, shiiiiit!" — is that of the sled coming down hard on the ice. In place of the sweet sound of blades cutting ice, there are several new sounds. The capsized sled crashes through each turn, tearing at the sled, and ripping the brakewoman from her seat. While the driver is usually (luckily) under the cowling, worried sick about her teammate, the brakewoman is left to fight it out with the mountain.

The pull of gravity is tremendous. On her sides, the brakewoman hangs on for dear life. It feels as though two very large hands are prying her fingers off the side bars. Then there is the sound of her helmet grinding against the ice. It is a constant "ssccchhhhh" sound that never lets up, except when the sled follows a new curve, sliding to the opposite wall. For a brief moment, sled and woman are separated from the ice wall. There is a moment to catch her breath before the sled leaves that turn and crashes again against the opposite wall.

Shoulders are on fire from the ice burn to any part of the body that is hanging out of the careening sled. Gritting her teeth and pushing against the ice with her head as the sled races down the mountain at 60, 70, 80 miles per hour, the brakewoman fights the track — a useless effort — with neck strength in an effort to save her shoulder from more ice burn or worse.

The only other sound is the grunting, the sound of exhaustion and pain while waiting for the ride from hell to end. And, finally, as the sled travels through the finish curve and slows to a stop, silence falls again. Then the brakewoman can fall in a heap, listening to her own breath. (This is assuming that she has not been knocked unconscious or that nothing is broken and/or bleeding.)

Oh, thank God. It's over. There is rustling in the front of the sled and the worried driver begins to stir, trying to find her way out of the ropes. Her voice is muffled through her helmet. "You OK?" she calls out, still not really seeing her brakewoman.

"Thank God, it's over," the brake will say. Footsteps approach, paramedics check the sled's passengers, and then track workers flip the sled upright again. A track coach will ask, "You OK?" and we will nod.

Then we would go back to the top and try again. We had to because we had to get it right. We had to prove to the FIBT (the international federation for bobsled) and IOC (the International Olympic Committee) that we were competent, qualified drivers and brakes, and the only way that was going to happen was to go over and over again.

During the 1995-96 season, the women's team of eight took its lumps. The total damage was a broken collarbone; two broken ribs; a broken foot; four grade-two concussions; one grade three; an emergency root canal; an injured sternum; torn liga-

Jill Bakken trained year-round for a sport she loved. She always knew she would strike gold (photos by Alexandra Allred).

ments and cartilage; a torn rotary cuff; a broken hand; numerous back, head, shoulder, and leg injuries; a knee surgery; and countless bruises.

When women's bob-sledding debuted in the 2002 Salt Lake City Games, Jill Bakken stood as the only original member of the first-ever U.S. women's bobsled team. She had endured it all — no uniforms, no sleds, no equipment, funds, or federation friends. We learned that bobsledding was much more than just jumping into a sled and going for a ride. It was about training, lifting weights, pushing a bob, enduring countless bumps and bruises. It was about friendship, teamwork, and companionship. It was and is about guts, nerve, knowing when to walk away, suck it up, blow it off. It's about crashing, hoping, praying, believing, and celebrating. For us, it had always been about embarking on a journey that would help our daughters to progress and flourish. So, when Bakken and teammate Flowers crossed over the finish line to win the gold medal, it was the most empowering and rewarding feeling in the world.. we can't even imagine how Bakken felt! And while the rest of the world rewarded Flowers the great honor of being the first African American to win gold in the winter Olympics, Bakken stepped respectfully into the background. Again.

For eight long years, Bakken had endured it all and walked away with even more. Today, she stands as the greatest female pioneer in bobsledding and we are eternally grateful for all her tears, blood, and sweat. She dared to be different and struck gold. In the words of our dear sister Andra Douglas of the New York Sharks, we have to be different so others can be normal.

Just Give Me the Damn Ball!

When we first met Andra Douglas of the Women's Professional Football League, she was trying to find a place to hold practice for her professional football team.

"If it weren't so ugly, it'd be funny," she says. "You should hear all the reasons no one is willing to give us field time. And it's not like I want it for free. I'm willing to pay. We want to pay for [field use] but no one is willing. We've called local colleges and high schools, rec centers ... and it's always, 'We just seeded the fields,' or 'We can't rent to professional teams,' or 'We don't have proper lighting.' It comes down to this: No one wants to give a field to a bunch of female football players."

Douglas was scrambling trying to find somewhere, anywhere, to accommodate tryouts for the new season. When we spoke to other team owners around the league we discovered most were having the same problems. Without positive public image of the league, business and park owners were reluctant to support local teams. On the flip side, because the league had no serious backing from business, the media and public perception was that the WPFL was a bit of a joke.

Throughout modern history of women in sport, becoming a media darling has meant corporate dollars and sponsorship, which equates to topnotch coaches, training facilities, and equipment. Perhaps one of the greatest bodybuilders of all time was a woman named Bev Francis, who, because of her masculine appearance, could not win the contest for sponsorship against the more feminine-looking, less-muscular competitors.

Anna Kournikova, the most downloaded athlete in history, has never won any major competition, but because of her undeniable beauty, she remains the most popular player on the tennis circuit. Michelle Akers, reportedly one of the greatest soccer players of all time (and widely respected/feared by her competitors) never really became the poster girl that Mia Hamm,

Julie Foudy, or Kristen Lily did. It's the whole goddess thing again, but as Coach Dee Kennamer of the Austin Rage wonders, "What does any of this have to do with football?"

In 1994, in response to a directive by the United States Olympic Committee (USOC) that each federation must have at least 10 percent representation of its minority sex, the U.S. Bobsled Federation held tryouts for the first U.S. women's bobsled team in history. Eight women made that team.

Here we were: the first female bobsledders. We were on our way. But on our way where? To what? We had no money, no traveling coach, no sleds, no idea what we were doing. Money was scarce, and all of the incoming money was earmarked for the men's team. Initially, the big question was how to raise money.

To be clear, the entire fund-raising issue is frustrating and complicated for USOC-sanctioned teams, i.e., all sports for both genders. In the case of the U.S. Bobsled and Skeleton Federation, its teams are chronically underfunded. Naturally, competition within the federation for scarce bucks created tensions, and the outcome for the women's team was trying. We were told we must raise our own money, but we must not approach sponsors already supporting the men's team. And we must not approach sponsors not supporting the men's team because those sponsors were being courted by the men's team.

We were in the same position the WPFL would find itself in almost a decade later. We needed to raise money for four $10,000 sleds (and $10,000 is quite inexpensive for a bobsled), not to mention gear for eight women, and a coach's salary. Without positive public images, corporations were slow to come forward, and without the support of big-name sponsors, the media didn't take us very seriously.

Adversity lies in the path of all female athletes to some degree. What if Babe Didrikson-Zaharias or Wilma Rudolph or Jackie Joyner-Kersee had listened to the nay-sayers? Or Mary Lou Retton, who became the first American gymnast ever to win gold in the individual all-around and score a perfect "10" on the vault? "I'm a very positive person," Retton says. "If I'm in a group and there's a nay-sayer, I leave the group because I don't want that person bringing me down." Attitude is everything.

What if Women's Sports Foundation executive director Donna Lopiano had listened to the nay-sayers? Lopiano participated in 26 national championships in four sports and was a nine-time All-American in softball, a sport in which she played on six national championship teams. She is a member of the National Sports Hall of Fame, the National Softball Hall of Fame, and the Texas Women's Hall of Fame. She has coached college men's and women's volleyball, and women's basketball, field hockey, and softball. And she is currently number 95 on *The Sporting News'* list of "The 100 Most Influential People in Sports." (2000), and *The Sports Business Journal* lists her among the "Top 10 Female Sports Executives" in the nation. Talk about determination.

Initially when Alex made the Austin Rage football team, it was for a story for *Sports Illustrated*, it was for the fun of it, the adventure and, always, to show her little girls that Mommy could do anything if she put her heart and soul in to it. But, as the Powe family vested itself with the Austin Rage and the WPFL — for nothing Karen, Michelle, or Alex ever does is less than a family affair — there was a certain feeling of dejavu. We couldn't help but think, "Hmm, we've been here before."

In bobsledding, funding was our major problem. For the first two years, most of us supported ourselves — often aided by our families — in the most expensive sport in the Winter Olympics, and most of us put ourselves in fairly serious debt doing it. In the 1995-96 season, some sponsorship was found for new personal gear for the women's team and to pay some travel costs for one of the four two-person teams. But everyone else was on her own for the travel, training, and other expenses. Individually, we each managed to find some help from interested individuals and companies. For instance, Powerbar and Verizon Wireless helped Alex and Michelle. Limited Edition of San Francisco provided 12 American flag jackets for the first women's bobsled team. These jackets were our only team uniform for two years.

Fund-raiser Earl Ashton (of Merrill Lynch) came on board in 1996, bringing parkas, snow pants, gloves, and spandex uniforms for the women. Ashton continues to support female sliders by raising money and sponsors for travel, lodge, racing fees, and equipment.

Also, in 1996, another financial advisor, Stew Flaherty, brought American Skandia Life Assurance Corporation to the table. Although the money committed by American Skandia was not enough to support all eight women on the team, it was a start, and — more importantly — American Skandia committed support through the 2002 Games!

That pledge of support took on even more importance when, in 1999, the word finally came down that women's bobsledding would be included in the 2002 Salt Lake City Olympic Games! Suddenly, everyone wanted on board.

Now that women's bobsledding is finally an Olympic sport, funding becomes even more problematic. Only the top two or three teams will receive funding from the bobsled federation or USOC. The women who are not supported will continue to support themselves or look for outside sponsorship; they continue to learn how to promote themselves. In order to slide more and be able to vie for one of the top positions, the women need sponsorship. To get sponsors, they have to slide. So, the athletes learn to be fund-raisers and business people, too. The interrelationship between sports and business is visible throughout the athletic world. Women's bobsledding and women' football are no exceptions. Unfortunately, the business side does not always run smoothly.

When the Women's Professional League was first conceived, owners of one of the northern teams stepped in to take care of media relations and corporate funding. Fourteen teams made up the league, and the coaches and players thought their time had come. Indeed, the timing did seem perfect. Fitness and fashion magazines were beginning to use professional athletes rather than models for their covers. The Williams sisters of tennis fame became cover girls for *Vogue* and spokespersons for Avon. Basketball, volleyball, and soccer players suddenly became part-time models, not to fulfill some dream they had to be in the fashion industry, but to be part of a movement that shows the ideal woman of the new millennium.

But for those athletes in the WPFL there came — nothing. They took the same lumps and bumps, breaks and bruises, gave the same hard-hitting, turf-pounding, crowd-pleasing (however small) plays as the NFL without the big checks, fans, or media coverage.

The following season, the owners agreed that someone else needed to handle the public relations and corporate sponsorship. A large, undisclosed amount of money was given to a group of businessmen in the West by the teams' owners. Passionate, dedicated sports fans who gave money from personal bank accounts "led with our hearts more than our heads," Coach Kennamer confesses, only to discover some months later that not only was there no media awareness and no corporate sponsors, there was no money.

A broken neck did not stop Chenell "Soho" Brooks from returning to the game (photo by Alexandra Allred).

With unpaid bills mounting and no acceptable explanation about where the money went, it looked as though the WPFL was going under. Owners met and discussed their future and, ultimately, split up. Just as there was once an ABL and WNBA basketball leagues, there are now two women professional football leagues. A mistake at best.

In the summer of 2001, the WPFL still had no explanation about the disappearance of its funds, had unpaid bills, and risked earning a less than stellar reputation. Some owners left, but Dee Kennamer and her partner, General Manager Donna Roebuck, were determined to hang on.

All of this is not a problem for most of the football players of the WPFL. What they care about it playing. "Just hand me the damn ball!" But, the reality is, this isn't the NFL. So, going back to square one, we found ourselves applying everything we learned about media relations, sponsorship, recruiting fans, corporate funding, and endorsements.

'Atta Girl! A Celebration of Women in Sport

The athletes and coaches recognize that until they get corporate funding, things will be difficult. Once upon a time, every successful women's sports organization was grassroots. The U.S. Women's World Cup is more popular than the men's and the players are America's sweethearts with a wide variety of book deals, posters, calendars, and public appearance bookings. There was a time, however, when they couldn't get anyone to pay attention to them. "I remember the days of cheap motels, low-fare travel," Mia Hamm laughs now thinking about the days. As she says, as they fine-tuned their skills as a team, they had almost total anonymity. Who knew who they were? Who cared about women's soccer outside of other soccer players and their families?

Just look at them now. At the last World Cup, there were over 80,000 fans in attendance. And on April 14, 2001, when the women's professional soccer league kicked off, it was backed by $64 million from investors and promised 22 games on cable, eight teams nationwide, and all of America's sweethearts from the U.S. World Cup team. For women's pro football, there were no major investors, no televised games, and no known sweethearts.

As the stands fill up, "Soho" knows how to motivate the crowd (photo by Alexandra Allred).

For the first season opening game between the Austin Rage and Houston Energy, there were 610 fans. You can't get more grassroots, but the men and women of the WPFL are determined. For now, it seems that the only people who care about women's football are friends and family, but already interest is picking up.

We wish Nancy Woodhull could have met Dee Kennamer and her coaching staff. We wish Woodhull could have seen that game between the Rage and the Energy. It would have done her proud. She was always impressed with the determination and will of the female athlete. "What I find surprising," she said, "is that so many young women have female athletic role models when so few newspapers and television newscasts offer consistent coverage of women's sports. That's further evidence, to me, that women have found alternative sources of information, outside the normal media, for information that they are passionate about. Marketers and media executives should be very wary."

Women's sports keep growing with or without coverage. Female athletes in nontraditional female sports are still sorely overlooked in most media. Case-in-point: women's boxing. While we watched our Austin Rager/pro boxer Ann Wolfe fight and win the IFBA (International Women's Boxing Association) title, we were intrigued with the post-fight talk. A well-known and respected commentator was saying that, since women are so new to boxing, it is difficult to really judge how good female boxers are or are going to be because there really aren't many comparisons.

"That's bull," says pro fighter coach Lori Steinhorst. "They're not new. They [mainstream media] just won't let them [the women boxers] in. Thank God for ESPN. HBO won't show any female boxers even though women have been fighting since the 1970s. Thank God for ESPN." Steinhorst laughs and adds, "There were actually female boxers in the 1800s, but no one wants to talk about that."

Public awareness is one of the main problems female athletes face. How can they promote themselves when it is so hard to get anyone's attention? Keeping an eye on the prize becomes difficult and confusing. The female trying to climb the ladder of success (whether in the corporate world or the sports world) must be part-businesswoman and part-public relations agent. This dual role is particularly taxing for the amateur female athlete who, instead of concentrating on her "job" of full-time physical and mental training, must take valuable time out to promote herself and try to win the sponsorship critical for all amateur athletes. Of course, this business/PR role is not limited to women: we have seen some of our bobsledding brothers struggling for individual sponsors, too. But the problem is certainly more prevalent in women's athletics and the barriers are sturdier.

To raise public awareness and support for female athletes (professional, Olympic, college, and high school), former diver Micki King founded the Women's Sports Foundation (WSF), along with tennis great Billie Jean King (no relation) and gold medallist swimmer Donna de Varona. WSF Executive Director Donna Lopiano expresses the feelings that drove the foundation's organizers: "What would be the reaction if there were no women on MTV? If there were no women in ballet, no women on Broadway, no women in the movie industry? You'd hear people saying, 'My God, this is terrible.' Well, my God, this was terrible. Women have been kept out of a lucrative career area by being kept out of sports." The function of WSF is to promote and enhance female sports and to act as an educational and advocacy organization for female athletics.

According to Micki King, the biggest promotional problem among female athletes is ignorance. Girls and women do not know how to market themselves; they still don't know the rules for getting noticed and, thereby, supported. This is exactly what we are saying to the women of the WPFL! Like us, King should know about lack of support. In 1960, she was 16 years old and searching for money to support her Olympic training, pool memberships, travel, and competition fees. Her father was a GM factory line worker, and from his limited income paid for everything. King approached her local paper, but "they wouldn't give me the time of day," she says. In high school, she was "allowed" to train in the school pool as long as she didn't get in the way of the boys who were training. She was not allowed to compete, however, and not allowed to earn the high school letter she coveted. She continued to train — on her own through college, although with no help from the University of Michigan. In fact, there was no women's team because, officially, it was "illegal" for women to dive at the University of Michigan. Because the men's diving coach liked her and saw the potential of greatness in her, he allowed her to train "unofficially" when the men did.

After King won her Olympic gold medal, the previously uninterested and unsupportive hometown newspaper sponsored a parade for her with "Welcome Home, Micki King" banners everywhere. "I didn't know that they knew I was gone," she says. "Where were they when I really needed them?" Her high school awarded her a varsity letter. And the university "claimed me as its own," she says. "I wondered, its own what?"

Only after she had obtained the unobtainable — an Olympic gold medal — did people take notice. But by then she (and her family) had already fought and won her battles alone. She had struggled — without public notice or interest — for money, for training facilities, for coaching, and had somehow prevailed. But female athletes (like male athletes) need sponsorship and support long before the actual Games: they need training time, facilities, coaching, sponsorship. And if that involves conducting themselves in the confident and assertive way Babe Didrikson-Zaharias did, so be it.

Didrikson-Zaharias understood the value of publicity in gaining the support she needed and she became a great self-promoter, often making predictions to the press before her meets. Her campaign began in the early 1930s when she wrote to a reporter, telling him about herself: "They said I was the athlete they have been waiting for," and, "They've never seen an athlete like me before." It was not unusual for her to report to the press how well she had competed and conclude her letters by saying, "Thanks for a heading." And, as always, she got it. Because of her exuberant, flamboyant, show-off style, and her great athleticism, she captured headlines.

Only when girls and women take opportunities to succeed will society see what they can really accomplish. And only then will society truly believe in female ability and stop requiring constant, case-by-case proof. And we can all help the girls and women in our towns realize their athletic dreams. To help us help, the Women's Sports Foundation has developed a nine-point guideline on how to make girls' sports a priority in every community:

1. Form an awards and grant committee.
2. Decide which awards programs best fit your community. The Foundation (1-800-227-3988) has programs in 15 categories providing grant money for communities to distribute. They range from spirit and courage awards to various player- or woman-of-the-year awards, plus awards for adults who do the most to encourage girls to take part in sports.
3. Determine which local and national grants programs your community would like to administer. Some of these programs are funded by major corporations. Sudafed, for instance, has a national travel and training fund; young athletes can receive up to $1,500.
4. Convene a committee meeting upon receipt of awards and grants materials.
5. Distribute award nomination forms and grant application forms to school, youth and adult sport clubs, and community agencies that conduct fitness programs for girls and women (such as YMCA, Special Olympics, and Girls, Inc.).
6. Collect nominations and applications prior to the deadline.
7. Select the recipients. Multiple awards can be given to ensure diversity, but it's important that selections are made with care so that the committee, the community, and the kids all feel good about who is chosen.
8. Announce the winners at a public ceremony that the media can cover.
9. Complete a report to the Foundation about the success of your awards and grants program. The Foundation then can track how its funds are being used, perhaps decide to throw in more money if its funds were used well, and offer suggestions to make the program even

better. That's what the Foundation is there for: to help educate communities and help the moms and dads who make these programs possible.

Speedskater legend Bonnie Blair says, don't be afraid to pick up the phone and brag about someone else. In fact, on one of her trips back and forth from Dallas to Austin, Alex carpooled with "Suicide" Sue Horton and began to talk to her about promoting herself. "What?" Horton laughed disbelievingly, "Call up the local paper and say, 'Hey, do a story on me?" Yes. Or, get someone else to. She chewed on this for a moment, then shrugged. "I've got nothing to say." No? Nothing except that she was undersized and turned down for a try-out with the Rage, but she refused to take no for an answer and is now one of the starters for the team. Nothing except that she was driven by a lifelong dream to play a sport that would not be available to her until she was in her 30s. Nothing except that this lifelong desire led her to a career in the fitness industry, and she now drives all her co-workers, friends, and family crazy because all she can talk about is football. Nothing except for the fact that she puts in more than 21 hours a week driving alone to make practices with her team.

For many of the pioneers in this book, they were fighting against discrimination and for the chance to show just what the determined female athlete could do. But for Jane Couch, her chosen sport was actually illegal. When Couch watched a documentary on women's boxing in the United Stated, she was instantly hooked. This was something, she says, she knew she had to do. But in her native England, it was illegal. Undeterred, Couch traveled and competed overseas, making a name for herself as a tenacious, always entertaining fighter with a huge heart. Her fight was not against a national governing sports body, but an entire nation not at all sure about what a female boxer was capable of. Today, because of Couch, women's boxing is beginning to take off in England. More and more women are stepping into gyms, taking boxing lessons and learning to take the punches!

Because of all the women who have laid the foundation for playing sports and promoting their sports, female athletes and women in all other walks of life are learning how to speak out and demonstrate extraordinary accomplishments in order to be acknowledged, in order to spark interest. What female athletes and nonathletes alike desire is simple: the same opportunities for advancement and promotion that men have, the same benefits, the same responsibilities. The tide is turning and it is so awesome to see, so empowering to watch that this is truly a cause to celebrate women in sport!

Sports role model and mentor Mariah Burton Nelson created the Frances Willard Society because, when she started out almost two decades ago, there were no mentors for her. By creating the Frances Willard Society, Nelson ensures that present and future female sportwriters have support and role models to talk to. Frances Willard, a suffragist and the first woman to write a nonfiction book about her sports experience, proved to be a great role model. Her book? *A Wheel Within A Wheel: A Woman's Quest for Freedom, 1895*. In it she writes, "I finally concluded that all failure was from a wobbling will rather than a wobbling wheel," when describing how she learned to ride a bike at the age of 53. Who could know more about the importance of supporting other women and encouraging each other to be the best we can be? Thankfully, Mariah Burton Nelson understood this and continues the work of Ms. Willard. (To join e-mail: FWS-subscribe@yahoogroups.com.)

When Alex informed her fellow "Frankies" (how members refer to themselves) that she was trying out for the Austin Rage, the support was overwhelming, including a personal note of encouragement from Ms. Nelson herself. Cool.

The Women's Sports Network, Power Play, and Girls in Motion all stepped forward, wanting to learn more, promote and encourage a sister stepping into a new sports arena. *Girls Life!* magazine has dedicated itself to promoting new, young athlete-hopefuls. The list is growing as the indisputable message of girl power reaches new generations.

As we watch this new era unfold, we can congratulate ourselves for our vision, determination, and courage in the face of resistance and, often, rejection. Michelle and Alex, raised by their parents as Ace and Sport, have a special greeting that reflects the spirit of women athletes. In place of the traditional "Hi! How are you?" we usually greet each other with the standard, "You go, girl!"

In 1996, the Professional Tennis Association announced that it would discontinue the practice of presenting equal purses (prize money) for men and women. "The decision was made on the basis of what is best for the tournament," said Geoff Pollard, president of Tennis Australia. The decision increased the total prize money for the men by 17 percent, and for the women by only 6 percent,[1] although the U.S. Tennis Association told us that in 1995 the difference in attendance between the men and women's matches was marginal.

At Wimbledon in 1996, the men's singles winner earned $628,000, while the women's singles champion received $564,000. In 1997, when the prize money reached a record $11.2 million, the Wimbledon men's champion received $676,450, while the women's champ got $608,805. Defending this discriminatory policy, All England Club chairman John Curry said: "We ... feel we have no good reason to change from where we are. ... It is still the public's view that they prefer the men's matches to the women's." We wonder where he's getting his information.

As far as the pay inequities: That means, explains Martina Navratilova, "a relatively obscure player, Richard Krajicek, who up to then could only have sold tickets in the Netherlands, [is] paid more than a superstar, Steffi Graf, who could sell tickets in Timbuktu."[2] In the spring of 2001, the proverbial tide had turned and it was payback time. While sales of tickets for the male players' matches slid considerably, players such as Anna Kournikova, the Williams sisters, and Martina Hingis were on the rise. In fact, the "act" to see was (and still is) the Williams sisters, and *Sports Illustrated* declared that women's tennis was the sport to watch.

In the world of tennis (and female sports in general) we have Martina Navratilova to thank. She defected to the U.S. from Czechoslovakia at a time when the top male player earned 50 percent more than the top female. But just as Babe Didrikson-Zaharias changed perceptions about female golfers, Navratilova changed perceptions about female tennis players and female athletes in general. She lifted weights and cross-trained. She won 167 singles events, including nine Wimbledon and four U.S. Open titles. She was the first female athlete to earn more than a million dollars in one year; in 1984, she won 74 consecutive matches and $2,173,556 in prize money — higher competitive earnings than any athlete in the world, except for three boxers. Throughout her career, she has earned more than 20 million dollars from tennis tournaments alone.[3]

When Lyn St. James realized that she had talent as a driver that would allow her to become a professional, she quickly found that she had little leverage. In an exceptionally expensive sport, she had to convince both officials and supporters of auto racing that she should not only be allowed to compete, but that she deserved to be bankrolled. What saved her, she told us, was perseverance. "I figured out in 1979, my first year as a pro, that I was going to have to sell. I owned an auto parts business, and I had to sell a lot of shock absorbers. And I had to sell myself as a potential moneymaker to companies which were really only interested in the bottom line." Based on her research, St. James concluded that she and the Ford Motor Company were made for each other: Ford was trying to sell more of their products to women, and St. James, an incredibly accomplished woman driver, needed a serious sponsor. She began a two-year telephone and letter-writing campaign to persuade Ford to sponsor her. When Ford finally signed her in 1981, she traveled 250 days a year as a spokesperson in order to keep her sponsor.

Thanks to women such as St. James and Navratilova, race car driver Sarah Fisher (now only one of a select few in the Indy Racing League) and tennis players Venus and Serena Williams (among so many) can pursue their sports. Much of the dirty work has been done for them.

Thirty years after Title IX was signed into law, we are beginning to see the results of what happens when we let girls and women play. We are moving closer to a generation of girls who cannot imagine NOT having full competitive opportunities — although 90 percent of schools and colleges are not yet in compliance with Title IX, and the NCAA says it will take another decade to reach full compliance. But it is not just the colleges that are playing catch-up ... or should be. In an age where girl power is everywhere, girls continue to face discrimination. There continues the policy where local high schools allow football and baseball to take top priority because local boosters deem them the only worthy sports. As money and sponsorships roll in for boys athletics, girls are prevented from using sporting equipment, fields, locker rooms, and access to qualified coaches. It seems implausible but it continues to happen. And, in one instance, while parents from a small Texas town protested loudly at games that their daughters were to be bussed across town to use the city recreational fields with no full-time coaches or suitable equipment, when it came time to approach the city council, only three stepped forward. Because it was a small town, most parents were afraid to make waves.

Slowly, the corporate world is helping us change the way we view women in sports. Today, there is a long list of companies who have donated large amounts of money for women's athletics and who send the message that women can and should be allowed to "excel on and off the playing field." And as Lopiano wrote in an article for *Women's Sports & Fitness*, "Other media entities are beginning to embrace female athletes as champions, heroes, and role models. Major corporations, such as State Farm Insurance, General Motors, Visa, and Kodak are using female athletes in large-scale advertising and promotional campaigns. The wonderful byproduct of all this is that the corporate commitment to female consumers is fueling gender equity in women's sports salaries."[4] In fact, while working on this book, we received a great phone call from Nike. It heard about the WPFL and wanted to help out. Another shift ...

It's a shift that can have global effects. What do we mean? Nike giving some corporate money to a women's football league is global? Exactly. Let us illustrate a great environmental story: In the early 1900s fishermen were getting sick of the sea otters springing their traps and decided their pelts were worth more than their lives. Otters were nearly wiped out and fishermen nearly starved.

It seems unlikely, but here is what happened. With the otters gone, the fish population grew out of control. The fish began eating all the sea kelp. Then, with no place to hide and nothing to eat, they were easy pickings for birds of prey that would swoop down and catch them. When the hunting finally stopped and the otters came back so, too, did the fish. It is sad, but not so unusual, to find the cause of imbalance in the environment is the very people who depend upon the ecosystem for sustenance.

There is a parallel between the story of the otters and athletics. Keeping women out of sports (or business or any field or endeavor) creates a social imbalance. When we encourage the participation of women in sport, we can restore the balance in society. As the popularity and worldwide acceptance of women in sport grows, cultures that have typically kept their women under close patriarchal control are realizing that they need to reevaluate their social structures. While some nations are being dragged into the new millennium kicking and screaming, more females from more nations are entering the Olympic Games than ever before. The impact is remarkable!

Imagine the talk and the dreams that arise in villages and towns around the world when women can see a woman training for and participating in sports. It is a beginning. Another shift, another hope to bring light to how women should be treated and how magnificent we are. When these women, who have been told all their lives that they are second-class citizens, see other women succeeding as athletes and businesswomen and leaders, their hopes and aspirations are raised. These brave and bold women are demonstrating not only that they, as individuals, are qualified and capable, but that women in general are capable.

What is especially exciting is the fact that Tori Allen, raised in Benin, Africa, has said she hopes to return to the village where she was raised to hlep build schools and homes. Imagine when she returns to her old stomping grounds, an accomplished world-class athlete and tells (she speaks French fluently) young girls and women of her amazing athletic feats and of all the support she received as a female athlete. As Allen notes in her foreword to this book, there is a responsibility to

Angela "Slim Shady" Brown takes pregame instructions and practices her trademark stu-stu-stutter step (photos by Alexandra Allred).

pass on all the knowledge and benefits she has received as an athlete. And, thankfully, Allen is not alone in this way of thinking. Peggy Fleming, Mia Hamm, Bonnie Blair, and Shannon Miller (among many) all discussed the importance of sharing the joy of sports.

These women are not exceptions to the rule. They are the rule, the rule of the new millenium — that women and men are equal, and that women are strong, capable, and ready. And as more women convince men of this simple truth, more women will begin to believe and embrace it, and it will become reality.

Until then, though, perhaps we need to adopt the ways of Didrikson-Zaharias. It certainly works for males. Watch teenage boys on any basketball court or in any gym. It's hard not to notice the bragging, the big-talking bravado that goes on. Mostly amusing, this banter goes back and forth, while two or more wager on someone's abilities and they good-heartedly challenge one another to some athletic feat. This is largely unknown in the female community. Bravado is a rarity. But wouldn't we have more attention from both media and corporate sponsors if we took a kind of Didrikson-Zaharias approach? Wouldn't it be hard not to be noticed on the court or in the gym if we loudly proclaimed our athletic prowess and predicted great athletic feats?

We tested this theory with a trainer from Accelerate Ohio. Working on a difficult treadmill routine, Alex was nearing the end of her training session and preparing to take a speed test. So she loudly proclaimed to the trainer that she would run 18 miles per hour on the treadmill.

Two things happened: 1) Alex ran the 18 miles per hour, proving once again that self-esteem and confidence are the ticket to success, and 2) the entire gym cheered her on. Some of the boys we had labeled as cocky encouraged Alex. All the trainers yelled, telling her to keep up her speed and, when she was done, everyone was smiling, and there were many congratulations and high-fives. In and of itself, this was a small feat (especially since many of the guys present could run 20 miles per hour), but it was huge in the sense that boys and girls, men and women stopped their own training to cheer one woman toward her publicly-proclaimed goal! And while the officials of the Iditarod race continue to debate the "safety" issues of allowing Rachael Scdoris compete, her own peers continue to cheer her on. Racers who have competed in the Iditarod themselves have recoginzed Scdoris' talent and are saying, "Yeah, way to go girl!"

As we continue to move forward, all the self-promotion, high-fiving, showboating we can do is all for the better. In a hard drive against the notoriously tough Houston Energy defense, Rage quarterback Sherri Schools threw a beauty of a pass to Angela 'Slim Shady' Brown. The receiver caught the ball with her fingertips and drew the ball into her chest, performing an amazing display of speed, grace and skill as she tiptoed along the sidelines careful to stay in bounds. She ran for a touchdown and the fans went nuts. Then, 'Slim Shady' Brown did the most magnificent thing. She stepped off to the side, facing the fans and raised her arms. Bending slightly at the knees so that she had this kind of a cool-guy bob and weave, she jutted her chin forward to the stands as if to say, "How do you like me now?" Man, it was pretty! And, she would do it again and again and again before the season was over.

Just give her the damn ball!

Notes:

1. "Thumps/You've Got To Be Kidding," *New Woman* (April 1996), 156.
2. Martina Navratilova, "Game, Set, Set, Set, Match," *The New York Times* (August 26, 1996), 15.
3. "Heroine Worship: Most Valuable Player, " *The New York Times Magazine* (November 24, 1996), 62.
4. Donna Lopiano, "Don't Touch That Dial," *Women's Sports & Fitness* (July/August 1996), 42.

Toting the Chain

It's the new millennium and you're thinking, all of this — Title IX and the days of telling girls they can't play sports — no longer applies to me! It does. And this dose of reality should make you both proud and determined. Be proud of the pioneers who toted that proverbial chain and fought so that you could be normal. Be determined that this will not happen to your daughters. Right now, there are girls teams trying to get equal playing time. There are teams of young women fighting to have a field to practice on, a coach to train them and/or equipment to play with. Right now. It is a dilemma that did not start yesterday and will not go away tomorrow. Not yet.

When U.S. speedskater Pooch Harrington participated in the 1960 Olympic Games at Squaw Valley, the temperature outside was -25 degrees F. A blizzard was brewing, dumping snow faster than the snow crews could clear the ice rinks (there were no indoor rinks then). Because skating was impossible, the U.S. speedskating coach sent the male skaters inside to clean their skates, stretch, and keep warm.

He sent the female skaters on a hiking excursion to the top of the ski jump. This coach had made it clear that he didn't want women on his team, so he routinely sent them on wild-goose chases just to keep them busy and out of his hair.

Angered by this newest and ludicrous chore, a member of the women's team — to protest the coach's ruling as unfair — picked a heavy chain that decorated a restaurant in the Olympic village. Amused with the symbolism of the chain and their first act of passive defiance, the members of the first-ever women's speedskating team began trudging up the mountain carrying the heavy chain over their shoulders, feeling a tiny bit vindicated. Some two hours later, as the storm worsened, the temperature dropped, and the wind and snow whipped them, the humor had worn off. The chain had become incredibly cold and heavy, but they couldn't put it down because it didn't belong to them.

Cursing their teammate's bright idea and every blistering step, they staggered on literally chained together until they were at last rescued by a park ranger. Although they may have been too tired and cold to realize it, the chain, as it became increasingly burdensome, had also become increasingly symbolic of their status and the sexism that confined them.

Despite the weather turning on them, the women's team had the right idea by handling adversity and discrimination with humor. At the time, they had no legal recourse, so attitude and determination were all-important. Women's sports history is filled with stories, like this one, of those who — through grit, determination, and positive attitudes — have won (and are winning) victories, not only for themselves, not only for other female athletes, but for all women.

We feel this way about our own bobsled athletes. The opening of Park City, Utah, was to be a joyous occasion. The site of the 2002 Olympic Games, Park City boasts only the second bobsled track in the United States and the only one on which, by most regards, any sane person would want to slide. Female bobsledders went to the opening ceremonies — having been promised the opportunity to slide and take part in the opening ceremonies.

What we had hoped for and what actually happened were two entirely different things. The brochure handed out to spectators did not even mention the U.S. women's bobsled team. What it did do, however, was name the youth program — an unofficial program to which the U.S. women's team had donated $5,000. This was $5,000 we really needed, but we felt so strongly about trying to involve youths, particularly young girls, in the federation that we bit the bullet. As a result of that donation, two members of our competitive team were not able to compete in Germany.

Worse, until women's bobsledding was added to the Olympic Games recently, the Utah Sports Authority — the folks (some of whom are women) who run the Park City track — refused to acknowledge women bobsledders, women who belong to an official USOC-sanctioned team. A sled which we had paid to have repaired and in running shape for the opening ceremonies lay untouched and abandoned, far from the repair shed. And, of course, no money was refunded. Sliding times were changed and then canceled. But because women weren't in the Olympics yet (even though a legitimate federation team), we didn't have all of the same rights as the men, and we didn't have anyone powerful enough to go to bat for us. The women athletes who were there had taken the semester off from school or taken leaves of absence from their jobs to stand around for two weeks and twiddle their thumbs. But always they showed up at the track with bright smiles, determined not to let the politics get to them.

"Every day I watched their hearts break, but every day they came with fresh hopes," said a spectator who attended the opening ceremonies. The women helped the men move sleds, retrieved equipment, and shoveled snow from the sled area so the men could work on their sleds. Of course, the beautiful irony here is that at the Salt Lake City 2002 Games one of the female sliders who had formerly acted as a sled dog for the men — Jill Bakken — was the first American slider to take gold! Atta girl! Despite the hard times, she never gave up. If anything, we believe it was that kind of adversity that made Bakken more determined to persevere. In doing so, she simply demonstrated the lessons taught by so many great female athletes before her so survived and overcame obstacles. Today, Bakken stands as one of those women.

A bit of a motley crew, my mother-in-law, sister-in-law, and I attended ESPN's *Friday Night Fights* to see some of the best female boxers in the world. Sheri, my sister-in-law, was still nursing my niece Abby, so little "Abby Lemons" came along as well — certainly not something you would expect to see at a professional boxing match. But this would be a night of many unexpected things, so Abby blended in perfectly. What was and is remarkable about that night was how everything discussed in this book came to life before my eyes: media images, stereotyping, breaking down barriers, motherhood and sports, supportive male role models, sisterhood, rivalry, and the beautiful imagery of female warriors giving it their all. It was a night in which Sheri, the girl-most-likely-to-place-a-daisy-in-the-muzzle-of-a-gun, was calling out boxing strategies to me. With more than a year of boxing lessons under her belt, this peace-loving, soft-spoken, homecraft-making gal could not only identify different moves but emulate them. As I sat between Sheri and another professional [male] boxer, I listened with admiration as Sheri would say things like, "Oh, see, she's backing up, making her opponent chase her. It makes her look bad for the judges." Seconds later, the boxer to my right would say, "She's making the other one run around, look stupid to the judges." Sheri was right on the money with almost every call. But, when arguably the best fight of the night went down, Sheri was gone — nursing little Abby in the ladies room. Oh, the irony. She told me later she knew she was missing something huge when she could hear the roar of the crowd from the bathroom.

What she missed was Sumya "Island Girl" Anani vs. "Gypsy" Jane Couch.

Seated ringside, we were just 10 seats away from training coach Lori Steinhorst who gave a nod and motioned that Couch would be going down by Round Three. Earlier, Steinhorst had predicted that Anani would come out a little slow but would be on fire by

Sumya "the island girl" (photo provided by Sumya Anani).

the end of Round Two. She didn't disappoint. With 10 seconds left in the second round, Anani seemed to get a burst of energy and began pummeling Couch. Round Three was brutal but Couch hung in. Then, some 20 seconds into the fourth round, a solid left hook dazed (if not temporarily knocked out) Couch and Anani went in for the kill. Anani's precision, skill, and power were overwhelming. Couch never had a chance from that point on and the match was mercifully called. The place

Honey Girl wows the crowd with a series of hook shots (photo by Alexandra Allred).

went wild. Women, men, and teenage boys were on their feet cheering on Anani. No sooner than it was clear she was the victor, she was blowing kisses and playfully throwing out T-shirts to the crowd. She signed an autograph, hugged everyone in the ring (including Couch), and waved happily. She had transformed from warrior to lady in the blink of an eye.

I was so excited because this was ESPN — the big time. Having spoken with so many female boxers, I was thrilled to be part of this celebration. It really was a celebration. As so many of the boxers said, even if they lost, they were still there on ESPN. The national recognition was all they really wanted. Even after taking a good whooping, Couch quickly showered, changed, and came back out to sign autographs and cheer on the new round of fighters. It really was a celebration. And, it was so exciting to see true fighters. It wasn't a showing like the Ali/Frazier fight in 2001. These were talented and trained fighters giving it their all for their sport.

It was also a celebration for women in sport as men and teenage boys cheered on the female fighters. There were genuine ooh's and ahh's as solid punches were landed and/or evaded. It was so powerful, so great, so gratifying and heart-warming. Then, DING! a round would end, the fighters would go back to their corners, the crowd would cheer and ... the ring girls came out, followed by wolf calls and lewd comments.

Honey Girl interviews with ESPN after her victory (photo by Alexandra Allred).

It was an unsettling feeling that would reoccur with every ring of the bell. While my mother-in-law pushed Abby around in her stroller, Sheri and I sat watching, cheering, and marveling at these amazing athletes. It was an empowering feeling. Then, the same men who were admiring our sister boxers leered at and called to the bikini-clad ring girls as they strutted their stuff. *Why were they there?* They didn't belong. Instead, Sheri called for men in Speedos! It would have been so much more appropriate. But all kidding aside, we wondered why any of it was necessary. A few rows behind us, a teenage boy loudly began comparing the ring girls to the female boxers — as though that were the real competition. The sadness we felt was so powerful that we often just avoided looking at the ring while the "girls" were there.

What was even more remarkable was the ring girls — at least this batch — were soft and jiggly. Sheri and I grumbled to ourselves that we would much rather look like some of the fighters than the ring girls. But our voices, like our sentiments, seemed to be lost in the sea of catcalls. Then Honey Girl came out. Melissa "Honey Girl" Salamone entered the ring wearing some kind of cave-girl outfit. Small-busted, narrow-hipped with amazing biceps and sporting six-pack abs, we couldn't stop looking at her legs. Muscular, lean legs with huge calves were all we could see and I swore loudly that if I could just have that body I would wear that same cave-girl outfit for the rest of my life! Forgotten were the ring girls, all eyes were on Honey Girl. Then, came the greatest catcall of all. A teenage boy gave a woof and said, "Man, now that's what an athlete should look like." Oh, yeah.

Sheri and I waved to the camera, drank a $4 Coke, chatted with people around us and spied all kinds of celebrities until the fight we had really come to see was fought. Ann Wolfe vs. Marsha Valley. Having been on the receiving end of Wolfe's power on the football field, I had really wanted to see her fight. Sheri knew her from the gym. The menacing Wolfe had actually held my nephew Joey and cooed at him. There was a whole different side to her. She was a mother, soft-spoken, gentle and sweet. In the ring, however, she was to be feared.

Even Valley herself had predicted Wolfe's "rocket right" would be a problem. It was. Repeatedly. And when the match was called — a TKO in favor of Wolfe — ESPN commentators later sat around and talked about the controversial match. Valley was never given a chance by some poor calls by the ref. However, the panel admitted, Valley would not have been able to withstand much more of Wolfe's hard and relentless blows. Mike Tyson's former manager even jumped in, talking about the questionable calls and Wolfe's "rocket right." It would not be until the following day when my husband and I watched a taping of the fights that the true extent of that celebration hit me. Never mind the ring girls and the wolf calls, my husband and I sat debating those controversial calls from the Wolfe vs. Valley fight. Now, there's cause to celebrate.

In an interview with ESPN before her death in 1994, the great Wilma Rudolph told how she was recruited from her small town in Clarksville, Tennessee, to attend Tennessee State, some 45 minutes away. Only 13 years old, Wilma had never been away from home. Even at such a tender age, no one had seen anything like Rudolf before. She was a phenomenon the coaches at Tennessee State couldn't wait to get their hands on and begin a mentor program. It was her first bus ride, her first adventure. "It was only 45 minutes away, but you would have thought I was going to Europe." Sports had opened a whole new world — a world beyond the racism and poverty of her youth. Just the burning desire to run had been enough to raise Rudolph, who had suffered from polio, from her bed and propel her on toward greatness.

In 1960, after the Olympic Games in Rome, Rudolph returned to Clarksville an American hero and three-time gold medallist. The entire town celebrated her homecoming, but before she would agree to a banquet in her honor, she insisted that there be no segregation. It was the first time blacks and whites sat together in Clarksville, and it would be a night the town would never forget. Sport allowed this young woman — at least for one night — to control her world and set it right.

But sometimes it isn't so easy to set the world right. Sometimes humor and a positive attitude aren't enough. Sometimes you have to listen to your principles, and do not what is easiest, but what is best for others, for yourself, for the future.

Years after the experiences of Rudolph and Harrington, Julie Croteau chose a legal battle when she had exhausted all other options. By then, the 1972 education bill, Title IX, had been signed into law, mandating full equality for women's school athletics (although it hasn't ensured equity). Croteau's lawsuit was the right course of action, enabling her to become a pioneer for women in baseball and to achieve some of her own aspirations. She has said that at the time she and her friends knew that they were right to be willing to fight for equity, and she is still sure today. And she says she "failed and succeeded publicly." While she lost her case in court, she won in life.

"Fight the good battle," she advises, "even if you can lose." And you may win in life, too. Croteau is a visionary. Also a visionary, who knows better about fighting against adversity and conquering the world than Nancy Hogshead-Makar? A world-champion swimmer, rape survivor, president of the Women's Sports Foundation, and long-term believer that the fight can make you who are you as a person. "If a young woman is being discriminated against," she lectures, "and she stands up for herself, this will be her biggest learning experience in her high school or collegiate career."

To say Lisa Hoyle entered the stunt world is misleading. She had to prove herself. She had to earn the right to call her-

self a stuntwoman. She recalls one day when she was standing on a movie set when a stunt coordinator asked her who
she was. "I'm a stuntwoman," she told him. "He said, 'Oh,
really? Who's your boyfriend?' It was just assumed that I was
there because of someone else. But you know what? I earned
this. I pounded the pavement, kept after it, and realized no
one could stop me from this."

Hoyle earned a reputation as a hard worker, someone who
could and would take the hits and the falls without a problem.
"I can adjust well to many situations. I'm a trooper and don't
complain, but I will stand up for myself." That's critical for
female athletes. Learning when, where, and how to fight means
so much to the success of all athletes. Even now Tori Allen,
with all her world titles, is having to fight for the right to pole
vault as a female athlete.

Attorney Ed Williams, former Olympian, co-founder of the
Athletes' Committee to the USOC, and an athlete-rights advocate, agrees that principles must be protected, even if the road
to equality is a rocky one. "You can't make any forward
progress," he says, "if you are not willing to fight difficult battles.
One recognizes the political reality that some cannot be won
right now, but that does not mean they should not be fought.
Some athletes choose to be leaders in these difficult situations.
The battle may not be won for several years." But, he points
out, legal battles set precedents and very often raise the awareness necessary to overturn earlier, discriminatory decisions. So
the battles must be fought.

Not knowing what to do about discrimination can keep
women from acting. Inequality exists in all sports and at all
levels — from elementary school to the national level. So, Williams stresses, girls must learn and understand the law before
they can decide if they are willing or able to take on court challenges. For instance, female athletes should be acquainted with
the American Sports Act of 1979, U.S. Code 36, Section 391.
Williams refers to this important legislation as "the foundation
of the U.S. Olympic Committee charter." Another important
document is the USOC Constitution, particularly Article IX,
which deals with the right of the athlete to compete.

Emphasizing Williams' advice to know the law, Woodhull (of the Media Studies Center) was quick to point out, "In years to come, historians of the women's movement may well define Title IX as the most important legislation in redefining women's ability to succeed in a broad variety of endeavors."

In fact, as long as we have been in sports, it was a surprise even to us just how many instances of discrimination there are among high school athletes in this country. So, why are so few Title IX cases filed? According to Dr. Ray Yasser of the University of Tulsa, Oklahoma, who specializes in Title IX cases, "There is a tremendous amount of counterpressure against parents and their kids getting involved in these kinds of lawsuits. There is fear of repercussion."

And the pressure is real. While the parents of three high school girls in Texas filed suit against a high school that prohibited the girls from using the high school fields, rumors circulated the small town that because of the girls and their parents, taxes would go up to cover the legal costs for the school. Because of the girls, other school activities would be shut down. Both Hogshead-Makar and Yasser agree that this is a common bullying tactic that is completely untrue. "But even so," Yasser says. "Who cares? You know, you have to make things fair for everyone. That's life. Schools have to face the fact that we are educating boys and girls.

"If this were happening to African-Americans, no one would think anything of marching into the office and demanding equality, fair play. This is no different. But what we have to get our parents and girls to understand is, they shouldn't be asking permission. This is their right."

It is about courage. Beyond knowing the rights that females have guaranteed to them under the law, both Williams and Yasser stress that girls and women must have the courage to take a stand for what they believe, the courage to be unpopular. Having a thick skin can be difficult. What was that Andra Douglas told us? You have to be different so that others can be normal. Williams and Yasser agree that while the law is often on the side of the women, most are too afraid to act, fearing repercussions. After all, Croteau became an outcast in her high school after her lawsuit. We know this all too well in the sport of bobsledding. Not all athletes are trailblazers. Not every athlete is going to be willing to speak out for the good of the team — which is frustrating for those who are.

Speaking out as an athlete is difficult, fearing repercussions from coaches, federations, sponsors, fellow athletes. We accept that not everyone is going to be a Billie Jean King, Karyn Bye or a Liz Parr-Smestad. But we would hope in the spirit of team, of sisterhood, of pride, that while one might not be able to speak out, she would always support those who do.

Particularly in women's sports which are fighting for equal status, such as Olympic status, women need to pull together as a whole.

Today, there still exist Olympic sports that maintain one-sex only. It is particularly hard to understand that if a sport already exists for one sex, why not include the other if the talent and the interest exist? We sympathize with those who wonder how a sport that already has a federation, funding, facilities, coaches, and equipment can deny privileges to a select group.

That pill is hard to swallow and the logic difficult to understand. And with only one woman on the executive board of the International Olympic Committee (IOC), the committee that decides the inclusion or exclusion of a sport in international competition, women's voices are weak.

We asked that one woman, Anita DeFrantz, what has to be done to get men-only sports expanded to include women in the Games (and women-only sports expanded to men). "A certain number of championships must be held for the IOC to review [the sport]," De Frantz says. "It is up to the women to champion their sports. Only the federations representing each sport can make requests to the IOC, so it is important that the women move the federations." But moving the federations is not easy.

DeFrantz does not take the role of "the only woman" lightly. She has labored to elevate women into the decision-making levels of the sporting world. In 1995, DeFrantz spearheaded the IOC policy mandating that women must make up at least

10 percent of the board by the year 2000, as well as 10 percent of the boards of all 197 National Olympic Committees. By the year 2005, DeFrantz intends to see that number rise to 20 percent. Donna Lopiano, of the WSF says, these numbers, although they seem small, will have profound and positive consequences.

DeFrantz is also responsible for a 1989 study of television coverage of men's and women's sports events in the U.S. That study, entitled "Gender Stereotyping and Televised Sports," proved to be very valuable, showing the overwhelming male bias in sports coverage. In 1994, a newer, updated study was conducted outlining the same problems. "Those two studies have significantly changed women's sports for the better," Lopiano says.

Currently, DeFrantz runs the Amateur Athletic Foundation (which manages Southern California's endowment from the 1984 Olympic Games), and serves on the IOC board, the Salt Lake City Olympic Organizing Committee, and nearly a dozen other foundation boards. In 2000, she made an unsuccessful bid to be the first female and only second American to head the International Olympic Committee. Although she did not win, it was a huge step for women in sports. She was the first female vice president of the IOC and vice president of FISA, the International Rowing Federation. She took the time from her incredibly busy schedule to speak with us. Her advice, succinctly stated, is: "Know when to fight and when to walk away." No one believes more firmly in the need for powerful female leadership than DeFrantz, and no one knows better when to fight.

In 1980, when the United States boycotted the Moscow Games, DeFrantz, then a rowing athlete, fought back. DeFrantz first heard about the boycott when a reporter from *Sports Illustrated* called her for her reaction. "They (*Sports Illustrated*) said, 'We're boycotting the Games' and I said, 'Who's we? What do you mean we? Where were we when I was out there busting my rear?'" The White House claimed to be held hostage by world events, in this case, by the Soviet invasion of Afghanistan; Carter administration officials said there was no other choice. "But I wondered," DeFrantz says, "whose lives would they really change? I'll tell you who, only the 500 U.S. athletes who didn't get to participate. It did nothing to change the Soviet [occupation] in Afghanistan. ... Meanwhile, a scientific convention was held in Moscow with representatives from the United States, and we continued selling wheat to the Soviets. It was all very wrong."

While the boycott and the Moscow Games proceeded without DeFrantz and her fellow American athletes, DeFrantz earned the Olympic Order Medal of Bronze for her leadership role in fighting the 1980 boycott. It was a fight that pushed her to the forefront, giving her a reputation that the International Olympic Committee took very seriously. DeFrantz recognizes she is where she is today because she had the courage of her convictions.

Her advice to women who are trying fighting athletic equality is to "move the federations," advice that is a double-edged sword. Without Olympic status, these sports will continue to get little to no support from their federations, and without financial support from the federations there can be no real international championships — meaning no Olympic status. As with the women who trudged in chains up a Squaw Valley mountain, the burden on women who currently compete in non-Olympic status national sports has become increasingly heavy. Many of these athletes, understandably, give up.

For example, in 1994, when the Modem Pentathlon Federation was informed that women would not be included in the 1996 Summer Olympics, the federation cut funds to the women. "We feel it was wrong [for women not to be included in the Games]," says Dean Billick, the federation's executive director. "There was no legitimate reason for it." But once the ruling was handed down, he says, the federation had to protect its resources for those athletes invited to the 1996 Games — the men.

What happened after that is no surprise. Female pentathletes were forced to stop training full-time so that they could return to work full-time. Many lost hope. "They lost their goals and stopped [training]," Billick says. The federation continues to pay for the women's travel and coaching expenses to international competitions, but the painful reality is that in a sport as demanding as the modern pentathlon, it is virtually impossible to be serious contenders with only part-time training.

The girls from a softball team in a small town in Texas understood that same dilemma all too well. They were constantly being told that any money spent on them would be taking money from the revered football program. In fact, one of the arguments frequently used against gender equity in sports (particularly at the college level) is that, in providing more opportunities for female athletes, we reduce monetary support for the sports that are the most popular (i.e., men's sports) and bring in the most money. That money, opponents of gender equity point out, is what supports all sports. The argument goes that if the football program loses money, then there will be less for everyone.

In fairness, we have rarely heard this argument from athletes themselves. It is usually the coaches, particularly at high school and college levels, who are still convinced that funding equal athletic opportunities for women will decimate their men's programs. Lopiano notes that while women's programs are being accused of taking money from football scholarships and/ or weakening all the other athletic programs, it is the "women who have less than 36 percent of all athletic participation opportunities, 33 percent of all scholarship dollars, 24 percent of sport budgets, and 23 percent of recruiting budgets."

Other little-known facts about "golden goose" athletic programs, i.e., football and basketball:

- At about 80 percent of all NCAA member institutions, football does not pay for women's sports or even for itself.
- Among the supposedly lucrative big-time football programs in Division I-A, 33 percent are running deficit programs averaging losses of more than $1 million annually.
- Ninety-five percent of Division I-AA football programs are running deficits averaging about $600,000 per year.
- Thirty-two percent of all Division I-A men's basketball

programs run deficits averaging more than $200,000 a year.

- Eighty-one percent of all other Division I men's basketball programs run annual deficits of close to $270,000.[1]

As Lopiano says, "There are no golden geese. There are only fat geese eating the food that could fund additional athletic opportunities for women." And as WSF President Benita Fitzgerald Mosley says: "If college presidents and athletic directors cut superfluous costs in men's football and basketball, enough funding could be available for everyone. Those well-funded sports simply have to give up small portions of their budgets so that both women and men involved in nonrevenue sports can have a chance to play. The point of an anti-discrimination law is to bring the disadvantaged population up to the level of the advantaged population, not to bring an already advantaged population down."[2]

Which brings us back to knowing when, who, and how to fight. Female athletes must educate themselves about the law, not only state and federal laws, but also bylaws specific to individual federations. They must have the facts at hand to negate the old, invalid arguments made by those who fear for themselves and oppose expanding athletic opportunities. Female athletes must be aware that discrimination (and the inevitably resulting harassment) exists at all levels, and they must be prepared for dealing with that discrimination.

We all must continue to encourage girls and women not to give up, and we should take pride in those who do not. As American Gladiator Sky says, "When I die, I don't want to die saying 'I wish I would have ... '"

Olympic fencer Cheris says the same. In fact, we could all learn a few lessons from this woman who refuses to acknowledge the word "can't." At our Accelerate Ohio program, the word "can't" hangs on a poster in front of the treadmill. There is a line through the word as though it were obscene. The message: We don't say "can't." But when you are running 16-plus miles per hour at a 30-degree incline, the word seems dangerously real. There are times when "can't" is the only word that comes to mind.

Yet, Cheris refuses to accept "can't." During the 1992 Barcelona Games, while Olympians traveled to Barcelona to prove themselves, Cheris and her colleagues were sent to Cuba. Epee, Cheris' form of fencing, was not yet an Olympic sport. That is when Cheris began her campaign. She was told over and over that epee would not become an Olympic sport. "I didn't hear that," she says. "If you believe in your sport, in yourself, you make the sport media-worthy, give demonstrations, write letters, call all the fencing clubs you can. ... It got to the point people were calling me saying, 'Elaine, please, stop the letters!'

"The easiest thing," she says, "is to say it can't be done. You must decide where you are going and do [whatever it takes to get there.]" But when we marveled at her very positive attitude, Cheris was quick to point out that it's not all about focusing on the positive. Learning to channel the negative can lead to success. "It's not about crashing through walls all the time. First, look for the door, asking yourself, 'Where am I going; where am I going?' When you've looked and find there are no doors, then you can work on making one." Negativity, she says, can work to your advantage, making you work harder and want it more. Wanting it and working for it may be the keys to success, but some doors have old and very stubborn locks. Cheris' point: Make new doors.

At a "peewee" bobsled competition the bobsled federation held for children under 16 years of age, two preadolescent sisters entered. They raced against 12 all-boy teams. At the end of the meet, the excited girls and their parents listened to the times of the boys' teams and tallied up the scores. The girls had come in fourth place!

Peewee championships where girls ruled supreme (photo by Alexandra Allred).

Then, right before their eyes, the judges changed the scores, placing the girls in tenth place. Welcome to bobsledding, girls.

Originally, bobsledding was a mixed sport that required women team members. Yet, as early as 1924, women began to be banned from competition. In 1940, the Amateur Athletic Union (AAU) reopened the sport to women. Katharin Dewey (granddaughter of Melvile Dewey, creator of the Dewey Decimal library catalog system) won the U.S. National Four-Man Bobsled Championship. In doing so, Dewey became the only woman in the history of bobsledding, or any other amateur sport, to win a national championship in open competition against men. Days later, the AAU reversed its decision and ruled that women could compete only against other women, stripping Dewey of her title and effectively banning her from the sport.

Just as the spirit to compete thrives in the current U.S. women's bobsled team, so it does in a new generation of bobsledders. Rather than quit, one of the sisters in the peewee competition turned to her father and said, "I guess I'll just have to come in first place next time." When asked why she continues to bobsled, she says, wide-eyed, as if there could be no other explanation, "Because I love it."

These are two girls we hope will ride the wave of adolescent peer pressure and continue to focus their determination into 'just give me the sled' and 'how do you like me now' attitudes. What so many do not understand — like the grown men who stripped two children of fourth place because of sexism — is that this is not a boys-against-girls story. We are all in this together, athletes striving for personal bests and to enhance our sports and ourselves.

In her article "The Girls Against the Boys," adventurer-turned-journalist Sarah Odell describes the frustrations she felt being excluded from the Team American Pride troop: a team that consisted of five members, one of whom had to be a female.[3] Despite its title, the article is not about girls against boys, but women striking out on their own. For Odell, when she was cut at tryouts, she and four other women created their own team — the first ever all-female team.

For what? The sixth annual Raid Gauloises (Challenge of the Warriors), said to be the most extreme race in the world. It is an event that demands that the teams hike, bike, climb, raft, and drag themselves to the finish line after managing 223 miles of incredibly crude terrain — in this case, in Borneo.

But before they could endure the extreme fatigue, leeches, reptiles, insects, torrential downpours, and sleepless nights, the first challenge for the women was to find a sponsor for the necessary $40,000 to fund the excursion. Team American Pride Woman found that support from Swiss Army Brands, and they were on their way ... to fatigue, leeches, reptiles ...

Often lost in the Bornean wilds, the women knew many were counting them out. Odell confesses to giving in to defeatist thinking — that is, until they discovered that the U.S. men's team had been disqualified. No longer were the women competing against their male rivals. Now it meant finishing for their sponsor, for America, for themselves.

The odds seemed insurmountable. One teammate fell with dysentery — Borneo's revenge. Hooked to an IV drip to hydrate her, the teammate rallied the following day, allowing the entire team to move on. Clawing their way through caves, biking up mountains, canoeing through the rapids, seven days and 22 hours later, the first all-female team and only the second American team ever to complete the Raid Gauloises crossed the finish lines. They didn't win, but it never was about that.

Anna Seaton-Huntington, two-time Olympic rower and member of the America 3 team, asked and answered the rhetorical question, "What did women prove?" by competing in the America's Cup race: "The 'real winners' are the people who cross the finish line first," Seaton-Huntington says. "That was not us. We did not sail flawlessly. ... But the women's team did exhibit an enormous amount of courage when we went out on the course totally green to face off against men who had been sailing in America's Cups all their adult lives.

"Most likely there will never be another [all-female] team in the America's Cup. But we hope that as a result of our efforts, there will be women on what would once have been all-male crews. As my teammates and I go on with our lives, as sailors, rocket scientists, mothers, hotel managers, or journalists, we will know that we have made inroads into a spectacular, once spectacularly male, sport."[4]

Our wanting to participate in sports does not mean we want to beat the boys, or join the "boys' club." We just want to be allowed to play also. We want to push ourselves to be better, to feel the satisfaction of accomplishment, to feel the sky is the limit, to learn the competitive skills needed in business. We want to demonstrate that, as Sameka Randall, the Associated Press' Ms. Basketball, says: "We can hang."

Notes

1. Donna Lopiano, "The Importance of Sports Opportunities for Our Daughters," Women's Sports Foundation, 6-7.
2. Benita Fitzgerald Mosley, "Entitled by Title IX," *Women's Sports & Fitness* (June 1997), 28.
3. Sarah Odell, "The Girls Against The Boys," *Elle* (November 1996), 196-201.
4. Anna Seaton-Huntington, "The America's Cup Race Is Over. What Did Women Prove?," *Glamour* (July 1995).

Entering the Boys' Club

Imagine standing in a locker room full of professional football players! We've all seen the scenes in movies or news clips of NFL or college players in their locker rooms. The team is decked out, complete with shoulder pads and that black stuff under the eyes. Some are standing, some are sitting on benches, hunched forward and listening as the coach talks on. Everyone is working on his game face. The speech is heated, intense, and motivating. It brings the seated players to their feet and those already standing to pump fists in the air, "Yeah, baby! This is our day!" There is a team huddle and a prayer. More motivating, "Go get 'em!" And, in this case, "Just give me the f-ing ball! I want the f-ing ball!" which leads players to pound on each others pads, pump each other up, and begin the team growl that carries out on to the field.

As Alex sits in the locker room of the Austin Rage, it occurs to her: This is real. It's not a movie. It's real, and it is so incredibly cool. Decked out in her official number 31 jersey, it's hard not to grin. It's hard not to comment aloud that the locker room stinks. It is sweltering hot, the team looks menacing, and the coaches looked somewhat annoyed that she, number 31, finds this all really incredibly cool! It's cool because it just is ... only later when she thinks back on it does she realize those were women. For just a moment, it hadn't mattered. It wasn't women's football. It was just football. And, perhaps the only thing that made that whole experience even better was the fact that the male coaches didn't view their players as women either. While helping special teams coach Preston Machock work on marketing projects for the Austin Rage and WPFL, Alex would often have to remind Machock the players were women (when discussing certain more delicate topics). Having coached football for high school boys and soldiers in the Army, Machock saw only jersey numbers and helmets.

But for many, this is a breach of the boys' club code. The boys' club, an area of society where male domination has had the effect of excluding women, whether intentionally or not, is still alive and kicking. Obviously, sport is one of those areas. The military is another.

Our father, Marc Powe, a retired career Army officer, sees a connection between women in sports crossing gender lines and the barriers he saw women cross during his service from 1961 to 1991. "When I entered the Army, there were not many women to be found," Powe says. "The [female] officers were invariably either nurses or administrators, while female NCOs [noncommissioned officers] always had clerical or medical duties. By the early 1970s, though, women had leapt over those fences. They had gained acceptance in a wide range of duties, including signal, military intelligence and military police specialties. For the first time, women were in the mainstream of the Army. Equally important, they were able to have careers that had been out of reach for so long. They could receive the same military education and training as their male peers and begin to aspire for the coveted senior ranks of colonel and general, although that was still a decade away."

Still, many male soldiers, whether officers, NCOs, or junior enlisted personnel, disapproved strongly. Dozens of reasons were offered by the Army's leadership (and that of the other services, which were also experiencing rapid changes in the roles of their female members) for why women could only go to this level or to that artificial limit.

Significantly, little of the serious concern being expressed was about physical capability such as upper body strength or monthly cycles. Instead, the discussions were about societal values. Congressional and public opinion was strongly against the idea of women in combat. The mere possibility that women might be in foxholes caused anxiety from Capitol Hill to the Pentagon to the Army in the field. "I believe that most male soldiers were genuinely afraid of what might happen to women if exposed to enemy infantry," says Powe.

"Sexist or not, few men wanted to think about their daughters, wives, or any other women subjected to the increasingly lethal weapons of the modern battlefield, let alone the possibility of capture, rape, and the like. There was plenty of defensive male chauvinism as well — the idea that 'If some woman can do what I'm doing, then that means I'm not as tough as I think I am.' But the fear about women in combat, in my view, was based on genuine concern for their well-being. And that has not been resolved yet. There are still significant restrictions on assignment of women to duties that would bring them directly into combat. That, in turn, means some artificial limits on what specialties and positions women can occupy."

On the other hand, Powe notes, women have come a long way in 20 years in the military services. The barriers to full equality are now relatively limited. For example, women can serve on U.S. Navy surface combat ships, but not in submarines. They can fly fighter aircraft, but not in fighter units committed to combat; and they can pilot Army utility helicopters at the front, but not armed attack helicopters. "These are distinctions with insignificant real differences," in Powe's view. As he sees it, once women were serving in the Army as equals to men in almost all fields, remaining inappropriate barriers began to fall by their own illogic. More will follow as time passes and pressure from women continues.

The comparison to the role of women in athletics and in the military is clear for Powe: Once women had gained recognition in the realm of sports, particularly in those activities which had been previously restricted to men (such as high-speed auto racing), remaining barriers were harder and harder to sustain. From this perspective, while full equality has not yet been achieved, the distance to travel is far less than the one already covered.

When we think about entering the boys' club, it seems as if few routes could be more challenging than for a woman driver entering the world of professional auto racing. Unlike the military services, there is no sense of shared national purpose. And there are no laws about equality of opportunity that govern professional athletics. So, when St. James decided to become a race driver in 1973, she was an anomaly. And she was not received warmly. She says of her driving career: "My entire career, it has always been, 'Who's going to work with the girl driver? Who's going to work with this bitch?' Many male drivers have told me, 'I couldn't do what you do.'"

But St. James has a philosophy that applies to her sport and that we think can be applied for all women entering the boys' club: "You have to live by the rules. You have to play by the rules. You have to win by the rules. Then, when you win enough, you can change the rules."[1]

Still the rules can be hard to live by, and the changes come slowly. (And sometimes, as discussed in the previous chapter, the rules are unacceptable and must be fought.) A healthy sense of humor is imperative for those entering the boys' club. Take, for example, the 1995 national championship women's bobsled race in Lake Placid. Sliders Michelle and her brakewoman Sharon Slader were among the teams entered, and on the morning of the race they arrived early at the bobsled shed. They were eager to see which sleds had been allocated for the women's race, ready to make whatever little adjustments their appointed sled would require to be race-ready.

As they stepped into the sled shed, their smiles momentarily turned to worried grimaces. But, they told themselves, everything would be OK. Most of the sleds were equally bad, with rusted and worn runners on them, so at least no one had a major advantage. No one that is except the team using shiny racing runners (lent to them by a male domestic driver). But Michelle and Sharon were still confident they could win.

Their first run down was a little rougher than they would have liked, and Michelle kept asking anyone who would listen why the sled had continued to bump the left wall. She was oversteering, she was told. Michelle knew she wasn't over-steering, but she wasn't experienced enough to know what the problem was. The problem, it turned out, was a broken right steering cable. Their sled, it was determined belatedly, was unusable. If Michelle and Sharon could come up with another sled before the second heat, they were told, they could stay in the race; if not, they would be disqualified. So they loaded the sled onto a truck and took it back down the mountain to get another sled (while the race was still underway). OK, they told themselves, this is not a problem. It's not as if another sled could be worse, right?

Wrong. A pile of faded red fiberglass and bolts held together by duct tape sat in the middle of the sled shed. The cowling (hood) of the sled was not completely bolted down and the words "Help Me" had been painted in large letters across the nose. The women exchanged silent glances. But there was no time to be afraid. They loaded the sled onto a truck and raced back up the mountain. Michelle and Sharon frantically duct-taped the cowling

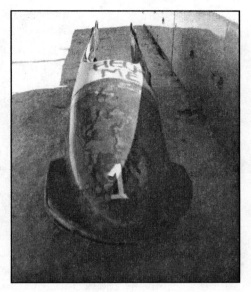

The "Help-Me" Sled (photos by Alexandra Allred).

down as best they could and pulled the sled to the starting gate just as their names were announced. There was no time to catch their breaths or to collect their thoughts; they just stripped off their jackets and hopped into the sled.

This run was smoother, no bouncing off the left wall. But Michelle kept wondering, "Why are my legs cold?" As they rounded the finish curve, she discovered why. The cowling was completely unattached (duct tape, it turns out, cannot withstand G forces) and air had been streaming through a 6-inch gap. But the tight finish curve caused the cowling to fly up like a car hood blinding the driver, Michelle. She finished the race, peering under the cowling and through her feet, and hoping that the cowling wouldn't fly off and kill Sharon. It didn't, and — amazingly — they won the race.

While this story is fairly typical of the kind of equipment U.S. women bobsledders had to use in the first years of women's sledding, we have learned to see the humor. We also wonder if Lyn St. James' pit crew would ever have allowed her to climb into a duct-taped 1980 Toyota Corolla for a race. We kind of doubt it.

Still St. James, like us, like so many female athletes, had to prove herself over and over to men. Each time she demanded her right and proved her ability to race, she silenced a few more of those critics who said, "Who's going to work with this bitch?"

Oh, but how those attitudes are being forced to change. On the birth year of the new millennium, race car legend Mario Andretti sounded off about two female race car drivers — Lyn St. James and Sarah Fisher, who was to race in the Indianapolis 500 for the first time. He said, "They've never proven they can be competitive. Until they win something, I don't consider them a factor." [2]

At the tender age of 20, Fisher is just getting warmed up. A significant number of male racers have needed time to "mature" and "develop" on the racing track before they could win, but Fisher was being held to a different and more difficult standard. That made it all the more precious to her when she received a symbolic induction into that boys' club. "Everybody was there. But the coolest was when Mario Andretti came over and said, 'Hey racer, how ya doing?' He told me he was proud of me for how I had qualified for the race the day before. It was really great. You know, I was part of them, one of them."

This is music to the ears of Micki King, who, like Lyn St. James was one of the first to break through the equity barriers. As a gold medal-winning elite athlete (1972 Olympic Games, springboard diving), a military officer (retired Air Force colonel), a diving coach, and a leader in advancing the rights of women athletes, she's been butting heads with Mario Andretti-types for a long time. "Certainly," she says, "I can understand that people would be threatened by an unknown breaking into their world. For me, it was quite different. I had better luck getting into the boys' club, as you say, because I had credentials (her gold medal)."

But there were plenty of barriers of her own to break down. While coaching at the Air Force Academy, King became the first woman ever to coach a man to an NCAA championship in any sport. She also was named NCAA Division II Coach of the Year three times and coached 11 All-Americans, including two women cadets who won three national titles between them.

But she says the only real discrimination she experienced was from reporters who wondered how she would coach the male cadets differently because she was a woman. Frustrated by the repeated questions, King finally told a reporter, "Well, first I'm going to cut out the locker room talks since I'm not allowed in, then I think I'll paint the diving board pink with a pink trim around the pool." She made her point.

One of the most intimidating places for women to "invade" is the men's locker room, particularly given the discomfort both sexes feel with too much skin or too much physical contact. (Marc Powe, who is a pretty liberated guy, still shudders over the fact that his physical examination upon retirement from the Army was administered by a woman doctor. "Turn your head and cough. Hmm. How long have you had this hernia?" Arghhh!!!)

There is no doubt in the minds of some sports reporters that men feel threatened when women enter that bastion, that last safe and fortified place for men — the locker room. Julie Tache, reporter for 510-AM Sports Radio in Charlotte, North Carolina, says that when she asked some NFL players if her presence in the locker room bothered them, the answer was yes. "Most said they would feel more comfortable if I weren't there, but acknowledged I had a right to be there," Tache says. "Even though they realize this, it doesn't change how tense or self-conscious those same players feel when I am around, something few male reporters may experience." One outcome, Tache notes, is that if two reporters, one male and one female, ask the same question, they may get different answers, "especially depending on where they ask it."[3]

On the other hand, there may be real benefits in having the two different perspectives provided by men and women reporters, says Lisa Winston of *Baseball Weekly*. She identifies two major differences in the way she covers issues from her male colleagues: "One is that I don't reduce the player to a set of stats. The other is that I'm always polite and respectful to the player I'm interviewing."[4] Winston says that she is amazed at the brazen way some male reporters simply demand that the athlete instantly meet the reporter's need for an interview. She wonders if this is a basic difference between the style of men and women, or if it is peculiar to the milieu of sports.

We believe that there is a stylistic difference between men and women in all domains that has to do with empathy and cooperation. In essence, we think that women see things in terms of the need for cooperation in almost all cases, whereas men more frequently see things competitively. That is not to say that men cannot pull together; obviously, they do. And women, through the medium of sports among others, have learned from their male colleagues more about competitiveness and assertiveness. Nonetheless, we like being women and enjoy greatly the kind of cooperation we are experiencing. And we think that men could learn something from us on this topic.

But why, some might ask, would you want to enter the men's domain — that crusty world of sports journalism and its associated, symbiotic relationship with the jocks? We're talking real jocks in real jocks. Leave well enough alone, some might say.

No one knows that better than former *Washington Post* sports reporter Christine Brennan. Brennan had made herself a regular in the locker room of the Washington Redskins. One day while conducting an interview, she heard "Hey, Christine!" She turned to see about 10 Redskins, wrapped in towels or already clothed, huddled together in the middle of the locker room. "They parted like the Red Sea," she recalls, "to reveal [strength coach] Dan Reiley standing totally naked, wearing nothing but a huge grin. I said, 'Uh huh, that's nice,' and turned back to my guy. His eyes were huge, and I just looked at him as if to say, 'Okaaay, we're going to continue this interview now.'"

When we asked Brennan about breaking into the boys' club, she was very positive. Sure, she acknowledges, there have been incidents. "I'm not going to sugarcoat it. But there have been incidents with male reporters as well. Think about this: There are about 1,000 female reporters covering sports today. Just tonight, there will be about 50 female reporters in locker rooms across the country." Brennan mentions the two questions she is most often asked.

Should women be in locker rooms? "That's like asking if women should be allowed to vote! It is very passe. We're here. Deal with it."

Yeah, but don't you get embarrassed walking into the locker rooms? "I say, 'Look, I chose this job.' Of course, I can [get embarrassed]. Does anyone ever ask a doctor about seeing naked bodies? It's my job. And going into a locker room is part of it. ... To be a female reporter you have to be a little deaf and a little blind."

Tache sees it this way: "The best days are still the ones where someone calls the media 'guys' and good or bad, I'm just like everyone else in the room."

What confuses everything and loses credibility for those professional women are the "sportscasters" who pose in semi-nude shots for men's magazines. This isn't empowering to anyone. It only reaffirms the "locker room" mentality.

Cris Dolan, CEO of Mainstream.com, has a childhood memory about a women's locker room at a country club. "I would hear women say they had to ask for their husband's permission [to do something]. I remember thinking how great it was to be

Cris Dolan sliding at the World Cup in St. Moritz (photo provided by Cris Dolan).

the husband. They had friends and did whatever they wanted. I thought it would be better to be a man than a woman. I thought the roles of men were so much more interesting. So I think I chose a career path that allowed me to be like the men."

Having carved her own niche into the system, Dolan would be the first to tell you that women's "roles" today are not less interesting. A former skeleton athlete, ranked third in the world, graduate of MIT, and one of the top troubleshooters in the nation for growing companies, Dolan is no slouch. But at the time, as a child, entering the boys' club seemed like a way to salvation. Now, so many women have begun carving their niches into the system, (i.e., the new female referees in the NBA) that women are beginning to be allowed to be both women and "one of the guys."

Being one of the guys in the guys' world can be very helpful, but also frustrating. Jamie Humphrey, one of about 400 women of the 4,000 students at the U.S. Naval Academy in Annapolis, Maryland, duked it out with the best of them. Literally.

As a graduate of the Naval Academy, Humphrey remembers the heavy course load, the strict discipline, and the difficult physical workout regimens required. The Academy maintains that all candidates must take a physical education class every semester and there are no exceptions for the women. They must run, lift, swim, and train just like the men, including boxing and wrestling. So while Humphrey bobbed, weaved and, yes, punched, she remained philosophical. "If this was going to be a gender-neutral Navy, we all had to be on equal ground and we had to get the same training. So, I was glad we were doing it," Humphrey says.

For Humphrey, being considered "one of the guys," freed her from being labeled. "When you get here, first impressions are very important. You get labeled real fast." With a male-to-female ratio of 10-to-1, it was important not to stand out as a female. Humphrey settled herself in nicely with the boys. But, she explains, it can be hard.

"We had a lot of female leadership because there were a lot of [women] seniors. Because we were [are] a minority of the brigade, a lot of the guys resent the women's leadership roles. They say [the women] got it because of the equal opportunity laws, not because they earned it." Did they? we wanted to know. Humphrey was quick to respond: "Well, I don't personally know all of them but, yes, they earned it. The ones I know I feel are qualified and, at the very least, equal to any of the men."

But to defend them too much would only place her in that precarious female category again. It is something she is still trying to figure out. She wished she could date, but was keenly aware of confusing her worlds. As it was, her undergarments caused enough problems.

As freshmen, cadets are led through a six-week boot camp in which they must learn the ropes of the Academy. That includes learning how to keep a room tidy, making beds, and folding laundry. Squad leaders are in charge of groups of 12 cadets, two of whom are usually female.

It is the duty of the squad leaders to inspect rooms and to impose discipline, which often translates into throwing items around, yelling, and forever burning the cadet's mistake into his or her brain. A misplaced shoe polish bottle can easily be thrown across the room or used to draw all over something. But when the stern leaders came into then-freshman Humphrey's room and found an out-of-place tampon box, they were reduced to blushing teenaged boys. They managed to say, "Uh, you really need to move that." "Move what, sir?" "That," said the squad leader, pointing awkwardly at the tampon box.

Her underwear was even more disconcerting. "They have a certain way you're supposed to fold your underwear," Humphrey explains, "but the men don't know how to handle women's underwear." Rather than tossing the improperly folded garments about the room, the squad leader sheepishly told Humphrey, "Uh, you need to fix ... that."

Then, there is that female thing that is still so frightening to the male population. For example, Humphrey says, squad leaders, also called "detailers," have been instructed that if ever a female cadet says she has to go to the bathroom, they must let her go! No questions asked. After all, it might be that time of the month. During one five-mile run, Humphrey realized she really had to go to the bathroom. Now, she easily concedes, if a male cadet had had to go he would have either be forced to hold it or to "go in the bushes," depending on the detailer's mood. "I said, 'Sir, I reallllly have to go.'" Without question, her detailer ran to the bathroom with her. "It's one of the ways guys are really discriminated against."

But these ways will continue until men learn to deal with women. The simplest things can be made difficult. Marine Major Ann Crittenden told us that she has learned at medal/promotion ceremonies to simply put her hand out and say, "Here, let me help you, sir," thereby relieving male officers of the apparently overwhelmingly embarrassing duty of pinning a medal on her chest.

Perhaps there is something to the power of the "female thing." Another interviewee suggested a funny way women could single-handedly fight crime. Imagine that a woman is alone in a dark alley. A mugger — a really, really big menacing-looking guy — approaches her. Suddenly, she pulls out a tampon, and not just the regular/slender style, but the super size. She waves it in his face, as he shields his eyes in terror. "Back off, buddy! I don't want to have to use this, but I will!" "Ahhhh!" he runs off, arms flailing in the air. Now, if we could just funnel that power ...

Seriously, though, entering the boys' club can be confusing. Role models can be hard to find, in and out of the sports world. But as more and more female role models break into the world of sports media, as more women break into all boys' clubs — whether sports or military or corporate — media-encouraged stereotypes will fall apart, and more and more women will be allowed to "belong."

As Lt. Gen. Carol Mutter, U.S. Marine Corps, says: "When you act like you belong, you are treated that way. If you act like you're breaking a barrier, or act too tentative or nonassertive, you can be treated negatively. So I have always acted like I belonged."

As we walk through more and more doors, there is a marvelous shift in the whole locker room atmosphere. Now, suddenly, we are moving back in time and dealing with the question of whether men belong in locker rooms.

After a WPFL game in which some frustrated players were letting off some steam, an argument broke out. The details are unimportant. Coach James Ubbins came flying into the locker room from where he had patiently been waiting outside while all the players changed. But he was NOT going to tolerate players behaving in this manner. The game had been good. He had eagerly been waiting to talk to his players, and he was not going to see the evening end on this note.

So blinded by anger, he never fully saw the five or so naked women who suddenly shielded themselves with jerseys. Actually, some could have cared less. But it brought up a slightly amusing and even more interesting dilemma — we have reached a stage in women's sports where the question must be asked whether male coaches and reporters should be allowed in the locker rooms of professional players. Ohhhh, what a deliciously wonderful turn of events. Vote whichever way you want but the fact that there is this question to ponder makes us deliriously happy!! Do we reallllly want boys in the girls' network?!?

Notes

1. Jill Lieber, "A Road Less Taken," *Sports Illustrated* (May 3, 1993), 53-55.
2. Tim May, "Fisher Gaining Recognition," *Columbus Dispatch* (May 26, 2001), D1.
3. Julie Tache, "Gender questions are part of answers," The Association for Women in Sports Media (Spring 1995), 4.
4. Lisa Winston, "Infiltrating the male domain," AWSM (Spring 1995), 1.

You've Come a Long Way, Baby!

At the announcement of Muffin Spencer-Devlin's "coming out," LPGA commissioner Jim Ritt had this to say: "I know there are still individuals who have problems with diversity, but we've come so far as a society that I don't see this as a topic that really moves people." Maybe not, but to have one of the Ladies Professional Golf Tournament's biggest players come out of the closet and publicly admit her sexual preference did two things for women in sports: It further fueled stereotypes about female athletes ("Yup, uh huh, I knew it!") and, at the same time, it elevated us to a new freedom from stereotypes.

There is a theory in sports psychology that women athletes may have more masculine traits and behaviors than women who are not athletes. Perhaps this is because competitiveness is still considered a masculine trait in our society. But whatever the reasoning the result is the same: Many female athletes are labeled butch, lesbian, man-wanna-be's, and/or deviant. Never mind that there is no evidence that there is a higher percentage of lesbians in sports than in society as a whole. (And never mind, that it shouldn't matter, anyway.) These labels are intended as insults, to discourage women from being "unfeminine" and, perhaps, to send a message to stop challenging men. It may sound like a ridiculous ploy, but it works.

Adolescent girls regularly drop out of sports rather than endure the taunts. And competitive athletes spend far too much time defending themselves against allegations about sexual orientation, avoiding or denying, when attention should be focused on their sports. Great athletes such as Billie Jean King and Martina Navratilova had as much media time devoted to their sexual preferences as to their amazing athletic abilities and legacies. Just as mothers are questioned about their dedication to their sports and the implied cost to their children, many women are suspect just for loving sports. In fact,

Navratilova says she is thankful no one knew she was gay when she first came to the United States at the age of 18. Had people known, she admits, she wouldn't be who she is today.

And the innuendoes are just as difficult for straight athletes, who don't want to be labeled gay. U.S. softball gold medallist Dot Richardson might not have her medal if she had listened to such labels. She admits it was hard to rise above the rumors. "I kept wondering, 'Why do I have to put up with this? Why does this keep popping up? What is wrong with me?'" She says many of her friends in high school quit sports because of the taunts and innuendoes, and she understands why they quit.

"I believe that the stereotyping of female athletes as lesbians has been one of the biggest hindrances to the development of women in sports," she says.[1] How many girls and women might have been athletic standouts, might have been gold medallists, might have developed true self-confidence, if they hadn't let others' opinions dictate their lives and cause them to quit sports?

As Coach Dee Kennamer went over the WPFL contracts with her new team, we reached a section of the contract that discusses how a player should conduct herself (in the best interest of the team) in public and to the media. At this point, Coach addressed the fact that there might be some reporters who will ask about the sexual preferences of players. Sadly, this was an issue that had to be addressed the prior year so Coach was feeding us the response she wanted her entire team to adopt: What does that have to do with football?

Sadder still is the fact that women's sports magazines are picking up on that very topic. *Sports Illustrated for Women* was offered two very different articles on women in the WPFL. One was about teamwork, camaraderie, and the pure joy of women on the gridiron. The second was an article about a specific player "coming out." *SI for Women* chose the second article. As Andra Douglas of the New York Sharks later wrote, this was very destructive to the image of women in football, women in sports, and potential corporate sponsors. It was unnecessary. As we have said before, there is a double standard even among ourselves as women that we must overcome. We must stop making sexuality a criteria for female athletes.

The females who do rise above the fray may accomplish great things, but they also pay a price. Allie Sizler, a high school standout basketball player, has been accused of being a lesbian. Sizler's mother told us, "Whatever Allie felt was OK with her father and me, but she said, 'Mom, I like boys.' I thought, 'OK,' but that really didn't matter. It was what was happening at school."

What was happening at school was a group of athletes, intimidated by Allie's athletic prowess, decided that she must be gay. No one girl could be that dedicated, that focused, that good, and be "normal." In fact, an ex-boyfriend started the rumor. Playing second fiddle to Allie's true passion — sports — was more than his adolescent ego could handle. There had to be something wrong with Allie.

Julie Croteau was routinely accused of wanting to be a man because she coached NCAA Division I baseball, accused of "getting off on the power of yelling at men." At the very least, such behavior was not considered "feminine."

Beyond appearance and femininity, there is also a standard — albeit a double standard — for feminine behavior. Sports psychologist Pat Bach points to Nancy Kerrigan, "whose poor behavior in winning the silver medal in the 1994 Olympics did not meet expectations for proper behavior," and who was roundly criticized by media, sponsors, and the public. But Bach wonders, "If a man had behaved so poorly, would sponsors have rejected him, too?" Every single day we can open the paper and read about what NBA or NFL star was arrested for some kind of violent or substance-abusing act. It gets one or two columns and bam! we don't hear much more about it. Our male athletes are notorious for misbehaving, yet they continue to get giant endorsement contracts. Boys will be boys.

While male professional athletes may behave badly on and off the playing fields; spit in the face of officials; abuse drugs and alcohol; drive while intoxicated; and commit spousal abuse, assault and murder, we continue to support and celebrate them. Simply put, Kerrigan didn't act nicely for a woman. Her behavior was out of the norm for "proper feminine behavior." But all bets are off for the men.

In fact, it was during the 2002 Salt Lake City Games that one of the biggest sagas unfolded. U.S. bobsledder Jean Racine (known on the circuit to be aggressive and cutthroat) dropped her best friend/fellow teammate at the last minute and replaced her with a larger, stronger brakewoman. But on the eve of the competition when her brakewoman pulled a hamstring, Racine went on the hunt for yet another

Olympian Jean Racine hits on the training sled (photo by Alexandra Allred).

brakewoman — the brakewoman of her main rival, Jill Bakken. This bit of information actually made breaking news during another sporting event. Racine was painted the villain of the 2002 Games and no one could get enough. Yet, in the previous Winter Olympics when the U.S. men's hockey team had trashed several hotel rooms — vomit spewed on walls, carpeting and furniture destroyed — that incident received little coverage. And during the 1994 Games when the U.S. men's bobsled team nearly unraveled after major partying and little sled prep time, people barely took notice. Although Racine's actions can be questioned, headlining her as the next Tonya Harding was unfair. Like Kerrigan, Racine's behavior was very 'unfeminine.'

During a game between the Austin Rage and New England Storm, the always volatile, always entertaining Lisa Mayers assaulted members of the Rage line. Shots to head and upper body were taken. When the play was dead, Mayers would slap someone down or shove someone backward, drawing a chorus of boos and hisses. Fans, coaches, and players complained vehemently to the refs. At 6'4" and 340 pounds., the Rage was having a difficult time dealing with this player. One could hope to wear her down physically, but Mayers also happens to be a star basketball player in her native Boston. She handled the offensive line and exerted little effort. "She's a wild woman," laughs teammate Jodi Burns. "But off the field, she's one of the nicest people you've ever met. She'd do anything for you. She is so nice." Popular with kids from local basketball clubs and fellow athletes, Mayers is also the perfect ticket for the WPFL. You either love her or you hate her. No one is quite sure what to do about her. "She's a crowd pleaser," agrees Burns. Whoever she is, she defies that "proper feminine behavior."

Babe Didrikson-Zaharias gloated to reporters that she was the best; she predicted before meets how she would fare (always the best); she told knee-slapping jokes to the boys in the pressroom. They loved her. Her fellow competitors were not so gracious. How could she act that way? Mothers began to warn their daughters away from sports, saying "You don't want to be like Babe."

The double standard for women actually works more than one way. Not only are women held to a standard of behavior higher than men's (i.e., "proper feminine behavior"), but they also are held to a lower standard of behavior. "The media like to portray female athletes as catty," says Hilliard. Take the challenge issued before the 2000 Olympics to three-time Olympian Janet Evans by 15-year-old Brook Bennett, saying, "She's scared." But there were no "cat fights." Instead Janet Evans was gracious before and after the Games, making it clear that she would not be dragged into any war of words.

That portrayal of "cattiness" is a far too widely held misconception. We have run across many statements that women (and, therefore, female athletes) are "back-stabbing, manipulative, and petty" or that you can't have a group of women together without having "cat fights." In our experience, the opposite is more often true. Female athletes tend to bond with each other more quickly and more closely than male athletes do, and to be protective of each other. Women are also more deeply disappointed when they feel a teammate has betrayed them or let the team down. This "pettiness" that many seem to view as a female trait is, in fact, the absence of a socialized male trait to be both ruthless competitors and good friends.

Too many girls do not learn the written and unwritten rules about sports, about how to be competitive on the field and friends off the field.

So, after the rift between the Austin Rage football players, the disgruntled parties went their separate ways. They didn't go quietly, however, leaving the coaching staff a little uncertain about how to handle the angry women. Later, when we spoke with Coach Preston Machock, he wondered aloud if the behavior he had seen earlier was a female athlete thing. Yes, it was, we told him. Two male athletes can have a raging fight and go have a beer together after the race or the game. Two female athletes will need a little time to work out their feelings. For Coach Preston, who has a long, impressive resume as a football coach, the female athlete deal was new. He wanted to know more, so we told him. This is who we are: complex and demanding individuals who expect a lot of ourselves and just as much from each other.

The blowup in the Rage locker room demonstrates why men often think that women are unable to get along in groups. This misinterpretation doesn't surprise sports psychologist Coleen Hacker. "Society or the dominant culture would prefer that women not participate in one-on-one sports," Hacker says, adding that gymnastics, golf, and figure skating are very popular for that reason. "Even tennis, because the opponents are separated by a net." Ironically, it was a tennis match — that most famous first battle of the sexes between Billie Jean King and former tennis champ Bobby Riggs — that finally allowed women to take their rightful place in the sports world and begin to knock down some stereotypical boundaries. (King beat Riggs, 6-4, 6-3, 6-3.)

Stereotypes aside, the reality is that women do get along in teams. What we have seen in women's team sports is very different from the men's teams. Many male team members recognize the difference and agree that there is a kind of easiness, friendship, and camaraderie among the women that the men don't usually share.

During the 1996-97 U.S. Bobsled Nationals, two women had come late to the camp and tested three days later than the rest of us. Those of us who had already taken the six-item test (30-, 60-, and 100-meter dash, five hops, vertical jump, and shot put throw) and made the points, spent the morning on sled-pushing drills while the two latecomers ran their 30-meter, 60-meter, and 100-meter dashes. At lunch break, we saw the women walking into the gymnasium to take the remaining three events.

Just that morning, we learned that one of the women, Liz, was pregnant with her second child. Five months pregnant, to be exact. Many of us were nervous for her. Five months is pretty far along to effectively run, hop, leap, and throw. We were all worried about how well she would do. Then, one of those things that you hear about in the best-of-sports-stories happened. Instead of counting Liz out, figuring she was one less competitor, the large majority of the women who attended the nationals, including women who had not met Liz before this day, went into the gymnasium to cheer her on. She needed the points, and we wanted them for her.

While we all nibbled on our chocolate chip cookies and milk (one of our favorite rewards for jobs well done), we cheered Liz through her vertical leap and shot put. Then, we overheard a testing official say she needed to hop 12 meters to make the team. She had already hopped twice and had only hit 10.65 meters. (This was far from Liz's normal score, but she was five months pregnant, for crying out loud.) We honestly didn't know if Liz — in her present condition — could hit 12 meters. Later it would be funny, later we would be teased by the male bobsledders: one by one, all the women put down their chocolate chip cookies and concentrated on Liz. As one male slider put it, "Now that's love when eight women all stop eating their chocolate chip cookies at the same time!"

Liz couldn't hit 12 meters — not five months pregnant. We all cheered and yelled and crossed fingers and toes, but in the end 10.65 would be her best for the day. And while Liz nervously paced the floor, we all gathered around the testing official. A few male bobsledders watched from afar.

"I get 429," one team member said, doing the math in her head. Liz needed to score 425 to make the team, and the testing official had tallied her score as 419 — not enough. Another team member nodded. "Yeah, I get 429, too."

After several recounts, the tester realized he had miscalculated; the score really was 429. And before he could even make it official, the gymnasium reverberated with whoops of joy. Liz was hugged from all sides. She hugged back hard, and there were many tears. Our teammate had felt our support, our concern. She had made the points just as much for us as she did for herself. We were all so proud.

Looking through the windows of the gym were three male sliders, grinning and shaking their heads. In the men's camp, the feeling is that every man out is one less guy between me and the 'A' team. But here was this group of women bobsledders hugging and whooping, the prized chocolate chip cookies forgotten. We took the teasing and felt a little bit sorry for the men for whom group support was so foreign.

There are also many wonderful stories of camaraderie between female and male athletes. Karyn Bye of the U.S. women's hockey team tells about growing up playing hockey as the only girl on the team. Not only did she become a full-fledged team member in the eyes of her teammates, she was also like a sister to many of them. "At one of our games in high school, the opposing team asked which number the girl was. They told them I was number 23. Number 23 was the biggest guy on our team [and he] had a beard."

The guys had fun with Bye, and there were laughs, but always they protected her. Since there were some players on other teams who set out to "hurt" her, Bye's own teammates would help Bye disguise who she was. She put only her initials on the team roster, so parents and players from other teams would not know who she was. Also, "My hair was real short. A lot of the guys on my team had longer hair than I did."

Record-setting race car driver St. James, spokesperson for the Women's Sports Foundation and Ford Motor Company, television commentator and author, told us about the very special connection she had with her pit crew, not the usual driver-pit crew relationship. Much to the frustration of her all-male crew, St. James was hopelessly modest. There were many times when she performed well in a race but questioned her ranking, not believing she had "earned" her ratings.

St. James recalls a particular competition, the Kelly Services Races, at which the top women racers were to be honored. Following the race, the number one woman driver would receive an award during a ceremony before the large audience. As always, St. James had underestimated her talents: she had expected to place fifth but, to her surprise, she had won! She also had started her period.

Wearing her white racing suit, she pulled into the pit and politely refused to get out of the car. While dozens of people raced into the pit area, her own crew yelled at her to get out. She shook her head. "Nope. I'm not getting out." Believing St. James to be playing the humble role again, the crew chief stuck his head into the car and began pulling her out. St. James grabbed his head and turned his face so he could see that her white racing suit was soaked with menstrual blood. "He said only three words," St. James remembers. 'Oh, my God!'"

Immediately, he rallied the crew and they pushed St. James' car out of the pit area and smuggled her into the locker room. Even as the sponsors were calling her name, her crew protected her from the crowds. Not another word was ever said about that incident, but her crew gave her a present — a black racing suit.

That sort of cooperation is also essential in the sport of bobsledding, where teams must work as units to move 450-pound sleds and lift them in and out of trucks. After we had proved ourselves to our bobsledding brothers, a few would help a little, by helping us move or repair sleds, by lending us equipment or walking the track with us. But they also — on a few occasions — stole the last brownie in the whole cafeteria off one of our trays. (They said they were watching our weight for us. Isn't that nice? But they also brought Alex, Chrissy, and Liz candy when they were injured in crashes.)

When we first began bobsledding, the original eight, we were the female version of the Jamaican bobsled team: starting with nothing and leading each other blindly through the maze of a new sport. But along the way, despite the obstacles, we encountered some tremendous gestures. In international competition, with our rented and dented sleds and no coach, the British and Canadian athletes loaned us equipment, and their coaches walked the tracks with us. The German coach visited Michelle in the hospital and gave us a tour of what was once East Germany. The Swiss translated for us and climbed into our sleds to make adjustments for us. And bodyguards for Prince Albert of Monaco helped us flip our sleds and set them correctly for prerace inspection. (We had no idea what to do.)

Women are able to bring that spirit of cooperation and camaraderie to sports and bring out those qualities in others around them. For example, our bobsledding brothers are not as generous with each other as they are with the women. They have admitted that the women broke the tension that had always hung over the training center and kept them apart. Women are more able to draw the fun out of sports. They tend to have a better appreciation for what sports mean.

That appreciation was demonstrated during the 1999 women's World Cup soccer game between the United States and Italy. An Italian player was hurt while the U.S. had possession of the ball, so the referee could not call time-out. But it was clear that the player was hurt, so a U.S. player passed the ball to an Italian player, giving the Italians possession and allowing the referee to call time-out. After the player was attended to, play resumed with a throw-in by the Italians. The Italian player with the ball returned the earlier favor by throwing the ball directly to an American defender, thus giving the U.S. possession again.

How we do love to watch women play sports! Correction, how we love to watch women excel in any athletic ventures. Heck, it's why we loved *Xena: Warrior Princess*. Do we really think there was a Amazon warrior roaming the world, righting wrongs and saving all of humankind? Well, we like to think so. And, it's why we like *Buffy, the Vampire Slayer*. In truth, it's pretty absurd to think there are all those vampires running around one small college town and no one outside the Buffy gang has noticed it. Instead, what we like is the message of a strong heroine and the supersonic stunt work!

Rather than holding information to herself, stuntwoman Lisa Hoyle has been only too happy to share tips with actresses such as Drew Barrymore, Cameron Diaz, Christina Applegate, Neve Campbell and Clare Kramer. "I've learned so much from my stunt coordinators, and I love the idea of sharing with others. It's kind of empowering that these women [actresses] can do some of the stunts themselves." In fact, actress/friend Clare Kramer isn't the only *Buffy the Vampire* actress to share in stunt work. Actress Michelle Trachtenberg who starred in *Harriet the Spy* with Rosie O'Donnell and now plays little sister to Sarah Michelle Gellar on *Buffy,* has done her own stunts with both productions. Not only has Trachtenberg learned from her stuntwoman but fellow actresses as well. "Sarah and I were both on the soap *All My Children*," she says. "So, we knew each other before I got the call for Buffy. She shows me things and teaches me bowling," she laughs. But, on set, when things get a little too intense, a stunt double is necessary.

"I accidentally punched Sarah's stunt double in the face," admits a sheepish Kramer. "Oh, I felt terrible. I left a big welt right between her eyes, but she was happy. It was her first injury!"

It's a different mindset. Something only that inner athlete could reach out for. "But I knew I had made it or really felt I had been accepted when I was made a member to the Women's Stunt Association," says Hoyle. "I was doing a stunt where I had to be hit by a car. Sandy Gimtel (stuntwoman/coordinator) drove the car that hit me, and she told me later that she had a really hard time hitting me. She said, 'I really like you as a person.' But after she hit me she told me she really respected me as a professional, too. She sponsored me to be voted into the group. It was such an honor."

Instead of cattiness, what we have found among elite female athletes is a strong sense of family, friendship, and bonding. One such example is the U.S. women's hockey team. Just as their soccer sisters had done for Joy Fawcett, the first-ever U.S. women's hockey team pulled together to help the assistant coach who brought her baby along for the World Cup tour. Each female hockey player grabbed something of the baby's (a bag of food, formula, diapers) along with her own possessions. In fact, as the team hustled to make a plane they were close to missing, Karyn Bye scooped up the baby boy and sprinted through the airport. No one thought any differently about carrying the baby and baby things than she did about hustling hockey equipment. They were a package deal. All for one and one for all.

Nickolaus Brown (wardrobe), Jamie Linn (stand-in), actress Clare Kramer and stuntwoman Lisa Hoyle celebrate after a successful day on the set (photo from the collection of Clare Kramer).

Coach Tara VanDerveer of the U.S. women's basketball team said the finale of the Olympic games, winning the gold medal, was the happiest and saddest day of her life. While she called her athletes "warriors ready for battle," they were also "family." The women worked, trained, and dreamed together. They traveled far, seeking personal goals and working together to gain the attention and respect they so greatly deserved.

They had to work hard to gain the public's respect. And most female athletes appreciate the frustration of being treated as jokes, called wannabes, and told plainly that we are "wasting our time." While the negativity itself has been draining, it has also served to pull women together. We have seen and been encouraged by women in our own and in other sports, and women in decades past, all fighting for their sports, for approval, and for acceptance.

But imagine this. You are in the Olympic Games. You are the anchor leg for the women's 4x100 relay. It's all up to you. Billions of people are watching you on television, tens of thousands are watching you from the stands. You're jiggling your arms and legs, trying to keep the muscles loose and warm. You're rolling your head from side to side. Your heart is pounding. You are running over the race in your mind, how you will take the baton, take off. The gun goes off! The race is on ... then, "Pssst! Your tampon string is showing!"

"What?" The USA's Gwen Torrence turned to face Pauline Davis from Team Bahamas. Davis was pointing down to Torrence's shorts. "Your tampon string," she repeated.

Mortified, Torrence tried to tuck it back inside the seam of her outfit. The baton was passed off to the second leg. Davis was shaking her head at Torrence. It was still showing.

Davis, then, actually crossed over her line into Torrence's lane to help. Imagine being in the middle of the biggest event of your life, and — with the event already underway — messing with a tampon string — yours or someone else's. Yet, here were Torrence and Davis huddled together in Torrence's lane, fixing a tampon string. Two women from opposing teams, the favorites for gold and silver. "It was so embarrassing," Torrence says. "I don't know why I was so embarrassed, but I couldn't help it. And everyone was saying, 'Why are those girls standing together? What are they doing?'"

By the time the third legs were coming around for Torrence and Davis, Torrence said, "Oh, forget it!" She got the baton, took off, and won the gold for the U.S. And the Bahamian team won the silver, making it the first time in the Bahamas' history that women medalled in any sport.

Later, reporters asked Torrence what she and Davis were talking about. Torrence laughs, "I told them, 'It was a female thing.'"

Upon reflection, it appears to us that those who imagine that girls or women as a group are petty or back-stabbing do not know much about women, and certainly not about women athletes. They have not experienced the exasperating, exciting, exhausting, exhilarating world of women's sport. We are sure that those who do not believe women can be happy in large competitive groups simply have not cried, sweated, and laughed together as hard as we have. Indeed, VanDerveer said that the end of her basketball team's Olympic quest for gold was like losing her family. Here is the point: women, at least in team sports, must be close to be successful. We must stick together individually to make progress collectively.

When Mary Ellen Clark prepared for what would be her last Olympic Games, the competition was tough. She knew it. She was recovering from vertigo, diving against girls half her age, including Becky Rheul. But instead of keeping all her experience and all her secrets to herself, Clark drew Rheul in. For Rheul, a first-time Olympian, it was an especially nerve-racking time. But rather than capitalize on that, Clark (Rheul's roommate at the Games) offered her advice about the competition and the audience. She warned Rheul not to let the crowd intimidate her, but rather, "Let the sounds be a blanket of warmth to soothe you." Rheul would later tell her mother that this advice worked. And anyone who watched the 1996 Games and the women's diving competition probably asked the question we did whenever Rheul stood on the diving platform: Why is she smiling?

What could possibly be so amusing at this point in her life? Didn't she have other things to think about, like not killing herself? But Rheul was taking Clark's advice to heart. She was doing what she loved most in life and the cheers of the home crowd only reminded her of that. Clair Rheul says of Clark, "She was willing to take the time to pass on her wisdom and share her experience. We really appreciate that and, hopefully, Becky will do the same at her next Olympics."

"This is what we need to keep good athletes going, to keep the cycle going. We are all very much a family. Both Becky and Mary Ellen come from large families, so during the Olympics we all sat together, and even Mary Ellen's parents told us it felt like we were one family. We were." In fact, with the Games long over, both divers continue to send each other notes and gifts. As trainer Radu says, when we learn to work together as a finely-tuned watch, all of us acting as perfect little pieces for the greater whole, then, we work well together.

In May 1994, bobsledder Jill Bakken had an enormous amount of schoolwork to plow through. School officials had not been happy that she had to attend a camp in May, just weeks before her final examinations and graduation from high school. All week we had trained, sweated, and collapsed onto our beds from sheer exhaustion. It was near the end of the week and Jill had completed only half of her schoolwork. Her team pitched in, helping set up essay questions to test her. We each studied certain subjects so that we could quiz her. While one teammate took physics, another took math, and another took history.

It was early Sunday morning and Alex sat alone in the cafeteria writing some test questions for Jill. Having spent all night brushing up on her post-World War II history, Alex was preparing some tough questions when a hand reached over her shoulder. A handmade card dropped onto the open book, and the unseen messenger was gone. A plain white piece of paper, folded in half, had been drawn on by Jill's loving hands. Little baby ducks, flowers, and wildlife decorated the cover. Inside was a very tender message wishing Alex a "Happy Mothers Day!"

It was Alex's first Mother's Day card ever. It was the second time she had ever been away from Kerri, then only 11 months old. Of course, the tears came and Alex turned in her seat to see if Jill was nearby. Standing outside of the cafeteria, Jill was pressed against the glass, watching Alex.

A sound from the other side of the cafeteria caught Alex's attention and she turned to see FIBT/Olympic official Joey Kilburn, who had been watching the entire exchange take place. He pretended to wipe a tear away from his cheek. He was not making fun. Clearly, he too was deeply moved by this silent exchange of affection. It was not long after that that Kilburn told us how struck he was by the kinship shared by the women sledders.

Whatever our social or sexual preferences, we are all women and we are all athletes. One does not suffer because of the other; in fact, each can be improved by the other. And there can be no better shining example, no better illustration about sisterhood, fair play, complete and utter selflessness in the name of sport, teamwork, and justice than the story of martial artists Kay Poe and Esther Kim.

It goes like this: two female athletes, one spot on the U.S. Olympic team for the 2000 Sydney Games. Best friends, training partners, black belts forced to compete against each other in the women's flyweight championships final fight that would make one's dream and break the other's heart. Only once in their young athletic careers had they ever fought against each other, and it was a fight so evenly matched that Poe won by the narrowest of margins. By all accounts, this would be an amazing fight.

Instead, there was an amazing act of grace that left everyone at the Olympic trials in Colorado Springs stunned and/or crying. Kim had reached the finals first. All her life she dreamed of going to the Olympics. Her father, Jin Kim, a martial arts instructor and coach to both Kim and Poe could not have been more proud or more twisted with conflicted emotions. Then, during the last fight in the fi-

Esther Kim with father Jin W. Kim (photofrom the collection of Esther Kim).

nals, Poe injured her knee. Kim was waiting for Poe when her father came in carrying the injured athlete. Poe's knee had swollen to the size of a cantaloupe, her kneecap dislocated. Both fighters were crying.

Kim asked her good friend Poe what she planned to do. "She told me she was going to fight and I just knew I couldn't fight against her. It wasn't right. It wasn't the way I wanted to fight or go to Sydney. So, I told her, 'I'm going to bow down to you.'" It would be an official act of forfeit that would disqualify the healthy Kim, allowing her friend the sole ticket to Sydney and the distinct honor of being called Olympian.

"Kay [Poe] tried to fight it, tell me 'no' but I told her I wasn't asking. It was what I was going to do, what I knew was right." As they walked out to the mat before the judges, Poe leaning on Kim for support, they were sobbing for their victory, for their loss, for their grief, pain, and friendship. One was winning, one was losing.

Everyone was crying — fans, coaches, other competitors — as Kim made the official bow down, forfeiting her dreams.

At the time she said she did not give up her dreams, she merely handed them over to Poe. [Incidentally, Poe did not win a medal at the games, but Kim's act of greatness so moved the President of the International Olympic Committee, not to mention the world, that she was invited as an Official Guest of the Olympic Games].

When we spoke with Kim almost a year later, nothing had changed. She had no regrets, no complaints. What she does have is the heart of a champion! If ever we could be judged by society through the act of one champion ...

Notes

1. Dot Richardson, "Sex, Lies and Softball," *Sports Illustrated Women/Sport* (Spring 1997), 42-44.

'Atta Girl! Our Heroines

Women's sports history has such a large archive of role models, of pioneers to whom we should give credit and thanks and from whom we can learn. Courageous, determined athletes who have dared to cross the line. Women who have dared to venture into no-woman's land. Women who have dared to perform dangerous, risky feats that few men would dare attempt.

In 1925, for example, a young American woman named Gertrude Ederle attempted to swim the English Channel. Only 18 years old, she had already broken world records, had an Olympic gold medal, and held 250 swimming records. However, the weather and frigid water temperatures of the Channel were too much for her on that day, and she was forced to quit after nine hours in the water.

As word spread that this "little girl" had attempted such a feat, the *New York Daily News* sponsored Ederle, offering her $5,000 to attempt the swim again and $7,500 if she succeeded. They even drafted her to be a correspondent and write her own story. "I want to be the first woman to swim from France to England. I know a woman can do it," she insisted.

As she prepared for her second attempt in 1926, and as her celebrity status rose, she became the topic of a very heated debate. Was she the symbol of a new, healthy woman willing to take on risks, striking out on her own? Or was she an example of the weaker sex overreaching? Surely, some reasoned, her failure would only prove the frailties of her sex.

Coated with three layers of grease, the top coat being a kind of thick car axle grease for insulation, Ederle plunged into the icy waters, setting out toward her goal. She swam behind a boat holding her father and sister and filled with reporters. Occasionally, people jumped into the water and swam beside her to keep her company. Her sister, father, and the reporters leaned over the side of the boat to sing her songs, entertaining and encouraging her along the way.

Sports historians estimate this kind of journey is perhaps one of the loneliest of the sports triumphs. Even with her supporters there, much of Ederle's time was spent in the darkness of the water, alone. Yet she was not alone. Ederle felt the weight of the world on her shoulders and recognized that many, many women were counting on her to complete this journey. Wall Street brokers wagered three-to-one against her, and one reporter with the *Daily News* proclaimed her actions were a reminder to us all that "females must forever remain the weaker sex."

The weather worsened and the winds picked up, making Ederle's strokes much more difficult. She was attacked twice by Portuguese men-of-war, which stung her horribly. But she told her family and coach, "I must keep going."

Fourteen hours and 34 minutes later, Ederle touched England's soil — a time that was 1 hour and 59 minutes faster than that of any man who had swum the channel. Billed as "woman swimmer, champion of both sexes," Ederle traveled to New York for the United States' first-ever ticker-tape parade and was greeted by a crowd of two million people. She did not lose her femininity because of her accomplishments.

Neither did Amelia Earhart. Earhart was the first woman to make a solo transcontinental round trip flight (in 1928), the first woman to fly across the Atlantic (also in 1928), and the first woman to fly solo across the Atlantic Ocean (in 1932), breaking down the stereotype that women were limited in their abilities. She was also greeted with ticker-tape parades. She won several flying awards in her lifetime, including the Distinguished Flying Cross.

There were no ticker-tape parades for Marcenia (Toni) Stone, who broke the gender barrier in baseball. She played second base for the Indianapolis Clowns of the Negro American League from 1953-1955, after having already played on men's semipro teams in San Francisco and New Orleans. After her professional baseball career ended, Stone continued to play in men's amateur leagues until she was 60 years old. But she got no official recognition and is not included in any of the exhibits at the Negro Leagues Baseball Museum in Kansas City. Stone said in 1993, "I just loved the game. But they weren't ready for me. ... But my heart was set. And I kept at it."[1]

These women first established the notion that females are physically capable of anything they want to do and paved the way for women today. Often facing male-dominated fields with no mentors and few supporters, these women were more than pioneers. They were adventurers, exhibitionists, and test pilots for what was to come.

Many of the greatest role models in women's athletics had accomplishments outside the world of sports. The celebrity status of such women lent credibility to their causes. Babe Didrikson-Zaharias was one such woman.

Her athletic feats are well known, but not so well known is the fact that she became an advocate for cancer treatment at a time when the disease was not well known or understood, when there was a real stigma attached to cancer patients. Many cancer patients tried to keep their illnesses secret. But not Babe. In 1953, at the height of her career — Didrikson-Zaharias was diagnosed with colon cancer and underwent an emergency colostomy. Remarkably, three and a half months after the surgery, she returned to the LPGA tour, and the following year she won the U.S. Women's Open by a record 12 strokes. After her victory, she said: "This should show people not to be afraid of cancer."

Didrikson-Zaharias was the first person to campaign against cancer, stimulating a national fund-raising campaign that was led by President Dwight Eisenhower. True to her nature, Didrikson-Zaharias hid nothing from the press or the people. She allowed the press to travel with her, keeping them apprised of all her ailments.

In 1956, Didrikson-Zaharias lost her fight — one of her few losses. After her death, Eisenhower made a public tribute to her, saying, "Babe took on the kind of fight that inspires us all."

This chapter's title, "'Atta Girl: Our Heroines," was initially dedicated to sprinter Wyomia Tyus. Tyus dedicated her last gold medal earned in the 4x400-meter relay at the 1968 Olympics to two fellow U.S. athletes who became overnight pariahs. During the 1968 Mexico City Games, as they stood on the medal stand, runners Tommie Smith and John Carlos raised their fists in the air as a silent protest to the treatment of African-Americans. It was a silent protest that got them expelled from the Olympic Village.

"All I did was win a track event. What they did lasted a lifetime," Tyus explains. Downplaying her gesture, and the fact that she grew up in a segregated school system, Tyus says simply she adjusted to what came her way. Now, she works with city kids in an outdoor program, taking them away from the city, trying to build self-esteem.

When asked if she considers herself a role model, Tyus laughs and says, "Only because people keep telling me I am." Again, she continues to minimize her contributions, naming others for credit. Then, she adds modestly, after some thought, "Maybe I am a quiet role model." As her coach Ed Temple from Tennessee State says, Tyus is "one of the pioneers for women and blacks."

Elaine Cheris not only trained herself to be an Olympic fencer, but runs a school for her sport as well. She staunchly believes that sports help children socially. Of her female students, Cheris says, "They're less likely to walk off with the first boy who blinks at them. Girls and boys learn to work with each other. They train like brothers and sisters; they scream and cry together. There is a mutual respect." And, absolutely, Cheris does not allow the battle of the sexes to take place in her school. Not only does she forbid any form of "hazing," but she also demands that her students praise each other. "You beat him 15-0. Now," she will tell her charges, "go over and tell him he really made you reach. Tell him he really made you work hard."

Cheris stresses the importance of pushing yourself to know your limits, always refusing to hear and be stifled by the negative. She always reminds her kids that winning comes from inside. And she serves as a role model for those who have been told or have believed that age limited their successes and dreams. At 50, Cheris thinks nothing of her age, or the fact that so few athletes male or female continue to compete so long. And she ignores those who would remind her of it (in the negative sense). She says, "People will give you a thousand reasons to lose. They don't really want you to, but they just tell you all the reasons you can't [win]." Can't. A word she just hates to hear.

Lisa Fernandez also refuses to hear the "C" word. As though the coach's words still burn in her ears ("You'll never be able to compete past 16"), Fernandez is determined to be a positive role model for young hopefuls. Two or three times a month, Fernandez offers softball clinics around the country. She gives inspirational talks, works with coaches, and remains an undaunted supporter of women's athletics. With a personal motto of "Never be satisfied," Fernandez continues to push all those around her to be the best they can be. What better role model?

Two other athletes who refused to be counted out are Wilma Rudolph and Althea Gibson; no list of pioneers in the world of sports would be complete without these two names. They stand as symbols of progress, not only for women, not only for African-Americans, but for all people. Both women came from very poor backgrounds and both broke down barriers for women and for people of color. Today, they are remembered as women of tremendous talent, grace, and sportsmanship, with the wills to be the best they could be.

Tori Allen (photo provided by the Allen family).

Today, at the age of 14, Tori Allen is a leader for young girls. She is a role model and an inspiration. Of boys, she recognizes that she doesn't need them to complete who she is or how she feels. In fact, she says they will only interfere with what she is trying to accomplish.

And just what is she trying to accomplish? When we first met Allen, she was just 12 years old but she knew what she wanted. Allen's response shows her leadership qualities: "I try to set goals a couple of years in advance. I'm 12 now so I'll be 16 at the next Olympic Games. I want to win gold and be the youngest female Olympian [in pole-vaulting] history."

Because she is two years ahead academically, she plans to graduate from high school that same year, use her money from endorsements, and invest. Then, she says she will turn her attention to rock climbing. As the reigning rock-climbing queen of the teen world, she wants to see the sport entered into the Olympic Games.

"It'll probably be up to me to get it in. ... I'll be 20 at the next Olympics and hope to compete in rock climbing and maybe pole vaulting. Then, when I'm 21, I will have graduated from college and will take my savings from my endorsements and open my own all-girl kindergarten. It's just always been my dream." Why all girl? "Cause I think it would be more fun. When you put boys into it, they cause trouble and break things. Girls are better."

Two years later when we caught up with Allen again, she was the same girl with the same goals... just much closer.

"I was undefeated as a freshman boy pole-vaulter and I won the freshman boys' county meet in pole vault. Now, I have a Title IX lawsuit against the IHSAA asking them to add vault for girls at the state level.

"I won several invitationals valuting as a girl so that was cool!"

During her summer breaks while most girls are hanging out the pool, Allen set a new record for her age group for USATF vault and, always the perfectionist, promised to do better at her next meet.

In climbing, Allen won both U.S. Juniors and Adult (again) in both speed and difficultly and bouldering for adults. Allen is also the only American to participate in the X-Games for climbing.

What's next? Allen is acting as a volunteer coach when she is in town and is lobbying to become the youngest female climber to take on the nose of El Capitan in Yosemite. World records? Title IX lawsuits? As always, we are left breathless by the pioneering spirit and the amazing talent of Tori Allen. Remember the name and check the web site (www.toriallen.net) because she is the future of women in sport!

Both race car drivers St. James and Sarah Fisher are also ready to accept the responsibility of being role models. "If I really dig down, I can accept it," St. James says. "It's hard to understand why I would be considered a role model. I think of role models as people who do something you want to do and want to try — something accessible. So, I wrestle with that, but I hold it in high regard."

St. James is a role model, and her actions on and off the racetrack attest to how seriously she takes that responsibility. In her 20 years of racing, St. James has set 31 national and international records She was named Indianapolis 500 Rookie of the Year in 1992. She was the first solo woman driver to win a professional road race, the first woman to exceed 200 miles per hour on an oval track, and the first woman to compete full-time on the Indy circuit.

Off the track, St. James has established the Lyn St. James Foundation and Driver Development Program, the goal of which is to help new female race car drivers and business executives develop skills for winning, skills needed in racing and in living. She is also the author of a car maintenance manual for women.

St. James serves on the consumer advisory board for the Ford Motor Company and on the board of the Colorado Bullets, the first all-female professional baseball team and is a past president of the Women's Sports Foundation.

Fisher is only now entering the world that St. James turned upside down. And for many of the seasoned drivers and racing commentators, Fisher has a solid future. Acting as role model is just one of many things she seems to excel in. "I just know how it feels to break into something fairly new to women, I know what it feels like not to be wanted just because you're a girl. But I also know what we are capable of. So, I'm proud to be a role model if it's gonna show girls they can do anything and be the best!"

Mia Hamm (photo by Tony Quinn).

Mia Hamm takes the charge of role model very seriously. In fact, when we met her she was preparing to receive an award from the Women's Sports Foundation, but she made time to talk about girls in sports. "This is all very overwhelming for me on a personal note, but I see it for what it is. This is — all of this — is so important. It is important to celebrate our successes and share with each other."

Marion Jones could not agree more. "It's an honor." While women such as St. James, Navritralova, King, and Hamm had no real female role models for their sports, Jones has a long and impressive ancestry for women's track and field. Instead of referring to her own efforts to break down the barriers, she credits much of her success to her role models, saying she is a product of what she watched, admired, and dreamed about. "I was already running. I loved to run. The women before me just showed me how. They gave me something to shoot for, and I am so grateful. I guess it's my turn. If a little girl can look to me in that way ...that's OK," she says as she flashes a smile.

Do it well. Keep your eye on the prize. These once seemed like such simple messages, messages all children would try to emulate. Right?

When celebrity trainer Tony Little was asked to attend a school assembly in southern Florida to receive an award, he thought energizing kids and getting them motivated about success would be a piece of cake. When he stepped up to the microphone, he called out to the kids, ready to get them fired up. It is, after all, what Little does best. "How many of you want to be successful in the world?" he yelled. To his disbelief, only about 50 percent of the kids answered him. "What is this?! They just sat there," he says. "It was one of the worst days of my life. I realized these kids don't care. They have all the stress of the world, but they don't have the dreams or support from their families like we had."

That is all the more reason to have strong, positive role models and all the more reason to celebrate them, so our children can see the value in hard work and determination.

When Lori Steinhorst moved to a small Texas town to be with family, she suddenly found herself restless and not entirely thrilled about her circumstances. Instead of leaving, however, she decided to make the best of her new home and focused on two things: her passion for sport and children.

Granddaughter to Golden Gloves Champion Ivan C. Fortein, Steinhorst grew up watching her grandfather work out in the basement. He filled her ears with great athletic stories and, however unwittingly, built the foundation upon which she stands today. "He would try to teach my brothers how to box. He'd knock my brothers down, and they wanted to leave. He'd knock me down, and I'd get back up again and want to do it over, do it right."

Admittedly, as a boxer she is average. But as a coach, she is outstanding and has so much to offer her community. "I just looked around and said, 'This is a poor community. This is the way I can give back.'" Give back, indeed. She teaches for free. For Steinhorst, giving back to the community through children and boxing seemed as natural as eating and breathing. As the author of the book *When the Monster Comes Out of the Closet* (Rose Publishing), the true personal account of a child molester, Steinhorst expresses her commitment and dedication to the idea of helping children. And the boxing community is all too willing to help.

"It's great. Larry Holmes, Hector Commacho Jr., Joe Frazier, Kathy Collins, Diana Lewis, Sumya Anani, Debra Nichols ... they've all sent pictures to my kids. We have local sponsors who help the kids buy their equipment. And what I get for reaching out to these kids is the expression on their faces. When I see the excitement in their eyes or the smiles on their faces, it really touches my heart."

But Steinhorst is doing so much more than she gives herself credit for. Maybe one of her students will grow up to be a boxing champion. Maybe not. It doesn't really matter. What does matter is the image that she is sending her young charges. As a woman, as a coach for such a traditionally male-dominated sport, Steinhorst is proving how strong, empowered, and awesome women can be. She serves to remind us all how incredibly important it is to serve as role models. Her motivation is not money — she gets nothing in monetary value — but the love of sports, her community, and the children.

There are also a great number of male coaches who coach for love of the sport and respect for the athlete. Gender plays no role.

It is all the more fun to watch the coaches of the Austin Rage work with their players. They are paid nothing. They have given up 10 to 12 hours a week to stand in the scorching heat and run drills, explain plays, watch runs, and ready their team for a winning season. During all the practices Alex attended, while other players were constantly taking water breaks

Coach Trey Ranson warms his team up (photo by Alexandra Allred).

or trying to find relief from the heat (true, they were all wearing pads and helmets in very hot and humid weather), the coaches never took breaks. Drenched in sweat, they stayed out on the field until they were sure the team had it right.

Collectively, these coaches are a handsome group of men who would fill your heart with dread if you had to pass them on the street corner. They wreak jock. There is an air of confidence with them that could be confused with cockiness but, as we got to know them, discovered it was truly love of the sport, appreciation for the female players, and knowledge of what they are doing.

All have impressive backgrounds in coaching and/or playing the game. They have done the locker-room scene, taken the hard hits, felt the sweetness of victory and pain of defeat. They know all about trash talking, injuries, post- and pregame analysis, and they accept the Austin Rage players as they are — football players. Just as Sarah Fisher must feel about her pit crew as she prepares for the Indy 500, members of the WPFL looked to their predominantly male coaches with gratitude. It was not until Alex was placed on the injured reserve list with broken fingers that she truly recognized their position as role models.

With such caring, self-sacrificing people as examples, the Tori Allens and Sarah Fishers of the world may be our up-and-coming role models. Tori's mother, Shawn, told us that Tori has always been a competitor and, unlike her friends, is not particularly interested in boys. Sports make her happy. Sports challenge her. Sports push her to limits. No surprise, this attitude carried over to her schoolwork and friendships, making her a faithful and trustworthy friend. "She approaches life with a real teammate attitude," says Shawn Allen. She is a straightforward, strong-willed, independent-thinking young woman with a set of goals she intends to accomplish — to make sports history and to get a college education. She has no time for drugs, unwanted pregnancies, the trivialities of boyfriend troubles, or petty arguments with girlfriends. Even by creating a web site (www.toriallen.net), her intention was to share with athlete hopefuls and to get more people interested in her sport.

It is for this very reason that Rachael Scdoris has dedicated herself to talking to the media and kids everywhere she goes about being an athlete, being legally blind, and having the courage and convictions to fight for what you want in life. "Kids can be cruel if you're different. It's important to find your passion and hang in there." And, she says, to have a supportive base. Role models are extremely important. When Olympic runner Marla Runyan — also legally blind — contacted Scdoris and began talking to her, Scdoris became even more focused as an athlete. To have a woman Scdoris admired "more than anyone on the planet" contact her and discuss athletics and obstacles was incredibly empowering. (To learn more about Marla Runyan, visit www. marlarunyan.com.)

As you have probably guessed, one of our favorite role models is Jackie Joyner-Kersee. We admire her for her athletic feats and the grace with which she'd win and (rarely) lose. We admire her because she was able to find her way out of a bad neighborhood by her own grit and determination and once she became a success, she returned to that very neighborhood, setting up a place for young people to get away from the streets. She found success and has created the opportunity for others to follow her. Like so many of our foremothers, Jackie Joyner-Kersee is a pioneer, paving the way for disadvantaged youngsters to find their way up. When we finally met this impressive woman, we were humbled. She speaks like she runs. She is elegant, focused, and concise.

Like Little, Joyner-Kersee lectures to young people about "keeping your eyes on the prize." And like Little, she says too many young people have their priorities turned around. The prize is not the gold medal: It is the hard work, doing the best you can do, and fulfilling your dreams. In many ways, talking with Joyner-Kersee was similar to a discussion we had with ex-pro football and baseball player Bo Jackson. "To this day," Jackson says, "the most important thing I have is my education. It is the one thing no one can ever take away from me." Like Joyner-Kersee, Jackson tours the country, educating kids on the importance of health and exercise.

Joyner-Kersee pounds the point of "being the best you can be." Over and over she counsels young athletes to ask themselves, "What can I do to be the best? How can I make this happen?" Believing in yourself, she says, is the key ingredient to success and happiness. Joyner-Kersee, herself, is known to competitors around the globe, to reporters, and to anyone lucky enough to speak with her as one of the kindest, most gracious women in sports. Her prize, it turns out, is that she has captured our hearts.

The night we met her, a young all-American long-distance runner was standing near Joyner-Kersee's waiting room talking to us. We spoke quietly among ourselves, careful not to disturb Joyner-Kersee while she prepared her speech. Suddenly, we heard Joyner-Kersee speak up.

"You're a long-distance runner?" came a voice. Shocked, the young runner looked to us for advice. Should she answer? Should she peek her head around the corner? We shrugged our shoulders at her. Joyner-Kersee spoke up, helping us in our awkwardness. "Wow, I really have respect for you. Shoot, I can't imagine doing that." The runner grinned and stepped inside to swap track stories with Joyner-Kersee.

Rachael Scdoris keeps company with some of her favorite athletes (photo by Ty Downing, www.downingphoto.com)

Later, as Joyner-Kersee went on stage to do her thing, the young runner was still beaming. It was a night that meant everything to an aspiring Olympian. Jackie Joyner-Kersee admires me!

During the Atlanta Games (her fourth and final Olympics) Joyner-Kersee would be an example of her own advice to "keep your eyes on the prize." A pulled hamstring meant her withdrawal from the heptathlon, an event she had dominated for the past decade. Despite her injury, she participated in the long jump (her favorite event and another she had dominated for a decade). In obvious pain, she tried in vain to jump to her own standards while thousands cheered. She could not and walked away with the bronze medal. Only later, in tears, did she say that this was her most moving Olympic experience. She realized that all those people didn't care if she won the gold or not. It hadn't mattered to them. It had only mattered that Joyner-Kersee showed them the heart, determination, and style of the champion she is. The prize was self-respect.

Throughout our interviews, as we have asked girls who their female role models are, we have been repeatedly struck by their uncertainties. Boys, on the other hand, seem to have no difficulty clearly identifying sports figures they admire. We learned that many male athletes credit their mothers. Indeed, we learned that boys can have positive, strong female role models as well, but it is a hard message to get out. For example, Reggie Miller of the Indiana Pacers knew that he would be a basketball star, and eventually an Olympian, after he watched his sister win a gold medal in the 1984 Olympic Games. Cheryl Miller, the first woman to dunk a basketball in regulation play (in high school), is his sister. "She made 105 points in one game," he smiles, "but who's counting?" Little brother Reggie, that's who.

We need to do a better job of making women more recognizable role models for both sexes. We need to publicize the incredible feats women have accomplished — for both boys and girls. As corporations such as Nike and Reebok change their course of advertising, things are bound to improve. And already they have. The Gap had a really upbeat jeans commercial that shows little girls doing martial arts. It's a strong message to kids of all ages depicting powerful images of the beauty of sport and sportswomen. But cartoons and reading materials for kids still have predominantly male lead characters. Why?

My mother the football player – Dawn Arnecke grabs a water break and a hug (photo by Alexandra Allred).

Because studies have shown that in order to catch the attention of both boys and girls, boy leads are necessary. "Boys generally won't watch programs or ads with strong females, but girls will watch shows with either strong males or females," says Tom McGee, vice president of Doyle Research Associates, a Chicago-based children's product marketing firm. The same can be found in children's books. Leading roles are given to males the majority of the time. In fact, Dr. Mary Trepanier-

Street of early childhood development at the University of Michigan-Dearborn found in a creative writing workshop among elementary students that female characters were "mostly princesses and teachers." All the more reason for books such as *My Mother Is A Football Player*. As Dr. Trepanier-Street says, "Exposure to different options is crucial."[2]

By creating and celebrating our own super heroes, the perception children have of female athletes is changing. One such hero is Karyn Bye, of the gold medal-winning 1998 U.S. hockey team. After her games, Bye makes it a habit to shake hands with fans. It is just part of the "giving back" attitude so many female athletes have. On one occasion, while she was shaking hands with fans, she noticed a little boy she had seen many times before. Every time she came near him, he sat perfectly still and stared at her, never daring to say a word. Bye would try to get him to talk, but he would only stare at her. (Although, according to his mother, he would talk excitedly about Bye the moment she was gone.)

A few days after one of these encounters, Bye received a phone call from the little boy's mother. The child idolized Bye, the mother said. It was his birthday, and she wondered if Bye could come as a surprise. Bye obliged. Can anyone picture members of the NBA or NFL showing up at an unknown child's birthday party?

When the little boy answered the door and saw Bye, he burst into tears, unable to speak. His hero had come to wish him a happy birthday, and he was overcome by emotions — joy, surprise, embarrassment. Bye said, "I didn't know what to do. I was hopping from foot to foot saying, 'OK, let's play!'" But the boy was so overwhelmed that he couldn't do anything.

"I haven't heard from him in about five years," she says good-naturedly, "I guess he grew up and thought, 'What am I doing wasting my time with that girl?'" While it is entirely likely that a boy did outgrow his hero-worship of a female hockey player, Bye continues to be a strong role model to everyone who knows her.

Another amazing role model was Nancy Woodhull (of the Media Studies Center). Yet she also was inspired by role models. Woodhull chose, as her two most influential female role models, Billie Jean King and Betty Friedan.

"The first story that I covered as a reporter about a woman trying to change things for women was Billie Jean King in the early '70s," Woodhull remembered. "King was trying to open the tennis circuit, get women playing in bigger tournaments, and give them access to bigger financial rewards. A couple of things happened for women journalists who followed and wrote about her. First, we were influenced and affected by her undaunted strategic approach to equality. Also, covering the story gave a lot of women journalists an opportunity because King was a page one story, and editors believed only women could cover her story well. Billie Jean was both a learning experience and a professional opportunity.

"Billie Jean King's professional rise was almost simultaneous with the reverberations from Betty Friedan's book *Feminine Mystique*, which were really being felt by women in a positive way. I wouldn't meet Betty until 25 years later when we started working together on how the press covered women. She had the same undaunted strategic and brave approach to dealing with women's issues that Billie Jean King did."

Like King and Friedan, Woodhull was a great heroine, championing women's rights and educating the public. Labeled "feminists" (the dreaded "F" word), Friedan and Woodhull intimidated many over the years — Friedan with her exploration of "the woman problem" and as co-founder of the National Organization for Women (NOW), and Woodhull with her aggressive work as a journalist and women's advocate. As senior vice president of the Freedom Forum, executive director of the Media Studies Center, chair of the national advisory board for the National Women's Hall of Fame, vice chair of the International Women's Media Foundation, and co-founder/co-chair of Men, Women and Media, Woodhull settled herself into the gutsy role of activist. To some, that's scary stuff.

But just as Woodhull was labeled with the "F" word, she taught us a thing or two about labeling. While we were busily writing this book, we were thinking of female athletes from "serious" sports such as soccer, hockey, skiing. In our minds anyone who was a cheerleader or drum majorette was certainly a flower. No storm would ever be a majorette, right? No one except Nancy Woodhull, lead majorette of the Matawan Regional High School. And she wasn't just a majorette; she wasn't just a lead majorette. Woodhull was a majorette with style, twirling batons that were on fire (while teachers stood by with fire extinguishers).

Later in life, after her majorette days were over, Woodhull's two passions were the Media Studies Center and her teenage daughter, Tennessee. Of the media, Woodhull said she was striving for her work at the Media Studies Center to be "a catalyst for helping the press be as good as it possibly can be." Of her daughter, Woodhull said she hoped that her work as an activist would be "a catalyst for my daughter, whatever profession she goes into." Demonstrating her passion, Woodhull named her daughter after an early suffragist, a strong-willed woman named Tennessee Woodhull (no relation). That Woodhull's sister, Victoria, was also a strong-willed woman and a suffragist, who actually ran for the presidency in 1870. These women spoke out for women's issues long before it became fashionable.

Nancy Woodhull continued that legacy — for her daughter, for all daughters — and did much to change perceptions about and acceptance of women in all forums. There are thousands of unsung heroines around the country — women, like Woodhull, who are part of the storm. Women such as the owners of the Austin Rage (and so many of the other professional women's football teams). Women such as Tina Cormier, a former player and current owner who stands over an open barbeque pit, working the concession stand in 108-degree weather, not seeing one play her football team is making, trying to make sure the fans have a great time so more women can play football. "One day," she says, "I would love to see our players do this full time. When I was playing, I wish there had been enough money that I didn't have to go to work the next day. Maybe one day ... I'd love to see girls playing football in high school so our pool of talent would be bigger, better."

"I just read about a high school that has girls playing football," general manager Donna Roebuck pipes in and we wonder, will this take off?

"It will in our lifetime," offers team owner Kathy Smith. "Because people like us are paving the way." She looks over to her field of players and nods, almost as though she is verifying what she sees to herself. "It'll happen. People just have to see the product. Is the product good? Absolutely."

Sports history may not have included some of the pioneers named in this book and the thousands like them, but what an impact they have had. Tori Allen is single-handedly trying to change pole vaulting and to introduce rock climbing as an Olympic event; Allie Sizler was being recruited by colleges at age 15; women like Dee Kennamer, Donna Roebuck, and Andra Douglas have sacrificed personal savings to let other women play football and live a dream; Greg Williams introduces mathercise to his kids. These people send the real message to little girls: you do matter; you can make a difference.

Hilliard put it rather poignantly when she wrote, "Female athletic role models are touchable icons who live down the street. Their presence is a motivating force for girls, sending the message that playing sports is not only an acceptable thing to do, but it's a status symbol."[3]

When we asked the super-cool, super-buff Brandi Chastain if she had any idea of what the fallout from her removing her jersey on field would be, she could only say she was still amazed by the response. Who knew that, after one of the most emotionally and physically draining soccer games of all time, when Chastain made the goal heard and seen around the world, and in a moment of complete and utter delirious joy, that the simple action of ripping off her shirt and flexing would create posters, books, public appearances, magazines covers — and the most coveted reward — a role model. "When I did it, I never, ever thought about 'What's going to happen if I do this?' I just did it. It just happened."

Thank goodness it did, because when she ripped off her shirt, exposing a muscle-toned, sports bra-wearing goddess-like physique, the female athlete was redefined: intense, beautiful, mus-

cular, and totally cool! When
her team ran on to the field in
celebration, we all celebrated,
too. When asked about being
a role model, Chastain says,
"We're all role models. We
were role models before we
stepped on to the field, winners or not."

She was not alone in
lending her valuable time to
this project. But it was still
amazing to us when we
picked up a ringing phone to
hear, "Hi, this is Micki King,"
or "This is Christine Brennan.
I just got your message. Am I
too late?" Women who have
very busy travel and public
appearance schedules (usu-

Marion Jones will forever be one of our
greatest heroines (photo courtesy of Vec-
tor Sports Management/Marion Jones).

ally for a fee) agreed to speak with us because they appreciate
how important this message is for women and men of all ages.
Women like Marion Jones, Mary Lou Retton, Janet Evans, Mia
Hamm, Bonnie Blair met with us or called out of the goodness
of their hearts!

American Gladiator Eason (Sky) stayed up until midnight
chatting on the phone with us. We sat at the dinner table with
Karyn Bye and Cammy Myler, swapping stories, and laughed
with U.S. track hero Wyomia Tyus. We conspired with Janet
Evans to write a gag autograph for a friend of ours. We actually forgot an important question for Mary Lou Retton because
of her infectious, deep-belly laughter. And we were thrilled to
find that both Evans and Retton are as charming and truly
nice as they appear to be in television interviews.

In so many interviews with female athletes and activists,
we snickered and giggled, swapped stories, exchanged telephone numbers, and listened intently to all of these women
talking about something they believe in: the wonderment of

sports, the confidence sports give girls, and the camaraderie of female athletes.

We had not one but several sports agents comment on how lucky we were to find so many female athletes and celebrities willing to talk with us. "If you were trying to do this with a group of elite male athletes, it would have never happened," we were told. "Every one of them would have wanted money."

But perhaps we owe our deepest and greatest appreciation to Nancy Hogshead-Makar. Not because she made sports history and showed men and women the world over how powerful and aggressive a woman could be in sport. Not because she showed how smart, dedicated, and creative a female athlete is. Not because she dedicated her life to making equal opportunities to little girls and little boys, women and men in sports, business, education, and life. But because she showed the world the kind of raw courage that comes from a survivor. She survived rape and let other women know they could come back from emotional and physical pain and suffering, reclaim their lives and become stronger than ever. How do you thank a person for that kind of selflessness?

We said this chapter was initially dedicated to Wyomia Tyus, but we know that she would happily share the title with Dr. Hogshead-Makar. In one moment of time, she was trapped in the cruelest of storms — one she would not only weather but conquer to reclaim her life and better those around her. We are eternally grateful that she did!

Notes

1. "A League of Her Own," *Sports Illustrated Women/Sport* (Spring 1997), 26.
2. Helen Cordes, "Raising Confident Girls," *Child* (September 2001), 76-78.
3. Wendy Hilliard, "The Trickle-Down Effect," *Women's Sports & Fitness* (October 1996), 55.

'ATTA BOY!!

It was the opening game of the new season and at top billing was the Moonbeams vs. the Clouds. This may not mean much to people around the map, but for 7- and 8-year-old girls in the Columbus, Ohio, area, this was big stuff. And, as history does have a way of repeating itself, an unpleasant encounter erupted again. Only this time, it involved the commissioner of the league who was ready for a particular dad and he was looking at being ejected not only from the game but the entire park.

At the end of the game when many parents gathered around the head referee and commissioner to see exactly why the father was not thrown out of the park, our dejected ref sighed in defense. "I don't know anything about 7-year-old girls. I only know soccer." He wasn't up for the challenge of facing irate parents, confused little girls, and frustrated coaches.

To fully understand the predicament of this particular afternoon, one would have to had endured two previous seasons with a father who berated little girls on the other teams. This man would holler at children from the opposing team. And when he was challenged by another parent, he would become volatile with the adults. He ranted at the Moonbeam coach, accusing him of cheating while his own daughter was known throughout the league as a very poor sport, calling other children names and crying when the ball was stripped from her.

In defense of the head referee, we are sure that when he initially came on board he really did believe he was just handling soccer games. But to be in his position, he needed to know much more. He needed to know how the mind of a 7-year-old girl works. For each time an adult is allowed to rant and rave, to shout insults at a child and loudly protest a referee, the not-so-subtle message of poor sportsmanship is being passed on to

'Atta Boy! The support of a great coach will carry throughout an athlete's life (photo by Alexandra Allred).

our children — both boys and girls. But the behavior of this particular father and the reaction of the commissioner and ref brought up another interesting issue. Is it enough to just love sports when coaching children and, specifically, females?

While interviewing ESPN sports shock jock The Fabulous Sports Babe, she questioned why so many men are still coaching women's NCAA sports. "Why are so many men coaching when there are so many qualified women?" she asked. "Why are coaching positions still dominated by men?"

Conversely, women coaching men is also widely criticized. Micki King faced this when she coached men's diving and Julie Croteau, the first professional baseball player, was routinely accused of wanting to be a man because she coached men's NCAA Division I baseball. Either way, it is exclusionary thinking. As much as we wouldn't want qualified women to be overlooked, nor do we want or need qualified men to be ignored. The truth is, even as our baby boomers bask in the glory of Title IX, the majority of little-league coaches are men. Whether it is because they have more time, feel more comfortable stepping into the arena of sports, or like the role of coach more than women, it is predominantly men who are coaching our children. And it is these men, these coaches, who are the first to expose girls to the world of sport.

Long ago, we were asked if this would be a man-bashing book. Our answer is simple: in order to properly celebrate our female role models, we must also celebrate our male role models. We need to teach them more about the importance of self-esteem building and nurturing tactics for budding athletes. Gold medallist and professional soccer players Mia Hamm and Brandi

Chastain both insist they are who they are today as athletes and motivational speakers because of the kind of coaching they received. Because men are ever-present in the sports world, it is important to embrace their roles as coaches and trainers so that we can strengthen relationships with winning results on and off the playing field. In talking to some of the greatest female athletes in the world, all agree that male coaches and trainers are very much a part of the game and very necessary. As Jackie Joyner Kersee points out, "Learning to communicate with men carries over into the business world, personal relationships, and team building."

And as we enter into the traditionally male-dominated sports, we must rely on the expertise of the male athlete. In our early careers in bobsledding when it was not an Olympic event and women were not welcome on the mountain, we found support from a few very special men. While we trained in Calgary, Alberta, three-time Olympian Greg Sun (Trinidad) and two-time Olympian and bobsledding official Joey Kilburn walked the track with us early in the morning and late at night explaining each of the turns in the mile-long mountain. These men taught the trade secrets of driving, equipment, and bobsled care to the U.S. women. Without the time and contributions of these men, it could have been much more painful and costly than it was.

The same can be said of women's professional football. As the new roster was named for the Austin Rage football team, there were many women who had never set foot on a football field before and knew little (if any) rules of the game. Not only was it important that the Rage coaches taught the nuances of the sport, they had the daunting task of making these women believe they were football players.

In what can only be described as a particularly frustrating day for many of the rookies, Coach Trey Vickers would walk over to the players, make some grand announcement and walk off again. Example: repeatedly he would say to Alex or two other defensive ends Paige Ropac and Tameko Scott, "Don't ever let the shadow fall on your shoulder." Each and every time the three women would look at each other for assistance only to be greeted with shoulder shrugs. "What the hell is he talking about?"

At one fateful practice, Paige and Alex stood on the sidelines, helmets tucked under their arms watching 'Meko' as she let the shadow fall on her shoulder. Translation: As a defensive end, when Meko was down in her three-points stance before the snap, she should have been on the outside of the line. She should have made sure that the offensive lineman was to the inside of her stance so that she would be able to go around the player, to the outside of the play. Should there be a reverse, she would be in position to see it. Instead, like Alex and Paige, Meko was eager to get her hands on the quarterback. Only the dreaded Ann Wolfe had other plans. As a running back, she waited for Meko to move into the inside, headed for her quarterback. Then, running with steam engine precision, she hit Meko so hard, so fast, so mean, so brutally that both Paige and Alex gasped. Their faces momentarily contorted as they watched Meko — a very powerful player — crumble to the earth.

Coach Trey looked back to the cringing defensive ends and shook his head. "I said, 'Don't let the shadow fall on her shoulder.'" Ahhh.

Even as Paige and Alex did papers, rocks, scissors to see who would run the next play, a very powerful message had been sent to Coach Trey's players. They weren't girls to be pampered or babied. They were football players. They were there to take hard hits and learn hard lessons.

It is hard to imagine not including men in women's sports. As fathers, they have been some of our greatest cheerleaders. Bonnie Blair's father was telling people she would win an Olympic medal when she was only 12. Blair says she thought "he was nuts." Then, at the age of 16, she began to taste success and wanted more. She began to believe her father. Thus was born the United States' greatest Winter Olympian. Tennis sensations Venus and Serena Williams were trained, molded and guided by their father — almost to a point where he has been criticized for his enthusiasm. And while Coach Trey Vickers' daughter is still too young to understand what he is doing, Vickers is ensuring that women have a place in all sports and sending the message to his daughter that he supports her.

Karyn Bye's father has been her biggest supporter from the very beginning. In fact, he was responsible for starting Bye's hockey career. One evening when Bye was just 7 years old, her older brother was sick and could not attend his hockey practice. Bye's father asked her if she wanted to put on her brother's equipment, go to his practice, and see if she could fool anyone into thinking she was her brother.

The motivation and support of a coach continues on and off the football field (photo by Alexandra Allred).

"Whenever any of the guys would come up and talk to me (thinking that I was Chris), I would turn my head away and ignore them. After a while, they figured out it was me, but I had so much fun at that practice that my dad signed me up for hockey the following year." How great that Bye's father never thought to limit her. Look at her now — gold medallist with the first-ever Olympic women's hockey team.

Initially, Rachael Scdoris' father was not supportive. Yes, she is an amazing athlete, level-headed, determined, and strong. But, because she is so young and because she is legally blind, Jerry Scdoris had some reservations about his only daughter becoming a competitive dog sled racer. Racers can gain speeds up to 20 miles per hour. That, combined with an icy trail, harsh weather and the very real possibility of getting lost or slamming head-on into a tree, is enough to make anyone nervous. But racing is in her blood. Her father runs Oregon Trail of Dreams, a dog sled service for tourists in Oregon (www.sleddogrides.com) and is also a competitive racer.

It was impossible to keep her out of the kennels, her father says. She was riding in sleds since she was a toddler and had learned to harness them before she could read. Eventually, the day came when Rachael's persistent begging paid off and her father relented. But, he confides, "She didn't know it, but I followed her that day." Racing on foot, Scdoris' father secretly ran behind his daughter as she made her first solo trip with the dogs. What a moment it must have been to realize his daughter was a chip off the ol' block and while she really didn't need him, he was there all the same. 'Atta boy!

Husbands coaching wives, brothers daring sisters, whatever the relationship, male influences among female athletes cannot be underrated. It is only because of parents, coaches, and supporters of female athletics that our spirits survive. It is this very special group of people who hold things together when the appeal of the sport is lost or self-doubt sneaks up on us. How many times has an athlete asked, "Why am I doing this?" only to be answered by her coach, spouse, or parent? The first chapter of this book asks, "Why Am I Doing This?" In it we examine the range of emotions athletes experience and point out some of the numerous rewards sports bring, including better health, fun, and companionship. There are times, though, when the athlete cannot find the answer to her question, or, at least, not an appropriate one. How many times has an athlete thought about bailing out only to be reeled back in by her father, friend and/or coach?

Men Are From Mars, Women Are From Venus was and is a national best seller. A talk show, countless radio topics, magazine articles, and other books have spun off from this concept. Since the dawn of man and woman, there has been a miscommunication. We don't get them. They don't get us. But through sport, men and women are learning to better communicate. And, thankfully, it is happening at earlier and earlier ages for girls.

When the Moonbeams came to be, two of the best father/coaches known to Little League teamed up. Shawn Lanning, a single father of one, and Don Jackson, a married father of three. Although the Moonbeams have never won the NCAA championships, what they have learned from these two men has more far-reaching implications than any shiny new trophy could offer.

Although these men are very busy in their personal and professional lives, time seems to stand still when they are running drills, conducting practices, coaching games, and planning team picnics. Lanning is a soft-spoken coach who is truly an overgrown kid himself. He continuously makes bets with players to inspire them to work and play harder. He's been drenched in water and silly putty, bombed with water balloons, smeared with body paint, pinched, tickled, chased, jumped on, and tackled. Jackson is Lannings nemesis. He has a booming voice and a commanding demeanor. He's all business, far more serious, easily aggravated when an easy goal is missed, and, like Lanning, is adored by his girls. Where Lanning has taught the girls that sports can be fun and team play is the best way to play, Jackson has taught the girls to accept criticism and demand more of themselves. Jackson is also the same guy who will run on to the field and sweep a little girl into the air, spin her around and loudly praise her for making a semi-decent play. From these men came a gift that will carry forward for the rest of their young charges' lives. It is OK to cry, fight for the ball, be aggressive, lose, win, and share. And, while it is more fun to win, Lanning and Jackson have taught their Moonbeams how to lose with dignity and bond with teammates.

That is why sports are so wonderful. Sports afford the opportunity for people to cheer for you. It allows men, in particular, who can be uncomfortable bonding in other ways, to relate to their daughter, sister, or spouse. Our own father grew up in a household of all boys, joined the military and commanded hundreds of men in battle and in Army posts. This was not someone who did idle chitchat. But on the soccer field he could relate to us.

The same could be said of the male coaches of the WPFL. They all know football. They eat, sleep, and breathe football. Most have played at the collegiate and/or professional level. And the one place they could definitely identify with the female players was on the field. In fact, it was curiosity about female football players that brought both James Ubbins and Melvin Modesty to a tryout. They just wanted to see ...

For them, it would be the beginning of something great. They hope. Like so many of the men in this chapter and in women's sports on the whole, the coaches of the WPFL see great potential in their athletes. As Coach Ubbins insists, "I see so much potential with this league and these players. You know, most of these women never played before, and I see a lot of talent. I think in a few more years when we have some real experience under our belt, we can really go far. If the NFL would get on line with us, we could turn this into something full time." Nothing would make him happier. We drew some snickers from other players when describing Coach Ubbins as "crusty." Indeed, this former tobacco-chewing, hard-ass Marine is crusty. And he relates perfectly to his football players.

While this chapter is dedicated to the men who have supported women's sports, it is also a show of thanks to all the coaches, families, and fans. We have demonstrated time and time again how athletes themselves become great cheerleaders (case in point — how many were willing to talk to us), but it is the families, friends, and coaches who have carried most of the athletes.

Bonnie Blair is convinced that her family gave her the winning edge. They became known as the Blair Bunch during her multiple Olympics, and their support for her won support and admiration from around the world. During the Calgary Games, there were 25 family members present. At the Albertville Games, 45 family members came. In Lillihammer, there were 60. And for her final speedskating competition during the 1995 World championships in Milwaukee, Blair had 300 family members present. How could she possibly lose? She says, "There wasn't any pressure because they were there for me all along." Even if she had lost, she still would have won.

As sports becomes more and more prevalent in our society and we continue to hero-worship people who can slam dunk, we need to try to remind our children what is really important: Hardwork, dedication, sportsmanship, honesty, fun. There are parents and coaches who don't value their athletes as stars (with or without a victory), who think winning is all that matters, and who promote winning at all costs. As we saw in the games of the Moonbeams vs. the Clouds, there can be a negative influence by family members as well.

For Clair Rheul, mother of U.S. diver Becky Rheul, it wasn't enough that she had taught her daughter about sportsmanship; it wasn't enough that Becky was a champion (both in body and soul); Clair Rheul wanted more for all young athletes. Too many times she had seen the pressures of a coach or parent destroy the purpose of sport and the drive of a young child.

For this reason, she created a handbook outlining guidelines for parents, coaches, and athletes at the school where Becky dived (Villa Madonna Academy). Clair Rheul sees to it that everyone at Villa Madonna — athletes, parents, coaches — gets a crash course in sportsmanship.

The handbook reads as follows:

Parent's code

Parents embark on a unique journey as they allow their child to enter the world of sports. This world provides the student with an arena for exercise, competition, and learning about life. It provides the parents with the opportunity to teach, communicate, and build character and self-esteem in their child. While winning a game can be exciting and inspirational, Villa Madonna parents are expected to help teach students that winning does not define the importance or worth of either the school, the team, or the individual player.

Villa Madonna's Sports Pledge for Parents

- I will always be supportive.
- I will never coach from the sideline.
- I will never yell negative remarks at players, other teams, or referees.
- I will never seek to humiliate or embarrass.
- I will never reserve acceptance and praise for athletic performance.
- I will help the athlete to set realistic goals.
- I will provide a shoulder to cry on when needed and a "high five" when earned.
- I will teach sports etiquette and good sportsmanship.
- I will educate the athlete regarding team loyalty and responsibility.

- I will help the athlete to communicate with the coaching staff in a positive way.
- I will support the coaching staff.
- I will relinquish the responsibility for my child's participation in the sport to the coach for the period of the contest.
- I will follow the line of communication to resolve problems as set forth in the Rules and Guidelines of Coaches.
- I will always cheer the athlete and the team.

Coach's Code

In many respects, a coach's responsibility is similar to that of a teacher, but in some ways, it is even more challenging because he or she is attempting to modify the behavior of both mind and body. The school and parents are depending on the coach for the welfare of the student as well as for developing proper attitudes and physical skills. The coach often is in the position during pressurized and competitive situations to demonstrate moral leadership. The coach is often in the unique position of being liked, trusted, and respected in an informal atmosphere. In effect, a coach can bridge the gap between home and school life. At Villa Madonna, our coaches are expected to accept responsibility as well as the rewards of the furthering development of a student.

We have adopted the "National Youth Sports Coaches Association Code of Ethics Pledge" which states:

- I will place the emotional and physical well-being of my players ahead of any personal desire to win.
- I will remember to treat each player as an individual, remembering the large spread of emotional and physical development for the same age group.
- I will do my very best to provide a safe situation for my players.
- I promise to review and practice the necessary first-aid principles needed to treat injuries of my players.
- I will do my best to organize practices that are fun and challenging for all my players.
- I will lead, by example, in demonstrating fair play and sportsmanship to all my players.

- I will ensure that I am knowledgeable in the rules of each sport that I coach and that I will teach these rules to my players.
- I will use those coaching techniques appropriate for each of the skills that I teach.
- I will remember that I am a youth coach, and that the game is for the children and not the adults.

Athlete's Code

Athletes who participate in organized school sports have a tremendous opportunity for growth. Athletes develop their strength, coordination, endurance, and specific skills related to the sport they play. But athletes would be missing the greatest gifts sports have to offer if they limited themselves to physical prowess. Athletes who have gained the most from sports have allowed their minds and spirits, as well as their bodies, to grow as they experience the wins and losses of organized sports. Those who have challenged themselves to be the best they can be, not just in the game, but during practice as well, will develop characteristics they will use throughout their life. Sports, if allowed, will teach athletes about never giving up, about taking pride in all they do, about feeling joy or empathy for others, about making friends, but mostly sports will teach athletes to believe in themselves.

Villa Madonna's Sports Pledge for Athletes

- I will always be a good sport, whether winning or losing.
- I will always show respect for all players, coaches, and officials.
- I will never use obscene language or gestures.
- I will support my team in a positive way, whether playing or on the sidelines.
- I will not argue with my coach or officials.
- I will give my best effort and attention at practice and during games.
- I will play fair and follow the rules of the game.
- I will remember that sport is a game and I will have fun playing.

Thank you, Clair Rheul. These are lessons all athletes and supporters of athletes should learn and follow. We are all connected to one another and should support one another.

The truly beautiful thing about sports is what men are learning from women. When Rich Young took on the job as coach for the New England Storm of the WPFL, he had no idea what he was getting into. Having coached at the high school, college, and professional level in men's football, this was — as they say — a whole new ball game. "Not in the professional sense. I think the women take this game, the learning process and play time, a lot more seriously. But ... they're different. I'm having to adjust."

Coaches Melvin Modesty and James Ubbins understand this statement. Slowly, they are learning how female athletes process information. "Calling her a dumb motherf— isn't necessarily going to help her along," grins a sheepish Ubbins. "You treat the female athlete with respect and that's what you're gonna get back," agrees Modesty. "They work harder, try more, and give more when you treat them with respect and dignity." Certainly, for these coaches, this will carry over into their professional lives.

When we met the big man himself at his own Arnold Schwarzenegger Classic, Schwarzenegger said this of the female athlete, "I am always humbled by the female athlete. She is so strong. She teaches us [male athletes] so much about sport, life, inner strength, and physical stamina. She has been our greatest teacher."

'Atta boy!

Postscript: Playing with Rage

by Alexandra Allred

When I read the book *The Girls of Summer*, about the U.S. women's soccer team, I cried. Actually, I kind of embarrassed myself on a plane coming back from Austin to Columbus, Ohio. I sat sniffling over a sports book, trying to look cool while tears streamed down my cheeks. I was crying because ... well, it's so hard to aptly put into words. And, here I am a writer.

I cried because I was and am so proud of those women. I cried because I was impressed by the undying support of their families and the amazing determination and grit of the players. I cried because this was the beginning of something really great for women in sport, and I cried because I was so envious. Imagine playing a sport you loved before the thunderous crowd of thousands! Imagine standing on a podium with the national anthem playing and wearing a gold medal around your neck. I'll never have that. We (Michelle Powe, Liz Parr-Smestad, Jill Bakken, Elena Primerano, Chrissy Speizio, Laurie Millet, Patty Driscoll, Nancy Lang, Sharon Slader, Krista Ford) did what we did for women's bobsledding but for many of us, the success of the fight was a little too late. I cried because so much is changing, and I'm so thankful to see the change.

Women of today are empowered, strong, independent, and fearless. As we have discussed, even Hollywood is changing its format. There are fewer damsels in distress and more heroines. It is a new and exciting era for little girls.

Once upon a time, there did not seem to be a place for us. We missed out on so many opportunities that we are only now figuring out. As Lopiano of the Women's Sports Foundation says: "Sport has been one of the most important sociocultural learning experiences for boys and men for many years. ... Sport is where boys have traditionally learned about teamwork, goal setting, the pursuit of excellence in performance, and other achievement-oriented behaviors — critical skills for success in the workplace. In this economic environment, the quality of our children's lives will be dependent on two-income families, so both parents should have the advantage of experience in sport."[1]

But now, not only are we benefiting, we are the athletes to watch. Women's track and field, ice-skating, gymnastics, soccer, basketball, and softball are some of the most sought after venues at the Olympic games. The fitness industry is booming as female bodybuilders and fitness pros are changing what the ideal female physique looks like; our notion of what qualifies as beautiful is changing. Leading actresses and top models are looking for muscle definition. The reality is that our young girls will always be confronted by images of sexy women. It is OK for us to appreciate beauty, but we shouldn't feel the need to emulate artificial images in order to be worthwhile. We must give girls the chance to grow up into confident, healthy, happy women, secure in who they are. There is a new trend that offers even more encouragement. In a recent poll conducted among U.S. teens, the word is Pamela Anderson is out and Jennifer Lopez is in. What? Smaller breasts with buffed bods and rounded thighs are in? Ya-hoo!

That confidence is multifaceted; it comes from many sources, and it shapes so many aspects of our personalities. We must continue to encourage girls into sports, teaching them competitive skills and confidence in school and business. And we must take responsibility for the images of femininity and female attractiveness we are sending to our children, so that we can teach them confidence in their own self-images and self-worth. Sports are so important for girls and women because they teach us to be proud, not only of our abilities, but of our bodies. Let's face it: in the real world we don't get the benefits of oil, special lighting, and dark makeup to shade and deceive. We can't spend all of our time posing in front of mirrors, cameras, or our dates. If we try or if we spend our lives comparing ourselves to others, we will be miserable. The reality is we get what we're born with. Through sports, we can spend months and years making our bodies — and minds — healthy and strong. That is enough.

This is what we want girls to learn, to emulate. My own daughters, Kerri and Katie — 8 and 6 years old, respectively — went with me to so many interviews (as well as my workouts). They believe that it is completely normal for a mother to teach kickboxing, fight competitively, bobsled, play football, and do back flips on a trampoline. Doesn't every mother? Well, shouldn't she?

So, it was nothing new for them when they came with me to an Austin Rage game. They couldn't appreciate all the wonderful things that were happening in the stadium that night and how much I truly enjoyed seeing them sitting on a bench next to female football players, donned in their gear, chatting away. They were playing on the grass between the team and over 600 fans, cheering wildly for Mommy's team. It was really cool!

When we first arrived at the field, I surveyed the injured reserved list. Miranda "Bam-Bam" Hernandez (the baby of the team) injured her back; Ana Rosales strained ligaments around her rotary cuff; Anna Lee was wearing a knee brace suffering from a torn ACL along with Sekethia "Ski" Tejeda and Lisa Jessup. Coach Trey also walked up, surveying the lot and gave a look of disgust to both Jessup and Tejeda. "You've lost weight," he accused. He eyed baby Bam-Bam suspiciously. He didn't like his players losing weight, and I was so suddenly struck with the beauty of this scenario. Even better, as the women reluctantly acknowledged losing weight, I could see Kerri and Katie scanning their bodies. The coach was saying he liked them bigger. Bigger.

As Kerri and Katie munched on their hot dogs and sipped their soda from the concession stand, they watched as KJ Scheib and Velma Pickens doubled-teamed the 6'4" 340 pound Lisa Mayers from the New England Storm — a battle that would go on all night. They listened while injured-reserved cornerback Bobbie James paced up and down the lines, chattering away. Seriously, ESPN needs to put a mic on this woman! In between plays, Dori Livingston, Demetra Logan, Sherron Day, and Chenell "SoHo" Brooks would turn to the crowd, chant with them and encourage the adorable elementary school girl cheer-leaders (complete with pom-poms) who yelled their little lungs out. April Green was on fire, Kim Mott tore up the line and both Angela "Slim Shady" Brown and the dynamic Tokie Ogita scored beautiful touchdowns. But it was the Air Jordan, ga-zelle-like interception of Sue "Suicide" Horton toward the end of the game that left the entire team chanting, "Sue, Sue, Sue, Sueiiiiciiide!" It wasn't a game. It was a celebration.

After the game, after both teams reunited in the middle of the field to shake hands and congratulate each other on a good game, after the Gatorade was poured over the coach, the play-ers ran over to the fence dividing field and stands. They hugged family members, signed a few autographs and posed for pic-tures. As they headed back to the locker rooms, there was a picture perfect silhouette in the darkness. With the lights from the stadium hitting their backs, a mother and son walked away side by side. Sheri Dillard-Davis, still in her shoulder and thigh pads, cleats and jersey walked with her son. He carried her helmet and looked up at her while they talked. Before we en-tered the locker room I asked 5-year-old Jordon what he thought of his mom. "She's a star," he said in a quiet, confident voice.

It just so happens it was Coach Dee's birthday and the team/coaches surprised her with a cake. After the melee of singing and threatening her with a trip to the showers, a rather embarrassed looking Dee Kennemar addressed her team. Her words were so sweet, so sincere and so on the mark of women in sport that I committed it to memory.

"When I was growing up in rural Alabama, I saw my first football game when I was 4 years old, and I fell in love. I grew up watching Johnny Unitas (among others) and dreamed of playing myself. Now, 40 years later, I am living a dream. Thank you for being part of my dream."

Before leaving the field, general manager Donna Roebuck handed me a tape entitled 'Playing with Rage.' It was a pro-motional tape for the Rage. As soon as I got home I popped it in the VCR.

"You can't quit now! You're too far along into this to quit!" booms the voice Coach Dee. On screen, the viewer can see the lone figure of a football player. She might be asking herself, 'Why am I doing this?' and questioning all those internal and external pressures she feels. But the athlete within beckons and we hear 'SoHo' Brooks voice: "I have no fear. Once I get on the field, it's on."

Back in the locker room, SoHo is leading her team in a pump-'em-up chant. "Everybody get your rage on!!"

Sitting in her state trooper cruiser, Dori Livingston ponders how much longer she could do something like this. It is, she says, the opportunity of a lifetime and at the age of 35, she knows this is her time. On the field, she leads her team. "What time is it??" Rage time!

It is rage time? Since my ESPN 'Friday Night Fight' experience, I find myself checking the women's boxing web sites, such as www.womenboxing.com, frequently. I am a fan. But when I found boxer Sumya Anani, I was particularly struck by her words. Never mind being wowed as a boxing fan. She writes, "We live in a patriarchal society, so to be empowered and to empower other women means not catering to men." Over the phone she tells me that this means believing in ourselves, our abilities, and following our own passions rather than listening to what society dictates to be proper feminine behavior. It means, she says, to follow our hearts and good will surely follow. Then, "Bear's" beautiful voice creeps in, focusing my attention back to the tape. Suddenly I was watching Jennifer "Bear" Barrington, sitting cross-legged on a football field, decked out in pads and uniform, holding a guitar. Barrington is a tough-talking, incredibly intense player who loves to hit hard and take people down. But strumming her guitar, she is transformed. She sings a song she wrote herself:

"Brick by brick, just one piece at a time, I am building a wall — a wall I can call my own."

The camera scans all the players, holding hands, readying themselves for game time. NFL player Ricky Williams makes a surprise appearance on film saying he would like to watch women's football to see the contact and collisions.

"Hit somebody!!" roars Coach Dee's voice. But back in the locker room, the head coach has her hands cupped around the

Jennifer "Bear" Barrington (photo from the collection of Jennifer Barrington).

face of Jennifer Monsevais. "You must control your emotions when the whistle blows." And to Monsevais, this doesn't mean 'no crying.' This means, don't lose your cool and knock someone's head off when the play is dead. Wait until it's showtime again. Like so many of the women of the WPFL, she is fierce. But sitting prettily at her office desk, Monty the Monster says, "When you put your helmet on, the girlie stuff goes away."

In between dialogue from various players, I see the faces of warriors I have grown to love. These women have endured injuries (and we're not talking little boo-boos), travel woes, financial setbacks, public scrutiny, child-care issues, and work schedule problems to make a dream come true.

During the game against the New England Storm, I had noticed Dori Livingston pacing back and forth like a caged tiger. She was always moving in one of two ways: on the field she was a Sherman tank on the move, off the field she paced. Unlike most of the other players who stood, waiting and watching, Livingston's energy could not be contained. But it is Livingston on tape who confesses she would transfer to a desk job to make playing football possible. It is hard to imagine.

There is talk of dreams of the future and the friendships made. "The very first practice," says Coach James Ubbins, "I thought 'What a mistake.' What do I think now? What an investment!"

Finally, 'Bear' Barrington speaks to us. It is after a game. It's freezing outside, and she looks as though she has done battle. Players file into a locker room behind her as she mugs the camera, almost confiding this secret information to us. She says, "These girls are great. Spending time with them and getting to know them has been incredible. I've needed this for a long time."

We all have, Bear.

Then, as the camera pulls away, she is there on the field, singing to us again. While she sings, we see the images of mother-athletes walking off the field holding the hand of a small child, high-fiving each other, and yelling in each other's ears. There is the obligatory Gatorade thrown over the coach, lots of hugs, lots of hard hits, and I start to cry again. It's the *Girls of Summer* all over again. Only this is a Field of Dreams. I cry because I am so proud of these women [and men] for their vision, determination, and grit. I cry because, as Coach Ubbins says, I see a lifelong investment and, I guess, I cry because I needed this for a long time.

Every night when I put my kids down, they get a story and a song. Thanks to "Bear" you've got your song. As for your bedtime story it should go a little something like this: Be different so others can be normal, dare to dream, reap the rewards, don't ever, EVER let the shadow fall on your shoulders and always, play with rage!

"TOUCHDOWN!"

Notes

1. Donna Lopiano, "The Importance of Sport Opportunities for Our Daughters," Women's Sports Foundation, 1.